John F. Davis

Chinese Miscellanies

a collection of essays and notes

John F. Davis

Chinese Miscellanies
a collection of essays and notes

ISBN/EAN: 9783337825461

Printed in Europe, USA, Canada, Australia, Japan

Cover: Foto ©Andreas Hilbeck / pixelio.de

More available books at **www.hansebooks.com**

CHINESE MISCELLANIES:

A COLLECTION OF

ESSAYS AND NOTES.

By SIR JOHN FRANCIS DAVIS, Bart., K.C.B.

" Collectanea—Scripta quæ ex pluribus excerpta locis in unum lecta sunt."

LONDON:

JOHN MURRAY, ALBEMARLE STREET.

1865.

PREFACE.

THE increased facility of access to China and Japan—
the combined result of successful war and diplomacy
—has augmented the interest which distance and difficulties had tended to keep down. Both countries may
now be reached in little more than six weeks, English
law is administered under a Royal Commission on
the coast of China, and money coined with the Queen's
image and superscription.

The few short Articles contained in this Volume may,
from their variety, serve for the amusement or information of various readers. Some are printed for the
first time, and the rest appear with the kind permission
of the proprietors of the *Edinburgh* and *Quarterly*
reviews, and others.

The fears formerly entertained of European nations
in both China and Japan, from the idea that their
principal object was territorial possession, must have
been greatly allayed by the moderation which has
attended our military successes. In the former country,
we and our allies, the French, took Peking, the capital,
and then (very unlike Oriental conquerors) left the city
to its owners with only the indispensable guarantees

for treaty engagements; in the latter, murderous acts of treachery and violence were fitly punished by allied armaments, which withdrew when atonement had been made. Thus both Governments, tho one an absolute though weak sovereignty, tho other a feudal oligarchy of discordant elements, have been compelled to yield to combined foreign pressure. The aim of the motto on our China medal—*armis exposcere pacem*—has been attained; and now our best policy is to hope for the internal prosperity and efficiency of both Governments as the most desirable security for our treaty rights. With all their faults they are, in their integral character, better than the mock Christian[1] Taepings of China or the rebellious and assassin Daimios of Japan.

Great as have been our exertions and success, the result was influenced in no small measure by the friendly union and combined action of the Western nations—the coalition of civilization against barbarism. The following relates to the year 1844 :—" So perfect and complete was the acknowledgement on every side, that each was negotiating for all, that we received officially certified copies of the French and American treaties from M. de Lagrené and Commodore Parker in China, while the Chinese copies were sent us in like manner by Keying. The whole of these negotiations had, however, been preceded by official communications from Hongkong to the respective ministers

---

[1] It has been plain, from the first, that they were no more like   Christians than Mahomet was like a Jew.

of copies of our English treaties already concluded, with all collateral information relating to them."[1] Had the same weights been thrown into opposite scales —had jealousies and mutual counteraction been the rule—advantage would certainly have been taken of it ; for the Chinese did their best at first to alienate the French from us, though they were speedily disabused by our honourable allies.

This cordial co-operation may be traced without difficulty to the generous and wise policy with which Great Britain extended the commercial and other rights, which she acquired by her original and *unaided* war, to all other nations.[2] Having been the first to inaugurate the freedom and community of trade at home, she followed up that wise policy abroad by the noble and generous (and no less wise) course of fighting and negotiating, not for herself only, but for the whole civilized world. It is thus that peace and mutual good offices are perpetuated for half a century between the most powerful nations ; and that, for just fifty years, England and France, instead of wasting each other's strength only to end where they began, have combined their forces and fought side by side as close allies in all parts of the world.

---

[1] " China during the War and since the Peace," Vol. ii., page 89.

[2] " La Grande Bretagne dans un esprit généreux, digne du caractère de la puissance qui la première a ouvert la Chine à l'Europe, stipule aussi pour d'autres nations la liberté de faire le commerce dans les cinq ports, sous les mêmes conditions que celles qui furent accordées à la Grande Bretagne."—*Chevalier Bunsen.*

CONTENTS.

Page

I. Calculating Machine—Common Tartar Characteristics of
Russians and Chinese   1

II. Huc's Travels in Tartary, Thibet, and China...   7

III. The Rise and Progress of Chinese Literature in England   ..   50

IV. The Roots of the Language, with their Threefold Uses   76

V. The Drama, Novels, and Romances   ...   91

VI. Address to the China Branch of the Royal Asiatic Society ...   112

VII. Chusan in British Occupation ...   127

VIII. Analysis of a Work on Husbandry and Botany   163

IX. Valley of the Keang to the Port of Hankow ...   175

CHINESE MISCELLANIES.

I.

CALCULATING MACHINE.

COMMON TARTAR CHARACTERISTICS OF

ERRATA.

Page 61, line 4, *for* Parker *read* Parkes.

Page 169, line 12, *for* longan *read* loongan.

both originated in the facilities afforded by the binary division into halves, quarters, eighths, and sixteenths, or eight, four, two, and one.

Their numbers are *generally* written in words at length, that is, unlike the Arabic system of numeration, where the powers or values of the numbers increase or diminish decimally, according to position. This inconvenience is got over in calculation, and the denary arithmetic adopted, by the assistance of a little apparatus called a *Suàn-pán,* or calculating dish, having balls

B

CHINESE MISCELLANIES.

I.

CALCULATING MACHINE.
COMMON TARTAR CHARACTERISTICS OF RUSSIANS AND CHINESE.

WITH reference to the science of numbers, it has been observed of the Chinese arithmetic, as well as of their weights and measures, that they proceed universally on the decimal scale, and that decimal fractions are their *vulgar* fractions, or those in common use. It is remarkable that the single exception to this exists in their *kin*, or marketing pound-weight, which, like our own, is divided into sixteen parts; and it is most probable that both originated in the facilities afforded by the binary division into halves, quarters, eighths, and sixteenths, or eight, four, two, and one.

Their numbers are *generally* written in words at length, that is, unlike the Arabic system of numeration, where the powers or values of the numbers increase or diminish decimally, according to position. This inconvenience is got over in calculation, and the denary arithmetic adopted, by the assistance of a little apparatus called a *Suán-pán*, or calculating dish, having balls

B

of wood or ivory strung on wires in separate columns, of which one column represents integral units, with a decimal increase and diminution to the left and right, as in our system of numeration. Each ball above the longitudinal division of the board represents five, and each ball below it stands for one. They sometimes write down numbers in abbreviated marks, and place them, like our Arabic figures, in numerical order; but still, in arithmetical operations, the above machine is always used, and seems never to have been superseded.[1]

The following extract from the letter of a late literary nobleman, written some years back, will show his high opinion of the Chinese machine on actual trial:—"I am very desirous of learning from you how I can acquire information on the manner of performing the operations of arithmetic with the *Swàn-pàn*. I have one of them which came from China, and I can use it with great facility for addition, but subtraction is more difficult, and I cannot discover any convenient rule for multiplication or division. I have searched many works on China and on mathematics, without being able to find any explanation, although one writer says that its use is 'well known.' I am informed by Mr. Dunn, and by others, that the Chinese perform with it all the operations of arithmetic with equal rapidity and accuracy; so that they must, I conceive, have some simple and almost mechanical process like that for addition. The practical utility of the *Swàn-pàn*, as used by them, ex-

---

[1] China, vol. ii.

ceeds, beyond all comparison, the far-famed calculating machine [1] of Mr. Babbage, and is such that the mode of working ought to be generally known, and the instrument itself should be generally adopted. It would save much time and trouble, and would also have the advantage of verifying calculations which are made in the ordinary mode. It appears to me to be an object of great curiosity and importance. We have adopted so much from the Chinese already that this would be no great addition to the sum of our obligations."

The Roman abacus seems to have been used in the same way occasionally for arithmetical purposes, but with loose stones in longitudinal divisions, instead of the much better mode of stringing balls on wires; but the denary numeration would appear to have been preserved, as with the Chinese. When commenting on the barbarism of the Russians in the time of Peter the Great, Lord Macaulay states that " their arithmetic was the arithmetic of the dark ages. The denary notation was unknown. Even in the Imperial Treasury the computations were made by the help of balls strung on wires." With all due respect for such an authority as Lord Macaulay, it seems to be only reasonable to suppose that the balls strung on wires were nothing more nor less than the calculating apparatus (of which the very base is the decimal scale), borrowed by the Russians from their conterminous neighbours, and cognate Tartar race, the Chinese, who had the denary notation, and

_____

[1] Concerning which the late Sir
R. Peel asked, " Could the machine   calculate when it was to be finished?"

constructed their *Swan-pan* accordingly, when our British ancestors were content to walk about with painted skins.

Other Tartar features in the same account of the Russians assimilate them to the Chinese. "The ambassador and the grandees who accompanied him were so gorgeous that all London crowded to stare at them, and so filthy that nobody dared to touch them. They came to the Court balls dropping pearls and vermin."[1] This is, though exaggerated, not very unlike *some* Chinese mandarins, but more like pure (or impure) Tartars.[2] It is further stated, that the young emperor "heard with great interest the royal assent given (in the House of Lords) to a bill for raising £1,500,000 by land-tax, and learned with amazement that this sum, though larger by one-half than the whole revenue which he could wring from the population of the immense empire of which he was absolute master, was but a small part of what the Commons of England voluntarily granted every year to their constitutional king." Thirty years ago, it was remarked in the same way, with reference to China, "Our own country has proved the fact of the largest amount of direct taxation being levied under a limited monarchy, and through the delegates of the people themselves; and the English House of Commons has done a great deal more than the Emperor of China could probably attempt with safety."[3]

The following arguments were addressed by me, soon

---

[1] Hist. of England, vol. v., p. 74. [3] China, vol. ii., p. 428.
[2] See Huc's Travels, *infra*, p. 13.

after arriving in China, in 1844, to the Emperor's
Minister Keying, in favour of legalizing the trade in
opium, and levying a duty on it. This has since been
done.

" Your Excellency is aware that, in the reign of the
Emperor Kien-loong, opium was subject, as a medicine,
to a duty. The extent of its consumption was then inconsiderable. Subsequently to that, the drug was prohibited, and penalties attached to its consumption; but
this prohibition, and these penalties, instead of pre-
venting, appear to have increased the consumption of a
noxious article in a wonderful manner, until the value
in money of the prohibited opium imported has come
greatly to exceed the amount of the lawful tea exported.
This is the experience of China. You will therefore the
more readily believe that the experience of England
has been the same in reference to all commodities.
Opium, having never been prohibited, is consumed in
small quantities, chiefly as a medicine; and the official
returns of the last year show that the whole quantity
used in England was only 47,432 pounds, or 355
peculs. But, in regard to many other commodities,
England formerly adopted the system of prohibitions
and high duties; and these only increased the extent
of smuggling, together with crimes of violence, while
they diminished the revenue; until it was at length
found that the fruitless expense of a large preventive
force absorbed much of the amount of duty that could
be collected, while prohibited articles were consumed
more than ever.

"The disposition of men in matters of mere sensual indulgence attaches additional value to what is difficult of attainment. If a commodity be plentiful by nature, its prohibition creates an artificial difficulty, and therefore an unnatural value. In China, since opium was prohibited, it has been greedily purchased at an enormous price; in England, where it has always been lawful, it is generally disliked, and seldom used, except as a medicine. England having for many years suffered from the evils of smuggling, as well as those of a preventive force, was at length led to annul the prohibitions against some commodities, and to lower the duties on others. The consequence has been that smuggling is no longer a gainful employment; and while the duties on useful and innoxious articles of trade have been diminished, the revenue consequent on their increased consumption has enormously increased. The total revenue of England for the last year was more than 150,000,000 taels," (about £50,000,000, in 1846.)

Keying was too polite to express any doubt of an amount so different from that of the Chinese revenue; but he evidently had no small difficulty in believing it. This unfortunate minister, having failed in negociation with Lord Elgin, was ordered by his unfeeling master to put himself to death; but the Emperor himself, with a juster fate, died two years after, of chagrin at the burning of his summer palace, in requital of the murder of English and French prisoners.

II

HUC'S TRAVELS IN TARTARY, THIBET, AND CHINA.

(From the Edinburgh Review.)

ABOUT the end of 1846, Mr. Alexander Johnston, son of the late Sir Alexander, and secretary to Her Majesty's Minister Plenipotentiary in China, was fellow-passenger on board the steamer from Hongkong to Ceylon with a French Lazarist Missionary, named Joseph Gabet. It appeared that M. Gabet was then on his way from China to Paris, intending, should circumstances be favourable on his arrival, to bring under the notice of the French Government the ill-treatment which he himself and a brother missionary had experienced at Lhassa, from Ke-shen, resident on the part of the Emperor of China at the Court of the Grand Lama. Some of our readers will recognise in this name that of the Imperial Commissioner who was opposed to Captain Elliot, in 1839, at Canton; and who, on account of the disasters which befel the Chinese arms, was disgraced, plundered, and even condemned to death by the Emperor, but has since, with marvellous expedition, contrived to regain nearly all his former honours and credit, and even a great portion of his former wealth, which was colossal, as we shall see.

Mr. Johnston found the narrative of M. Gabet so curious and interesting, as the most recent and authentic account of Thibet in its relation to China, that he noted down the principal heads at the time, and, on returning to his official post, presented the manuscript to our minister, who forwarded a copy in his despatches to Lord Palmerston.

Nothing more was heard about the matter until the appearance of the two volumes by M. Huc, the companion of M. Gabet in all his adventures. A more interesting as well as diverting book has seldom issued from the French press. The qualifications of a Humboldt are not to be expected in a missionary priest. And though it should contribute nothing to the geographer or *savant*, we might well be grateful for its information regarding countries nearly inaccessible to Europeans ; while this information is conveyed in such an inexhaustible strain of good humour and fun, as amply to repay the perusal of any class of readers. In these points M. Huc bears some resemblance to his English *namesake*, Theodore, as we may almost call him.

Some eight years before the late "Papal Aggression," his Holiness of Rome took a rather smaller liberty with the Emperor of China, by appointing a vicar apostolic to Mongol Tartary. The next thing was to ascertain, if possible, the extent and nature of this gigantic vicariat. However dreadful the intolerance and oppression under which Romish priests groan among us, they were a good deal worse off in the Celestial Empire ; and yet there, strange to say, they were as quiet as lambs, and the government seldom heard of them, except when some stray missionary was detected and packed off to the coast for foreign shipment. MM. Gabet and Huc, who happened to be residing a little to the north of the Great Wall, in Eastern Tartary, at the commencement of 1844, were appointed by their spiritual superior to make their way as well as they could through Western Tartary to Lhassa, the capital of Thibet, and the holy see of the Lamas. This might look, at first sight, like taking the bull by the horns. The reader will find, however, to his surprise, that all the opposition they experienced was not *ecclesiastical*, but *lay*—not religious, but political; and that, while they received every encouragement and hospitality from the Lama's government, they were baffled, and at length expelled, by the exertions of the Chinese resident or ambassador, Keshen.

In China a Romish bishop or priest was obliged to pass himself off, as well as he could, for a native, in the lay dress of the country; but they were now going to enter a nation of priests, and therefore prepared to disguise themselves as Lamas. Off went the tail, which had been cherished ever since their departure from France, leaving the head entirely shaven. A long yellow robe was 'fastened on the right side by five gilt buttons: it was drawn round the waist by a red girdle. Over this was worn a short red jacket or waistcoat, without sleeves; or, as they call it in Chinese, " a back and breast;" having a narrow collar of purple velvet. A yellow hat with broad brim, and surmounted by a red

silk button, finished off their new costume. Their only
attendant was a young Mongol neophyte, named Samdadchiemba, who is thus described :—" Un nez large et
insolemment retroussé, une grande bouche fendue en
ligne droite, des lèvres épaisses et saillantes; un teint
fortement bronzé, tout contribuait à donner à sa physionomie un aspect sauvage et dédaigneux." This
Tartar Adonis had charge of two camels and a white
horse, which, with a tent, and a dog to guard it, completed the equipment of our adventurous missionaries
for the desert. They had no other guide for their route
than a compass, and a map of the Chinese empire,
published in Paris.

The apprehensions expressed by the friends whom
they left behind, regarding what they might suffer in the
journey to Lhassa, were fully answered in the event. M.
Gabet well nigh sank under the extreme hardships of
this savage and nomadic life—first across an inhospit-
able desert, and then over mountains to which the Alps
are trifles. From plunder they escaped tolerably free,
though the Mongol robbers would seem to be the civilest
in the world. Instead of rudely clapping a pistol to your
breast they blandly observe, " Venerable elder brother,
I am tired of going a-foot, please to lend me your horse;
I am without money, do give me the loan of your purse;
it is very cold to-day, let me have the use of your coat."
If the venerable elder brother has the charity to comply,
he is duly thanked; but if not, the humble appeal is
supported by the cudgel; and, should this not do, by
something more coercive still. Very little better than

the professional robbers were any bands of Chinese soldiers with whom they might have the bad luck to fall in, and whose neighbourhood, therefore, they diligently shunned. During the war with England, on the north-east coast, these ragamuffin troops were so dreaded by their own countrymen that, when the process of civilized warfare came to be known and understood by the Chinese people, the latter often welcomed us as deliverers, and their satisfaction was increased when the public granaries were thrown open to them for nothing. This confirms the dictum of their philosopher Mencius : "If, when you invade a country, the people come to welcome you with supplies, this can only be because you are about to rescue them from fire and water."

Our missionaries had a characteristic account of the war with England from a Tartar, whom they met in the desert :—

" 'What, were all the Tartar banners called together ?'—'Yes, all. At first it passed for a very small matter ; every one said it would never reach us. The troops of *Kitat* [1] (China) went first of all, but they did nothing. The banners of Solón also marched, but they could not resist the heat of the south. The Emperor then sent us his sacred order . . . . On the same day we marched to Peking, and from Peking we went to *Tien-tsin*, where we remained three months.'—'But did you fight— did you see the enemy ?'—'No ; he did not dare to show himself. The Chinese protested everywhere that we marched to certain and una- vailing death.—'What can you do,' said they, 'against these sea mon- sters?—They live in the waters like fish. When least expected, they appear on the surface, and throw combustible balls of iron. When the bow is bent against them, they take again to the water like frogs.' Thus it was they tried to frighten us, but we soldiers of the eight banners are

---

[1] Thus, the Chinese town at Mos-   Polo always calls China *Kathay*. cow is called *Kitaigorod*, and Marco

ignorant of fear. The Emperor had provided each leader a Lama instructed in medicine, and initiated in all the sacred auguries. They would cure us of the diseases of climate, and save us from the magic of the sea monsters—what, then, need we fear? The rebels, on hearing that the invincible troops of *Tchakar* approached, were seized with alarm, and asked for peace. The sacred master (*Shing-chu*) of his immense mercy granted it, and then we returned to our pastures and to the charge of our flocks.' "

It is known for certain that when the British force had reached Nanking and the Grand Canal in 1842, the Emperor so fully expected a visit at Peking that he stationed a force at Tien-tsin, as stated by the Tartar, and made every preparation to decamp into Tartary himself. In the confusion of packing up, some dexterous persons contrived to rob the treasury of several millions, and to this day the culprits have never been detected. The parties considered responsible, however, were, with all their relations and connexions, made answerable for the restoration of the treasure to the third and fourth generation. Without adverting to this circumstance, M. Huc observes, in another place, that during the progress of the war with the English, "nous savions que l'empereur était aux abois, et qu'il ne savait où prendre l'argent nécessaire pour empêcher de mourir de faim une poignée de soldats qui étaient chargés de veiller à l'intégrité du territoire Chinois."

The most distinguished hero, sent by the Emperor to exterminate the English during our war, was a Chinese general named Yang. This man had enticed the unfortunate Mahommedan chief, Jehanghir, in the war with Cashgar, to trust himself in his hands, and then sent him in a cage to Peking, where, after amusing the Emperor, like a trapped rat or mouse, he was cruelly put to death. M. Huc heard the following account of Yang's tactics:—

"Aussitôt que l'action s'engageait, il faisait deux grands nœuds à sa barbe pour n'en être pas embarrassé ; puis il se portait à l'arrière de ses troupes. Là, armé d'un long sabre, il poussait ses soldats au combat, et massacrait impitoyablement ceux qui avaient la lâcheté de reculer. Cette façon de commander une armée paraitra bien bizarre ; mais ceux qui ont vécu parmi les Chinois y verront que le génie militaire du général Yang était basé sur la connaissance de ses soldats."

His tactics certainly did not succeed against our troops, and as he never made his appearance, it is supposed that he occupied his favourite place of honour at the tail of the rear guard, and led gallantly in a retreat. "Nous avons demandé," says M. Huc, "à plusieurs mandarins pourquoi le Batourou Yang n'avait pas exterminé les Anglais : tous nous ont répondu qu'il *en avait eu compassion.*"

We have a terrible description in these volumes of Tartar uncleanliness, and several of the details on this subject are quite unpresentable. The dogma of the transmigration of souls acts, it seems, with some as a protection to the vermin with which they are infested. The interior of their tents is repulsive and almost insupportable to those unaccustomed to the odours that prevail there. Dirty as the Chinese may be, their northern neighbours far exceed them ; the former at least have taken it upon themselves to settle the question, by calling the latter *Chow Ta-tsze*, "stinking Tartars," as systematically as they call Europeans "foreign devils."

This clever and indefatigable, but not too scrupulous, race, have nearly displaced the Manchows in their original country to the north-east of the Great Wall, and almost as far as the river Saghalien.[1] The Chinese are the men of business and shopkeepers in all towns, and have very little mercy on the comparatively honest and simple Tartars. It is impossible to help laughing at the stories of their ingenious rascality. They are in fact the *chevaliers d'industrie*—the *Scapins* and *Mascarilles* of Eastern Asia. M. Huc, in the following passage, gives an account of their tricks, which might have applied very closely to the way in which they treated our poor sailors in the south of China :—

"When the Mongols, an honest and ingenuous race as ever were, arrive in a trading town, they are immediately surrounded by Chinese, who carry them off home as it were by force. Tea is prepared, their beasts looked to, a thousand little services rendered. They are caressed, flattered, magnetised in short. The Mongols, who have nothing of duplicity in their own character, and suspect none in others, end by being moved and touched by all these kindnesses. They take in sober earnest all the professions of devotion and fraternity with which they are plied, and, in a word, persuade themselves that they have had the good fortune to meet with people they can confide in. Aware, moreover, of their own inaptitude for commercial dealings, they are enchanted at finding brothers— *Ahatou*, as they call it—who are so kind as to undertake to buy and sell for them. A good dinner *gratis*, which is served in a room to the rear, always ends by persuading them of the entire devotion of the Chinese confederacy. 'If these people were interested,' says the honest Tartar to himself, 'if they wished to plunder me, they would hardly give me such a good dinner for nothing ; they would not expend so much money on me.' It is generally at this first repast that the Chinese bring into play all that their character combines of villany and trickery. Once in possession of the poor Tartar, he never escapes. They serve him with

---

[1] "Maintenant on a beau parcourir la Mantchourie jusqu'au fleuve *Amour*. C'est tout comme si on voyagait dans quelque province de Chine."

spirits in excess, and make him drink till he is fuddled. Thus they keep possession of their victim for three or four days, never losing sight of him, making him smoke, drink, and eat ; while they sell his live stock, and purchase for him whatever he may want, charging him generally double or triple for every thing."

M. Huc puts in a strong light that appropriation to themselves of Manchow, or Eastern Tartary (the country of their last conquerors), which has been effected by the Chinese within something more than a century, and to which we have already alluded. In a map of this country, constructed by the Jesuits, Père Duhalde states his reason for inserting the Tartar names, and not the Chinese. " Of what use," says he, " would it be to a traveller in Manchouria to know that the river *Saghalien* is called by the Chinese *Hé-loung-Keang* (river of the Black Dragon), since he has no business with them, and the Tartars, with whom he has to deal, know nothing of this name ? " " This observation might be true in the time of Kanghy," says M. Huc, " when it was made, but the very opposite is the fact at present ; for the traveller in Manchouria now finds that he has to deal with China, and it is of the *Hé-loung-Keang* that he hears, and not of the *Saghalien.*" In our own colonies, the rapidly increasing numbers and wealth of the Chinese, where they exist, are apt to give them a degree of presumption which, with the aid of their vices, might make them troublesome, were it not for the wholesome dread they entertain of European power, wherever they happen to be really acquainted with it.

M. Huc explains how Thibet, and even Mongol

Tartary, to a considerable extent, is a nation of Lamas. He says he may venture to assert that in Mongolia they form at least a third of the whole population. In almost every family, with the exception of the eldest son, who remains "*homme noir*,"[1] all the rest of the males are destined to be Lamas. Nothing can be more obvious than the fact that, in China Proper, Buddhism and its temples are in ruins, and the priests left in a starving condition; while, on the other hand, the government gives every encouragement to the Lamas in Tartary. The double object is said to be thus to impose a check on the growth of the population, and at the same time render that population as little warlike as possible. The remembrance of the ancient power of the Mongols haunts the court of Peking. They were once masters of the empire, and, to diminish the chances of a new invasion, the study is now to weaken them by all possible means.

With this large proportion of the male population condemned to celibacy, M. Huc gives us the following reasons for his thinking that polygamy, under all the circumstances, is the best thing for the Mongol Tartars.[2] It seems generally to have existed in the pastoral and nomadic state.

---

[1] This is a distinguishing term for the laity, who wear their black hair, while the Lamas shave the whole head.

[2] M. Huc is here treating of the Mongol Tartars ; not of the Thibetians. Father Regis, in his memoir annexed to Duhalde, speaking of the polyandry of Thibet, states expressly that "the Tartars admit of no such irregularity." Turner, Moorcroft, and Skinner found a plurality of husbands common at Teshoo - Loomboo, Ladak, and on

"La polygamie, abolie par l'Evangile, et contraire en soi au bonheur et à la concorde de la famille, doit être considérée peut-être comme un bien pour les Tartares. Vu l'état actuel de leur société, elle est comme une barrière opposée au libertinage et à la corruption des mœurs. Le célibat étant imposé aux Lamas, et la classe de ceux qui se rasent la tête et vivent dans les lamaseries étant si nombreuse, si les filles ne trouvaient pas à se placer dans les familles en qualité d'épouses secondaires, il est facile de concevoir les désordres qui naîtraient de cette multiplicité de jeunes personnes sans soutien, et abandonnées à elles-mêmes."

The married state, however, is any thing but the conjugal, in the literal and derivative sense of the term. The husband can send back the lady to her parents without even assigning a reason. He is quits by the oxen, the sheep, and the horses which he was obliged to give as the marriage present; and the parents, it seems, can sell the same merchandise over again to a second bidder.

Our travellers in their progress westward had to cross the Yellow River more than once where it makes a bend northwards through the Great Wall and back again, enclosing in this curve an area of some three degrees square, the miserably waste and sandy country of the Ortous. Unhappily for the poor missionaries, this

---

the Himalayas. We found it too in Ceylon, as Cæsar had found it in Britain. Barbarous as the custom seems to us, and inexplicable by any supposed disproportion of the sexes, we perceive no more satisfactory explanation of its existence among the Thibetians, than among the Nairs in Malabar. There is no incompatibility, it is true, between polygamy and polyandry. The Nair, we suspect, does not limit himself to his coparcenary wife: and in the Mahabarat, although Draupadi is the wife of the Five Pandus brothers, some of them,—if not all,—and Arjuna especially, have several other wives. But, in case M. Huc found polyandry at Lhassa, in either form, the omission is unaccountable. It must have been as great a novelty to a European, as the rumour of Mr. Hodgson's "live unicorn."

ruthless and ungainly stream (which a late emperor
justly called "China's sorrow") was in its frequent
condition of overflow, and we have a pitiable description
of the miseries endured by themselves and their camels,
of all beasts the least adapted to deal with floods. The
waters of the Yellow River, pure and clear at their
source among the Thibet mountains, do not assume
their muddy tinge until they reach the alluvial tracts of
the Ortous, where they spread over thousands of acres
during the inundations, altogether concealing the bed
of the stream. Being from this point always nearly on
a level with the country through which they flow, this
defect of *encaissement* is the cause of disastrous
accidents, when the rapid stream is swollen by melting
snows near its source. The same velocity, which
charges the river thickly with comminuted soil, prevents its deposition on the passage until it reaches the
provinces of *Honan* and *Keangnan*, where the actual
bed of the river is now higher than a great portion of
the immense plain through which it runs. This evil
being continually aggravated by further depositions of
mud, a fearful catastrophe seems to overhang that
unfortunate region; at the same time that the constant
repair of the dikes taxes the ingenuity, while it
exhausts the treasury, of the Chinese government. Our
plenipotentiary offered to the minister Keying, a relation of the Emperor, the aid of English engineers in an
emergency where science could scarcely fail of beneficial results; but he shook his head, and said he dared
not even mention the subject.

The personal observations of M. Huc settle the question as to the real nature and amount of what is called the " Great Wall " towards the west :—

"We had occasion," he says, " to cross it at more than fifteen different points, and several times we travelled for whole days in the line of its direction, and kept it constantly in view. Often, in lieu of those double turreted walls which exist near Peking, we met with nothing more than a simple piece of masonry, and sometimes a modest rampart of earth. We even occasionally saw their famous wall reduced to its most simple expression, and composed solely of some heaped stones." [1]

It may be observed, with reference to the land frontiers of the Chinese empire on the west, that the authority of the Emperor, instead of abruptly encountering the hard outline of an entirely independent authority, is shadowed off by something of a blended jurisdiction. " Il existe dans le *Kan-sou*, et sur les frontières de la province de *Sse-Tchouan*, plusieurs peuplades qui se gouvernent ainsi elles-mêmes, et d'après des lois spéciales. Toutes portent la dénomination de *Tou-sse*, à laquelle on ajoute le nom de famille de leur chef ou souverain." (P. 36.) We find in another place that this prevails to the south-west, on the borders of Ava. " On the outskirts of the empire, towards the west, are a number of towns or stations,

---

[1] "Père Gerbillon informs us, that beyond the Yellow River, to its western extremity (or for full one-half of its total length), the wall is chiefly a mound of earth or gravel, about fifteen feet in height, with only occasional towers of brick. Marco Polo's silence concerning it may therefore be accounted for on the supposition that, having seen only this imperfect portion, he did not deem it an object of sufficient curiosity to deserve particular notice, without the necessity of imagining that he entered China to the south of the great barrier."—*The Chinese*, vol. i.

called *Too-sse*, or 'native jurisdictions,' where the
aborigines are more or less independent, and where
there is, in fact, a kind of divided authority, each
party being immediately subject to its own chiefs.
This is particularly true of the Lolós."—*The Chinese*,
vol. i.

It is an odd result of our war with China, that something of the same principle should have been established
by treaty at the Five Ports of trade on the opposite side
of the empire. British subjects are there entirely independent of the Chinese law, and governed by their
own consuls, who act under ordinances framed by the
governor and legislative council of Hongkong, confirmed by Her Majesty in Council. The inference from
the frequency of these " native jurisdictions " is, that
Chinese law, as administered towards foreigners, becomes intolerable ; so at least it proved at Canton.

It would be a pity to spoil the following passage by a
translation :—

" Notre aubergiste, un Chinois pur-sang, pour nous donner une preuve
de sa sagacité, nous demanda sans tergiverser si nous n'étions pas Anglais ;
et pour ne laisser aucun doute à sa question, il ajouta qu'il entendait par
Ing-kie-li les 'diables marins' qui faisaient la guerre à Canton.—'Non,
nous ne sommes pas Anglais ; nous autres, nous ne sommes diables
d'aucune façon, ni de mer, ni de terre.' Un désœuvré vint fort à propos
détruire le mauvais effet de cette interpellation intempestive.—'Toi, dit-il
à l'aubergiste, tu ne sais pas regarder les figures des hommes. Comment
oses-tu prétendre que ces gens là sont des *Yang-kouei-tse ?* Est-ce que
tu ne sais pas que ceux-ci ont les yeux tout bleus, et les cheveux tout
rouges ?—C'est juste, dit l'aubergiste, je n'avais pas bien réfléchi.'—'Non,
certainement, ajoutâmes-nous, tu n'avais pas bien réfléchi. Crois-tu que
des monstres marins pourraient, commes nous, vivre sur terre, et seraient
capables d'aller à cheval ?'—'Oh, c'est juste, c'est bien cela ; les *Ing-kie-li*,
dit-on, n'osent jamais quitter la mer ; aussitôt qu'ils montent à terre, ils

tremblent et meurent comme les poissons qu'on met hors de l'eau.' On parla beaucoup des mœurs et du caractère des ' diables marins,' et d'après tout ce qui en fut dit, il demeura demontré que nous n'étions pas du tout de la même race.''

These volumes contain the most detailed and complete account of the Lamas that we remember ever to have met with ; and they confirm, on the authority of these Romish priests themselves, the astonishing resemblance that exists between the external rites and institutions of Buddhism and those of the Church of Rome. Besides celibacy, fasting, and prayers for the dead, there are enshrined relics, holy water, incense, candles in broad day, rosaries of beads counted in praying, worship of saints, processions, and a monastic habit resembling that of the mendicant orders. Although our worthy missionaries call the images of Buddhism *idols*, and the Romish idols *images*, we do not think the distinction is worth much, and therefore may throw in this item with the rest ; the more especially as, on the summary principle of *inveniam viam aut faciam* the commandment against idol worship has been thrust bodily out of *their* Decalogue by the Romanists, as may be seen from any copy of the missal. It is remarkable that these very missionaries had an image made for their own adoration, from a European model, at a place on their journey where a huge image of Buddha had just been cast, and sent off to Lhassa. (Vol. i., p. 41.) Thus the object of their worship was a molten image, the work not only of men's but Pagan hands, employed indifferently for either Buddhism or Romanism.

It is at once curious, and an instructive lesson to unprejudiced minds, to observe that M. Huc, while he indulges in pleasantries at the expense of the Buddhists, entirely forgets how applicable his sarcasms are to his own side of the question. After describing an assembly in a college of Lamas, where the explanations given by the priests or professors on certain points of their religion proved as vague and incomprehensible as the thing to be explained, he adds, " On est, du reste, convaincu que la sublimité d'une doctrine est en raison directe de son obscurité et de son impénétrabilité." Let us only suppose M. Huc expounding to these Lamas the dogma of transubstantiation, and adding, in testimony of its truth, that St. Ignatius Loyola, with eyesight sharpened by faith, declared he actually *saw* the farinaceous substance changing itself into flesh. "Les hommes," observes our author in another place, "sont partout les mêmes!"

The jokes in which M. Huc indulges against the devotees and recluses of Buddhism are similar to what have been repeated a thousand times with reference to those of Romanism :—

"Ce jeune Lama de vingt-quatre ans était un gros gaillard bien membré, et dont la lourde et épaisse figure l'accusait de faire dans son étroit réduit une forte consommation de beurre. Nous ne pouvions jamais le voir mettre le nez à la porte de sa case, sans songer à ce rat de La Fontaine, qui par dévotion s'était retiré dans un fromage de Hollande."

The monasteries of the Lamas, resembling as they do in so many respects those of the Romanists, differ from them on some few points. The members are all subject to the same rule and the same discipline ; but they do not seem to live to the same extent in community, and exclusive rights of property prevail among them. Our missionaries passed some months in these establishments. Besides his Holiness the Supreme Lama at Lhassa, there are Grand Lamas, who derive their investiture from him, and descend from past ages in uninterrupted succession. With reference to one of these it is observed :—

"Si la personne du Grand Lama nous frappa peu, il n'en fut pas ainsi de son costume, qui était rigoureusement celui des évêques ; il portait sur sa tête une mitre jaune ; un long bâton en forme de crosse (*crosier*) était dans sa main droite ; et ses épaules étaient recouvertes d'un manteau en taffetas violet, retenu sur sa poitrine par une agraffe, et semblable en tout à une chape. Dans la suite, nous aurons à signaler de nombreux rapports entre le culte catholique et les cérémonies Lamanesques." (Vol. ii., p. 101.)

M. Huc afterwards recapitulates as follows :—

"La crosse, la mitre, la Dalmatique, la chape ou pluvial, que les grands Lamas portent en voyage, ou lorsqu'ils font quelque cérémonie hors du temple ; l'office à deux chœurs, la psalmodie, les exorcismes, l'encensoir soutenu par cinq chaînes, et pouvant s'ouvrir et se fermer à volonté ; les bénédictions données par les Lamas en étendant la main droite sur la tête des fidèles ; le chapelet, le célibat ecclésiastique, les retraites spirituelles, le culte des saints, les jeûnes, les processions, les litanies, l'eau bénite ; voilà autant de rapports que les Bouddhistes ont avec nous."

He might have added that they likewise have a goddess, whom they call *Tien-how*, literally *regina cœli*, "Queen of Heaven," but with a different legend.

Our author very naturally endeavours to persuade himself and his readers that by some process of *diablerie* these things have been borrowed from his own Church ; but why should we do such violence to the subject, when there is the much easier, more intelligible, and more straightforward course of deriving both from some-

thing older than either ; and remaining persuaded, as
most of us must have been long ago, that the Pagan
rites and Pontifex Maximus of the modern Rome represent, in outward fashion, the Paganism and Pontifex
Maximus of the ancient ? Strange to say, instead of
blinking the matter, a sort of parallel has often been
studiously preserved and paraded, as when the Pan-
theon, the temple of " all the gods," was consecrated
by Pope Boniface to " all the saints." Is it necessary
for us to compare the annual sprinkling of horses with
holy water to the like process at the Circensian games—
the costly gifts at Loretto to the like gifts at Delphi—
the nuns to the *virgines sanctæ* of old Rome—the shrines
of " Maria in triviis" to the like rural shrines of more
ancient idols—the flagellants (whose self-discipline
Sancho so dexterously mitigated in his own case) to the
practices of the priests of Isis ? In running the parallel
the only difficulty is where to stop. It is impossible to
look at the innumerable votive pictures and tablets which
conceal, without adorning, the walls and pillars of many
a church at Rome, and not to think of

" nam posse mederi
Picta docet templis multa tabella tuis." [1]

To instance a higher department of art—as the old
artist, in painting his Venus, is said to have combined
" each look that charm'd him in the fair of Greece," so
the Italian painters have sometimes immortalized the
features of their own mistresses in pictures of saints and
martyrs, intended to adorn churches.

---

[1] Middleton's Letter from Rome.

In its modern traits, as well as in its ancient, Buddhism maintains its resemblance to Romanism. Prodigies and miracles of constant occurrence come to the aid of the priesthood, and maintain their influence over the stupid multitude. Some of the instances adduced are palpable cases of ingenious jugglery; but M. Huc, with characteristic facility, believes in the miracle, while he attributes it to the agency of the devil :—

"Une philosophie purement humaine rejettera sans doute des faits semblables, ou les mettra sans balancer sur le compte des fourberies lamanesques. Pour nous, missionaires catholiques, nous croyons que le grand menteur qui trompa autrefois nos premiers parents dans le paradis terrestre, poursuit toujours dans le monde son système de mensonge ; celui qui avait la puissance de soutenir dans les airs Simon le Magicien, peut bien encore aujourd'hui parler aux hommes par la bouche d'un enfant, afin d'entretenir la foi de ses adorateurs."

Whatever Protestants may think and say of the means by which the Romish Church has maintained and extended its influence over the masses of mankind, it is impossible to deny the thorough knowledge of human nature on which all its measures have been calculated. The same causes which have aided it so long against the reforms of a purer faith are likely to aid it much longer ; and we really see very little chance of a change. The priestly array, the lighted taper, and the histrionic pantomime, are aided by smoking censers, graven or molten images, and all the paraphernalia by which so many temples of so many different religions have been before distinguished. We entirely agree with M. Huc, that the Romish Church has a fair field for proselytism in the vast regions where Buddhism at present prevails.

In external forms the transition is the easiest possible ;
and during his short residence at Lhassa he remarked,
—" Il nous semblait toujours que la beauté de nos
cérémonies eût agi puissamment sur ce peuple, si avide
de tout ce qui tient au *culte extérieur.*" [1]

If the new system cannot be made to supersede the
old, it may at least be grafted upon it, as experience has
already proved at our own colony of Ceylon ; for Romanism has sometimes been satisfied with a part, where the
whole was unattainable. In a recent work by Sir
Emerson Tennent, he observes of the early converts in
that island to the Romish Church, "there is no reason
to doubt that, along with the profession of the new
faith, the majority of them, like the Singalese of the
present day, cherished, with still closer attachment, the
superstitions of Buddhism ;" and he attributes the ease
of their external conversion to "the attractions of a

---

[1] In a book which had belonged was found this estimate, written on
to a Romish missionary in China the fly-leaf in Italian :—

" Numbers included under different known religions :—

Catholic Apostolic Church of Rome	139,000,000
Schismatic Greek Church	62,000,000
Protestant Church and its branches	59,000,000
Total of Christianity	260,000,000
Jews	4,000,000
Mahomedans	96,000,000
Hindoos	60,000,000
Buddhists	170,000,000
Confucianists and others	147,000,000
	737,000,000"

The number of Buddhists is Lhassa, and from the confines of
probably not over-rated, considering Siberia to Siam.
that they extend from Japan to

religion which, in point of pomp and magnificence, surpassed, *without materially differing from*, the pageantry and processions with which they were accustomed to celebrate the festivals of their own national worship." We may, however, charitably and reasonably suppose that the present emissaries of Rome would stop short of the complaisant conformity of their Jesuit predecessors, who, according to the Abbé Dubois, " conducted the images of the Virgin and Saviour on triumphal cars, imitated from the orgies of *Jaggernath*, and introduced the dancers of the Brahminical rites into the ceremonial of the Church."

After eighteen months of mingled residence and journeyings through the immense tract which intervenes between the neighbourhood of Peking and Lhassa, MM. Huc and Gabet reached the capital of Thibet in a very weary and exhausted state. The snowy range of mountains which formed the latter portion of their route was passed with a caravan, which is periodically collected as a protection against robbers; and the miseries and privations which they endured had well-nigh proved fatal to M. Gabet, though both travellers were in the prime of life—one thirty-two, and the other only thirty-seven. Scarcely settled in the lodging where they had installed themselves, troubles not less harassing, though of another kind, were to be encountered. " Après les peines physiques, c'était le tour des souffrances morales." As far as rested with the native government of the country, they might long have remained unmolested to exercise their zeal at the

head-quarters of Buddhism ; but obstacles arose in a
direction which they were hardly prepared to anticipate.
The minister of the Emperor of China resides at the
Court of the Supreme Lama, something like the
Austrian ambassador at Rome, but with a vastly greater
and more undivided influence. His spies were the first
to detect the intruders; and he succeeded at length,
notwithstanding the favour and kindness shown to them
by the temporal Regent of Thibet, in effecting their
expulsion from the country. The whole narrative is
extremely curious, and, in fact, gives a better insight
into the real relations existing between Peking and
Lhassa than any other source within our reach.

In addition to the numerous and striking analogies
which have been traced between the rites of the Lamas
and the Romish worship, M. Huc observes that " Rome
and Lhassa, the Pope and the Supreme Lama, might
also furnish points of resemblance full of interest."
The Thibetian government is altogether ecclesiastical.
The Talé or Dalé-Lama is its political and religious
head. When he dies, or, as the Buddhists say, trans-
migrates, his indestructible personification is continued
in a child, chosen by the great Lamas, distinguished as
Houtouktou, whose sacerdotal rank is inferior only to
that of the Grand Lama, and whom, therefore, we may
compare to the cardinals. The present Dalé-Lama is
only nine years of age, and his three predecessors had
none of them reached their majority; a circumstance
which seems to indicate foul play, and which was in
fact expressly attributed to treachery on the part of the

administration of Thibet, vested chiefly in the hands of a functionary styled Nomekhan, during the Grand Lama's minority.

A party at Lhassa opposed to this Nomekhan applied secretly, in the year 1844, for the interference of the Emperor of China, who is sufficiently ready to extend his influence on all occasions, in Thibet and elsewhere. The person selected to proceed as ambassador to Thibet, and overturn the ill-acquired power of the Nomekhan, was Keshen, who only about four years before had been ruined by the result of his negotiations at Canton : but whose energy and talents appear still to have been appreciated by the Emperor's government, and whose failure might possibly have met with palliation and excuse in the still worse failures of his successors in the South. On reaching Lhassa, Keshen took his measures in concert with those opposed to the Nome-kahn. That high functionary was arrested ; when, to avoid torture, he at length confessed to the guilt of having taken *three lives* from the Grand Lama, or, in other words, having caused his transmigration three times by violence. To this confession the seals of Keshen and the other parties were affixed, and it was transmitted by a special courier to Peking.

" Trois mois après, la capitale du Thibet était plongée dans une affreuse agitation ; on voyait placardé au grand portail du palais du Nomekhan, et dans les rues principales de la ville, un édit impérial en trois langues sur papier jaune, et avec des bordures représentant les dragons ailés. Après de hautes considérations sur les devoirs des rois et des souverains grands et petits ; après avoir exhorté les potentats, les monarques, les princes, les magistrats, et les peuples des quatre mers à marcher dans les sentiers de la justice et de la vertu, sous peine d'encourir la colère du ciel et l'indignation du grand Khan, l'Empéreur rappelait les crimes du Nomekhan, et le condamnait à un exil perpétuel sur les bords du Sakhalien-oula, au fond de la Mantchourie. A la fin était la formule d'usage : *qu'on tremble, et qu'on obéisse !* "

Such an unusual sight as this Imperial edict on the gates of their governor excited a general insurrection among the Thibetians of Lhassa. At half a league's distance is a College of Lamas, composed of some thousands. These armed themselves at random, and came down like an avalanche, denouncing death to Keshen and the Chinese. They carried by assault the residence of the ambassador, who, however, was not to be found. They next attacked those who had acted with him, and sacrificed more than one to their fury. They released the condemned Nomekhan, who, however, had not the spirit to avail himself of the occasion. "Il avait" (says M. Huc) "la lâche énergie d'un assassin, et non l'audace d'un séditieux."

The next morning, the Lamas were again agitated like a hive of bees, and again swarmed down upon Lhassa. But Keshen had profited by the interval, and his measures were taken. A formidable array of Chinese and Thibetian troops barred their passage ; and the Lamas, whose trade was not fighting, betook themselves to their cells and their books, and were glad to avoid the consequences of their temerity in an immediate resumption of their clerical character. In a few days, the Nomekhan, who had thrown away his only chance, was on his way " comme un mouton " to Tartary—while Keshen, elated with his triumph, showed a disposition to extend the penalties to his reputed accomplices in guilt. The ministers of the local government, however, thought that Chinese influence had done enough, and the ambassador had the prudence to forbear. The new Nomekhan was selected from the Lamas of the greatest eminence in the country; but as the choice fell on a youth of only eighteen, a Regent was appointed in the person of the chief *kalon*, or minister. This individual soon showed that his first care was to provide barriers against the ambition and encroachments of the Chinese ambassador, who had so boldly taken advantage of the weakness of the Thibetian government to usurp its powers, and extend the pretensions of his master the Emperor.

Things were in this state on the arrival of our two missionaries, who, after some weeks of unmolested residence, began to flatter themselves that they might pass unobserved. They were one day seated at their lodging in conversation with a Lama well versed in Buddhistic learning, when a well-dressed Chinese suddenly made his appearance, and expressed a strong desire to inspect any merchandise they might have to dispose of. They in vain declared they were not merchants: he was not satisfied, and in the midst of the discussion arrived a second Chinese, and then a third; after which, the number of visitors was soon swelled to five, by the appearance of two Lamas in rich silk scarfs. They all joined in a multitude of questions, addressed to MM. Gabet and Huc, and their looks were directed on all sides, in a minute examination of the contents of the dwelling. They at length

took their leave, promising to return, and left our
missionaries in an uncomfortable state, justly thinking
that the pretended chance visit looked like a concerted
measure, and that their new friends had very much the
appearance of either spies or swindlers.

When dinner was over, two out of the late five re-
appeared, and at once announced that the Regent
desired to see the missionaries ; "and that young man,"
—said they, pointing to their faithful Tartar attendant
Samdadchiemba, who eyed them with no very friendly
looks—"he must come too." The authorities must be
obeyed, and they set out together towards the palace of
the Regent. On their arrival, they were conducted
through a court and passages, crowded with Thibetians
and Chinese, to a large room, at the end of which was
seated the Regent, with his legs crossed upon a thick
cushion covered with a tiger's skin. He was a man of
about fifty, stout, and remarkably fair, with a most
intelligent and benevolent countenance. The strangers
were invited to seat themselves on a bench covered with
red carpet to their right. We must give what follows
in the original :

"Aussitôt que nous fûmes assis, le Régent se mit à nous considérer
long-temps en silence, et avec une attention minutieuse. Il penchait sa
tête tantôt à droite, tantôt à gauche, et nous examinait d'une façon moitié
moqueuse, et moitié bienveillante. Cette espèce de pantomime nous parut
à la fin si drôle, que nous ne pûmes nous empêcher de rire. 'Bon! dîmes-
nous en Français, et à voix basse, ce monsieur paraît assez bon enfant ;
notre affaire ira bien.—Ah ! dit le Régent, d'un ton plein d'affabilité,
quel langage parlez-vous ? Je n'ai pas compris ce que vous avez dit.—
Nous parlons le langage de notre pays.—Voyons, répétez à haute voix ce
que vous avez prononcé tout bas.—Nous disions: 'Ce monsieur paraît assez
bon enfant.—Vous autres, comprenez-vous ce langage ?' ajouta-t-il, en se

tournant vers ceux qui se tenaient debout derrière lui. Ils s'inclinèrent tous ensemble, et répondirent qu'ils ne comprenaient pas. ' Vous voyez, personne ici n'entend le langage de votre pays ; traduisez vos paroles en Thibétain.' Nous disions que, dans la physionomie du premier Kalon, il y avait beaucoup de bonté. — ' Ah ! oui, vous trouvez que j'ai de la bonté ? Cependant, je suis très-méchant. N'est ce pas que je suis tres-méchant ? ' demanda-t-il à ses gens. Ceux-ci se mirent à sourire, et ne repondirent pas. ' Vous avez raison, continua le Régent, je suis bon, car la bonté est le devoir d'un Kalon. Je dois être bon envers mon peuple, et aussi envers les étrangers.' "

This good-natured functionary assured the missionaries that he had sent for them merely in consequence of the contradictory reports in circulation, and without the least wish to molest them. After having found, to his surprise, that they could express themselves in the written characters of China, Tartary, and Thibet, and having satisfied himself as to the nature of their pursuits, he informed them that the Chinese resident was himself going to question them. He advised that they should frankly state their history, and added that they might depend upon his protection, for it was himself who governed the country. As he took his departure, the noise of the gong announced the approach of Keshen. The experience of our travellers made them anticipate a less agreeable interview in this quarter; but they screwed their courage up to the sticking place, determined that, as Christians, as missionaries, and as Frenchmen, they would not kneel to any body; and they bade their squire and neophyte *Samdadchiemba* confess his faith, if the occasion should require. The portrait of the celebrated mandarin must be given at full length.

"*Kichan*, quoique âgé d'une soixantaine d'années, nous parut plein de force et de vigueur. Sa figure est, sans contredit, la plus noble, la plus gracieuse et la plus spirituelle que nous ayons jamais rencontrée parmi les Chinois. Aussitôt que nous lui eûmes tiré notre chapeau, en lui faisant une courbette de la meilleure façon qu'il nous fût possible. 'C'est bien, c'est bien, nous dit-il, suivez vos usages ; on m'a dit que vous parlez correctement le langage de Péking : je désire causer un instant avec vous.— Nous commettons beaucoup de fautes en parlant, mais ta merveilleuse intelligence saura suppléer à l'obscurité de notre parole.—En vérité, voilà du pur Pékinois ! Vous autres Français, vous avez une grande facilité pour toutes les sciences : Vous êtes Français, n'est-ce-pas ?—Oui, nous sommes Français.—Oh ! je connais les Français ; autrefois il y en avait beaucoup à Péking, j'en voyais quelques-uns.—Tu as dû en connaître aussi à Canton, quand tu étais commissaire impérial.' —Ce souvenir fit froncer le sourcil à notre juge ; il puisa dans sa tabatière une abondante prise de tabac,[1] et la renifla de très mauvaise humeur.—' Oui, c'est vrai, j'ai vu beaucoup d'Européens à Canton. Vous êtes de la religion du Seigneur du Ciel, n'est-ce pas ?—Certainement ; nous sommes même prédicateurs de cette religion. — Je le sais, je le sais ; vous êtes, sans doute, venus ici pour prêcher cette religion?—Nous n'avons pas d'autre but. —Avez-vous déjà parcouru un grand nombre de pays ?—Nous avons parcouru toute la Chine, toute la Tartarie, et maintenant nous voici dans la capitale du Thibet.—Chez qui avez-vous logé quand vous étiez en Chine ?—Nous ne répondons pas à des questions de ce genre.—Et si je vous le commande ?— Nous ne pourrons pas obéir.' (Ici le juge dépité frappa un rude coup de poing sur la table.)—' Tu sais, lui dîmes-nous, que les Chrétiens n'ont pas peur ; pourquoi donc chercher à nous intimider ?—Où avez-vous appris le Chinois?—En Chine.—Dans quel endroit ?—Un peu partout.—Et le Tartare, le savez-vous ? Où l'avez-vous appris ?—En Mongolie, dans la terre des herbes.' "

The firm bearing of MM. Huc and Gabet was properly respected by Keshen, who, however, did not treat with the same ceremony their Tartar attendant *Samdadchiemba*, on finding he was a subject of China. He ordered him peremptorily to kneel, and in that attitude

---

[1] The Chinese generally take snuff out of a small bottle, but Keshen probably required larger supplies, and had a silver box or vessel at his side — " vase en argent."

obtained from him his history, which might have gone
far to compromise the unfortunate squire, but for his
connection with the two missionaries. Keshen's character appears to considerable advantage throughout this
narrative. Encroaching and overbearing towards the
Thibetian government, according to his supposed duty
to his sovereign, his personal demeanour to the two
travellers proved his due appreciation of the European
character, no doubt the result of his experience at
Canton. The lateness of the hour put an end to the
audience, and our missionaries had an immediate interview, followed by a supper, with their kind friend the
Regent, whose solicitude may fairly be attributed as
much to his jealousy of the Chinese resident as his
sympathy for the strangers. At this interview appeared
as interpreter, on account of his knowledge of the
Chinese language (the medium most familiar to the
missionaries), a certain Mahomedan chief of the Mus-
sulmans of Cashmere, resident at Lhassa. This little
incident shows our increased vicinity to the Chinese
empire, since Gholab Singh, ruler of Cashmere, became
our tributary, and bound himself in the treaty with
Lord Hardinge to transmit annually a dozen fine shawls,
and a certain number of shawl goats, in acknowledgment
of British supremacy.

The greatest cause of anxiety to the Regent, and the
circumstance most likely to compromise the missionaries, proved to be the supposed possession of maps of
the country, constructed by themselves. It would
seem, according to our author, that this fear originated

since the visit of our countryman Moorcroft,[1] who, *according to the Thibetians*, introduced himself at Lhassa as a native of Cashmere. They stated that, after a residence of some years, he took his departure, but was murdered on his way to Ladak. Among his effects were a number of maps and designs which he had executed during his stay in this country; and hence the fear of map-makers. The truth, however, is, that this fear has been of long standing, in China at least, where the common notion of an Englishman is that of a *bipes implumis* who goes about making maps of the country, with an express view to future conquest. Keying, the most liberal Chinese we have ever had to deal with, was in a perpetual fidget about the coast survey, carried on since the peace by that able officer, Captain Collinson, between Hongkong and Shanghae, and plagued H.M.'s plenipotentiary incessantly on the subject. It was useless to protest that nothing but the safety of our traders was in view; that the commercial treaty was altogether futile without the safe navigation of the seas by our merchant vessels; and it became necessary at once to cut the matter short by saying that the commanders of H.M.'s ships must obey any orders they received from their government in the prosecution of their lawful business.

[1] The time and place of Moorcroft's death near Balkh, as related by Professor Wilson, have been confirmed through repeated notices gathered by Barnes and others during our occupation of Cabul and the adjacent countries, and there is no doubt of the fact. Moorcroft's residence for twelve years, from 1826 to 1838, at Lhassa, without being heard of, directly or indirectly, by any European, whether in India, Nepaul, China, or Russia, is incredible on the face of it.

Maps of the country our missionaries had, but they were not autograph, nor even manuscript. A grand scrutiny took place before Keshen :—

"'We are fortunate,' said the travellers to the Chinese Minister, 'to find you here. In your absence it might have been impossible to convince the authorities of Thibet that we did not construct these maps ourselves ; but to a person of your information—to one so well acquainted with European matters—it is easy to perceive that these maps are not our work.' Keshen appeared greatly flattered by the compliment.—'It is evident at once,' said he, 'that these are printed maps. Look,' he added to the Regent, 'the maps, instead of being made by these persons, were printed in the country of France. You could not perceive that ; but I have been long accustomed to distinguish the various objects which come from the west.'"

Solvuntur risu tabulæ.—This incident was of more use to the missionaries, and relieved them more completely from the cloud which had hung over them, than anything else that could have occurred. The only fear and anxiety of the Regent himself was effectually removed, and from being virtually prisoners, and their baggage under seal, they returned in a sort of ovation to their lodging. It did not seem unreasonable for them, under all the circumstances, to hope that they might remain unmolested in the country. This appeared still more probable after their friend the Regent had allowed them to take up their quarters in a house belonging to the Government, where they established a chapel, and where they were visited by both Thibetians and Chinese, some of whom manifested no disinclination towards the Romish worship. Enough has been shown to prove that, in external rites, there is not a great deal of difference ; and there are, besides, certain

circumstances which give the Papal emissaries great
practical advantages over Protestant missionaries.
Whatever may be the evils or scandals attending
celibacy in the Romish Church (and Dr. Dens' miscalled
" Theology" proves its dangers in the confessional), it
has been very useful to them in the case of foreign
missions, and in the exploration of untried regions or
new fields of action.   The very undertaking we are considering could never have been accomplished by Protestant clergymen encumbered with the " impedimenta"
of wives and families. When a missionary is nomi-
nated from England, the prospect of a provision, sup-
posing him to be single, generally induces him to
marry, and he fixes himself down, say at one of the five
ports of China, for perhaps his life, with the very
moderate prospect of converting the empire from a place
corresponding to one of our seaports. If he dies pre-
maturely, which is often the case, the funds which
sent him out become charged with the maintenance of
those whom he leaves behind, and we need only look
over the accounts of the Propagation Society to see that
a very considerable amount of their funds (most justly
and unavoidably, we admit,) are swallowed up annually
in this way.   •

The interval of prosperity now enjoyed by our travellers, but destined to be too soon interrupted, was varied
by some interesting and unreserved conversations with
Keshen. His Canton recollections seemed to haunt
him. " Kichan nous demanda des nouvelles de Palmerston ; s'il était toujours chargé des affaires

étrangères." He gave them a graphic and perfectly true description of the absolute power of the Chinese sovereign :—

" 'Notre Empereur nous dit, Voilà qui est blanc. Nous nous prosternons, et nous répondons, Oui, voilà qui est blanc. Il nous montre ensuite le même objet, et nous dit, Voilà qui est noir. Nous nous prosternons de nouveau et nous répondons, Oui, voilà qui est noir.—Mais enfin, si vous disiez qu'un objet ne saurait être à la fois blanc et noir ?—L'Empereur dirait peut-être à celui qui aurait ce courage, Tu as raison : mais en même temps il le ferait étrangler ou décapiter.' "

Keshen was a high authority on this subject, for he had been one of the Emperor's privy councillors.

M. Huc persuades himself, naturally enough, perhaps, that the Chinese resident in Lhassa became jealous of the progress made by himself and M. Gabet among the Thibetians, and therefore determined on bringing about their departure from the country ; but any Chinese functionary in his position would have deemed such a measure necessary, and a mere act of prudence as concerned himself, considering he served a master who, as we have just seen, treats his servants in so truculent a style, even when they have reason on their side. Keshen had already been once condemned to death himself.

."Un jour l'ambassadeur *Kichan* nous fit appeler, et après maintes cajoleries il finit par nous dire que le Thibet était un pays trop froid, trop pauvre pour nous, et qu'il fallait songer à retourner dans notre royaume de France. Kichan nous adressa ces paroles avec une sorte de laisser-aller et d'abandon, comme s'il eût supposé qu'il n'y avait la moindre objection à faire. Nous lui demandâmes si, en parlant ainsi, il entendait nous donner un conseil ou un ordre ?—'L'un et l'autre,' nous répondit-il froidement."

They in vain urged that they were not Chinese subjects and therefore disclaimed his assumed authority

over them in Thibet. The conference was abruptly
terminated by their being informed that they must prepare themselves to quit the country. They went at
once to their friend the Regent, who, in words at least,
seemed to impress them with the notion that he did not
consider their departure absolutely depended on the will
of the Chinese resident. The habitual insincerity of
Asiatics renders them very ready to say anything that
may be agreeable to their hearers, and their love of ease
makes them willing to avoid unpleasant discussions.
It is very probable that the Regent was jealous of
Keshen ; but we cannot go quite the length of imagining, with M. Huc, that a ready compliance with the
determination of the Chinese minister on the part of
himself and M. Gabet became necessary, "de peur
de compromettre le Régent, et de devenir, peut-être, la
cause de fâcheuses dissensions entre la Chine et le
Thibet." We are persuaded that whatever circumstances
may occur to occasion a war between Thibet and China,
it will not be for such a cause as this. M. Huc must
before now have become sensible that he equally mis-
calculated in another quarter. "Dans notre candeur,
nous imaginions que le gouvernement Français ne verrait
pas avec indifférence cette prétension inouïe de la
Chine, qui ose poursuivre de ses outrages le Christian-
isme et le nom Français jusque chez les peuples étrangers, et à plus de mille lieues loin de Péking." China
has long exercised the same sort of power (or influence)
in countries very far west of Lhassa, and therefore more
distant from Peking.

It was certainly a stipulation in 1845, between M. de Lagrené, the French minister, and Keying, that the Romish religion should no longer be subject to persecution in China; and Sir John Davis lost no time in obtaining for Protestants whatever privileges were to be accorded to Romanists. In 1847, however, two Romish bishops *in partibus* were found in the interior, and immediately sent off to the coast, whence they found their way to Hongkong, indignant at what seemed to them so direct a violation of treaties. The Chinese government declared that the privileges in question were only intended for the Five Ports where Europeans were permitted to reside, and that they did not extend to admitting the teachers of Christianity into the interior.

We altogether concur with M. Huc on one point. If the two missionaries were to quit Lhassa, they might at least have been allowed to leave it in the readiest and easiest way. Within three weeks' journey was the frontier of Bengal, whence it was their wish to proceed to Calcutta. But no—Chinese fears and jealousies had decreed otherwise. The same absurd precaution which had caused certain emissaries from Russia to be conducted by a roundabout course from Kiachta to Peking, doomed our poor missionaries to *travail* from Lhassa through Alpine passes to the frontier of China, and from thence to Canton—a weary course of about eight months. They protested in vain, and declared that they would denounce this cruel measure to the French government. Keshen was inflexible, observing that ho must remember what was expected of him by the Emperor, and take care of his own head.

A good escort, however, was provided, and every care taken for the welfare of our travellers. A mandarin of respectable military rank, and fifteen Chinese soldiers, were charged with their safe conduct by Keshen in person, who, moreover, in a most edifying oration, recorded by M. Huc, pointed out their respective duties; and truly the undertaking before them was not a light one, as the description of the journey to the Chinese frontier (where the present work concludes) will easily show. In this almost impassable tract of country we may discover the real cause of the separation, for so many ages, of China from the Western world; for mountains of nearly the same Alpine character extend all the way from Tartary southwards to Yunnan and the frontiers of the Burmese Empire. The hardships of the present journey, undertaken under all possible advantages, killed no less than three mandarins, that is, their conductor and two others who joined them on the route. We must observe, however, that the former had been invalided from his duties on account of swelled legs and other, probably dropsical, symptoms, brought on by the abuse of stimulating liquors. We must give our author's description of this mandarin's separation from his Thibetian wife, as it is a specimen of M. Huc's style:—

"Avant de monter à cheval, une Thibétaine vigoureusement membrée et assez proprement vêtue se presenta : c'était la femme de Ly-kouo-ngan. Il l'avait épousée depuis six ans, et il allait l'abandonner pour toujours. Ces deux conjugales moitiés ne devant plus se revoir, il était bien juste

qu'au moment d'une si déchirante séparation, il y eut quelques mots
d'adieu. La chose se fit en publique, et de la manière suivante.—'Voilà
que nous partons, dit le mari ; toi, demeure ici, assise en paix dans ta
chambre.—Va-t-en tout doucement, répondit l'épouse ; va-t-en tout doucement, et prends bien garde aux enflures de tes jambes. Elle mit ensuite
une main devant ses yeux, comme pour faire croire qu'elle pleurait.—Tiens,
dit le Pacificateur des royaumes [1] en se tournant vers nous ; elles sont
drôles ces femmes Thibétaines ; je lui laisse une maison solidement bâtie,
et puis une foule de meubles presque tout neufs, et voilà qu'elle s'avise de
pleurer ! Est-ce qu'elle n'est pas contente comme cela ?'—Après ces adieux
si pleins d'onction et de tendresse, tout le monde monta à cheval."

One word more about Keshen. A most striking
trait of Chinese character is recorded by M. Huc, just
as he is on the point of departure. We have seen the
circumstances under which our missionaries took leave
of the imperial representative at Lhassa. Whatever
he might think or say on the occasion, *they*, at least,
had just cause to consider themselves treated by him
with unnecessary harshness ; if not for their removal
from Thibet, at least for their removal by the way of
China, instead of Bengal. Notwithstanding all this,
he drew them aside at their last interview, and said,
confidentially,—" ' I shall soon be on the way to China
myself ; that I may not be overcharged with effects on
my departure, I send two large chests by this opportunity ; they are covered with Thibet[2] cowskins' (showing us at the same time how they were lettered) ; ' I
recommend these two cases to your special care. When
you reach the relays at night, let them be deposited in
your sleeping apartment ; and when you arrive at the
capital of *Sse-chuen* province, deliver them to the care

---

[1] A play on his Chinese name. *poil*, figured in Turner's embassy.
[2] The Yak of Thibet, *bœuf à long*

of the viceroy.'" Thus, when a Chinese officer, a
countryman and nominee of his own, was going the
same journey, he preferred entrusting this treasure (for
such no doubt it was) to two poor European missionaries, whom he had injured, rather than to a Chinese
mandarin of respectable station, who was, in a great
measure, his own dependent. He had often said that
he admired and respected the European probity, and
this was a practical proof of it. M. Huc very justly
adds,—" Cette marque de confiance nous fit plaisir :
c'était un homage rendu à la probité des Chrétiens, et
en même temps une satire bien amère du caractère
Chinois."

Some time after Keshen's disgrace, there appeared
at Hongkong the copy of a Peking gazette, which
detailed the circumstances of his sentence, and gave
the amount of his registered property. The two
ministers commissioned on the occasion reported that
they found in his house, or at least in his possession,
682 Chinese pounds of gold, being about 14,560 English ounces; but of silver the enormous amount was
17,940,000 taels, which is more than six millions
sterling, or as nearly as possible the whole amount of
indemnity paid to England on account of the war,
including the ransom of Canton. Keshen might thus
truly be said to have " paid for the war." But, as if
this were not enough, his women were sold by auction
(Mr. Robins never had such an opportunity), and when
he reached the capital from Canton, he was without the
necessaries of life, though the emperor soon packed

him off to Elee, the Celestial Siberia.[1] After all this, it was rather cool, when his services were wanted, to appoint him resident at Lhassa; where, however, he soon contrived to do something towards repairing his broken fortunes, by helping himself to the gold and precious stones in which Thibet abounds. The two chests in charge of the missionaries were, no doubt, an instalment of his remittances to China; and he is now viceroy of the province of *Sse-chuen* (whither he sent the chests), one of the largest of the empire, being equal in area to all France. This strange history is not unlike that of many a minister of the Celestial Empire.[2]

Our missionaries make no pretension to learning; and are credulous in proportion. But their notices of what they saw are curious, and, we believe, truthful. We will conclude with two very extraordinary Thibetian customs, which we do not remember in Turner: though it must be observed that, while they did not reach Ladak or the Indian frontier, neither did Turner reach Lhassa or the Chinese.

"Les femmes Thibétaines se soumettent dans leur toilette à un usage, ou plutôt à une règle incroyable, et sans doute unique dans le monde. Avant de sortir de leur maisons, elles se frottent le visage avec une espèce

---

[1] M. Huc has the true version of the story. "L'Empereur, dans sa paternelle mansuétude, lui fit grâce de sa vie, et se contenta de le dégrader de tous ses titres, de lui retirer toutes ses décorations, de confisquer ses biens, de raser sa maison, de faire vendre ses femmes à l'encan, et de l'envoyer en exile au fond de la Tartarie."

[2] The unfortunate Keying, who negotiated the Treaty of Nanking, being sent in 1858 to stop, by negotiation, if possible, the progress of Lord Elgin, and having failed, was ordered to put himself to death, which he did, being upwards of 70 years of age.

de vernis noir et gluant, assez semblable à de la confiture de raisin. Comme elles ont pour but de se rendre laides et hideuses, elles répandent sur leur face ce fard dégoûtant à tort et à travers, et se barbouillent de manière à ne plus ressembler à des créatures humaines."

It is certainly something altogether new to find any race of women with the ambition " de se rendre laides et hideuses," but it must be an amazing simplification of the business of the toilet. The only wonder is that such a custom was ever submitted to, when, as M. Huc states, a certain Nomekhan, or Lama-king of the country, imposed it on the female part of the community, as a corrective of their morals and a protection to their virtue.

" Afin d'arrêter les progrès d'une license qui était devenu presque générale, le Nomekhan publia un édit, par lequel il était defendu aux femmes de paraître en public, à moins de se barbouiller la figure de la façon que nous avons déjà dite. De hautes considérations morales et religieuses motivaient cette loi étrange, et menaçaient les réfractaires des peines les plus sévères, et surtout de la colère et de l'indignation de Bouddha."

Nothing but a hierarchy, or rather, a nation of priests, could ever have succeeded in so monstrous a scheme of moral or religious discipline, more unnatural than the nunneries of Romanism. " One need not sure look frightful, *though* one's dead."

The second strange custom is a Thibetian salutation of respect, more absurd even than the " nose-rubbing," with which the Esquimaux greet their friends. M. Huc describes it by the terms " tirer la langue," which can only mean " putting out the tongue." We have read that the New Zealanders have a habit of expressing their hatred or defiance of their enemies by the same elegant gesture, and for such a purpose it might seem sufficiently significant and appropriate among savages : but how a people, at least semi-civilized, like the Thibetians, could ever have fallen upon such a mode of signifying *respect*, is altogether marvellous. It goes far at least to prove the purely conventional nature of all such signs, when the very *opposite* movements have been adopted by different nations to denote the same thing. If to uncover the head be, in Europe, a mark of respect, it is precisely the reverse in China : and though to salute with either the right or left hand be a nearly indifferent matter among us, a salutation with the left is so deadly an insult with Mahomedans in the East, as to have been instantly answered with a stab or a shot. For this reason, the native commissioned officers of our Indian army, in ·giving the military salute, confined it to the sword held in the right hand, and did not at the same time raise the left hand to the forehead.

Since the ruler of the Valley of Cashmere has become a tributary to the British crown, circumstances must occasionally bring us into contact with the Chinese government through Thibet. From the first conclusion of the treaty between Gholab Singh and the Governor-General of India, Lord Hardinge, with the foresight of a statesman, turned his attention to the accomplishment of two most desirable objects : first, the exact ascertainment and definition of the boundaries between Cashmere and the Ladak territory ; and secondly, the continuation of the same trade between the territory now dependent on the British government, and Ladak,

as had been before established by treaty between Cashmere and Ladak. We found, in fact, such a treaty
existing, by which tea[1] and shawl-wool were to be
transmitted to Cashmere and the Punjab by the Ladak
road ; and persons proceeding from Ladak to China, or
from China to Ladak, were not to be obstructed on the
way. That no means might be left untried, Lord
Hardinge engaged the services of H.M.'s plenipotentiary
in China, to communicate with the minister of the
Emperor, Keying, on the subject, and obtain, if possible, the appointment of Chinese or Thibetian commissioners to meet our own on the new frontier of
India. The land distances to be traversed in negotiation were enormous. From Canton to Peking was
1,200 miles, and from Peking to our frontier more than
2,000. Various and Protean were the shifts and changes
by which Keying, in Chinese fashion, endeavoured,
to elude all concern or responsibility in the matter.
Among others was this highly ungeographical objection : " The trading with Thibet would not be in conformity with the maritime treaty, as it is not included
in the Five Ports." When convinced of the real nature
of this *non-sequitur*, Keying admitted that the traders
on the Indian frontier might carry on a commerce
entirely distinct from that of the English merchants,
who repair to the Five Ports of China ; and he engaged
" faithfully to transmit to his sovereign the whole tenor

---

[1] Our manufactory of tea in
Kumaon is so promising, that we
may one day supply it to Thibet
and Chinese Tartary, where the
consumption is very large.

of the correspondence." He would hardly fail to do so, being aware that all Lord Hardinge's communications must at last reach Peking through Thibet, and betray any concealment of the subject. Three commissioners were appointed by Lord Hardinge in 1847, to enter the Thibetian territory, and endeavour to settle the frontier boundaries, if possible. Other objects were combined with the principal one. Lieutenant Strachey, one of the commissioners, was instructed to follow up his previous researches in Ngari, and penetrate through Gurdokh to the Lake Manasarowar, and so eastward, as far as practicable, through Darjeeling or Bhotan to the British provinces. That officer has printed an interesting narrative of his first journey, in 1846, proving the rigours of those Alpine regions to be precisely corresponding to the experience of MM. Huc and Gabet.

III.

THE RISE AND PROGRESS OF CHINESE LITERATURE IN ENGLAND,

DURING THE FIRST HALF OF THE PRESENT CENTURY.

CHINESE literature among us is almost entirely the growth of the present century. In the arrangement of the embassy of Earl Macartney, at the close of the last, not an Englishman could be found who knew anything of the language; and, when that nobleman was appointed to proceed to Peking, we were somewhat discreditably reduced to the necessity of engaging the services of two Romish priests to aid the important objects of the mission in the quality of interpreters. Sir John Barrow observed, with reference to that embassy, that its "intercourse and communications were committed to the timidity and ignorance of two native Chinese missionaries, who had been educated in the College de Propaganda Fide" at Rome. Then it was that the advisability of remedying this state of ignorance became first apparent. The English are not often disposed to waste their time and energies on anything that does not offer a fair prospect of advantage in some way or other; but when once they begin the progress is commonly rapid. Sir George Staunton, at that time a boy of twelve years of age, and attached to the mission as page to the ambassador, was judiciously devoted to the acquisition of that "great unknown," the Chinese language. There never was a stronger instance of the *omne ignotum pro mirifico.* It was then supposed that every separate character stood apart, independent and *per se*, and had to be committed to memory without any associating link to aid its retention. This absurd assumption of course repelled and revolted all approaches even to the threshold. Time and knowledge dispelled the delusion, and young Staunton made such progress in the course of a very few years as led to his obtaining a nomination to the East India Company's Service in China, at that time considered a certain and rapid road to fortune, and having then in its ranks one or two scions of the house of Baring.

The first fruit of Sir George Staunton's labours was a translation of the Penal Code of China, published in 1810. This system of criminal law received a high meed of praise from no less a judge than Sir James Mackintosh, who, in his critique in the *Edinburgh Review*, pronounced it to be well adapted to the existing condition of the Chinese people—the true test of the fitness of all laws. When Hongkong fell to us by conquest as a crown colony, I found no better way of governing the Chinese population (by far the majority) than by the "Penal Code," a copy of which always lay before the judge when Chinese were concerned. Every village was placed under the charge of its elders, who incurred considerable responsibility on account of those under their control.

The practical importance of the language being now duly estimated, another labourer appeared in the person of Morrison, who proceeded as missionary to China about the year 1808, and was soon engaged in the service of the East India Company as interpreter, remaining under their liberal patronage until his death in 1834. The quiet and leisure which this afforded him were favourable to study, and he improved his opportunities to the production of works calculated to teach the language, and therefore most wanted at the time. Some useful dialogues and a grammar were the forerunners of his chief work, the Dictionary; but the Grammar was undertaken too soon, consisting of phrases more English than Chinese in construction, and has been since far surpassed by the Grammar of Rémusat, which owed much to the " *Notitia Linguæ Sinicæ*" of Prémare, then a MS. in the King of France's library, but since printed. The Dictionary could not have been executed but by the liberal aid of the East India Company, who from first to last expended on it some ten thousand pounds, between its commencement in 1817 and its completion in 1823. All the characters had to be expressly cut in metal, and when the Dictionary was concluded this valuable fount remained in China to print numerous other works; above all, the " Chinese Repository," in twenty volumes.

The Dictionary of Dr. Morrison still remains as the greatest monument of literary labour in the cause of the Chinese language. There are six large quarto volumes. The first three are from the Dictionary of Kanghy, and follow the Chinese classification by the Roots. Had the plan been completed as it commenced, the work would have been an encyclopædia, but it proved too vast, and was curtailed. The two next volumes are according to the phonetic arrangement, or the *sounds* of the characters. The sixth and last volume is a not very copious dictionary, English and Chinese. I myself derived considerable occupation and advantage from correcting nearly the whole of the work for the press.

While this Dictionary was yet in embryo, or only begun to be compiled, I went out in 1813, more than half a century ago, to join the same station with Sir George Staunton; and it is now almost ludicrous to call to mind the meagre helps which then existed for learning Chinese.

Professor Wilson well described similar obstacles to our first students in Sanscrit. "The difficulty of acquiring the knowledge of a difficult language without any other appliances and means than grammars and lexicons in the language itself, and preceptors ignorant of English, and unfamiliar with our notions of elementary tuition, can be conceived by none but those who have been placed in similar circumstances."

The first step was to copy out the whole of Morrison's grammar in MS., and then the whole of his "Dialogues." The East India Company liberally presented me with two MS. dictionaries, one of them Latin and Chinese, and the other Chinese and Latin, both compiled by Romish missionaries, and copied by a Chinese convert. It so happened that in that very same year,

1813, a huge folio was printed at Paris by order of
Napoleon I., being the Dictionary of P. Basile de
Glemona. Notwithstanding its immense size, weighing
as it did, with the binding, between thirty and forty
pounds, the number of words was not very large; and
though it was duly sent out from England, I preferred
using the more handy dictionaries in MS. A new
labourer in the same field arrived about that time in the
person of the Rev. W. Milne. He soon attained to a
very considerable proficiency in the language, and not
long after printed a translation of the *Shing-yu*, or
Sacred Edict, which is, in fact, a complete exposition of
Chinese moral and political principles. Had Dr. Milne
long survived, he would have been a very distinguished
Sinologue, being a person of much talent and sound
judgment.

About the same time the Rev. Mr. Marshman, a
Baptist missionary at Serampore, turned his attention
to the same pursuit, and without the advantage of a
residence in the country acquired sufficient knowledge
to publish a very respectable work, called " *Claris
Sinica*," in one large quarto volume.

The embassy of Lord Amherst was despatched to
Peking in 1816, some twenty-three years after that of
Earl Macartney, and the impulse which had been com-
municated by the first mission became augmented by
the second. A new and practical turn was given to
Chinese studies. The translations which had been
made by the Romish missionaries of classical and
philosophical works were sufficient to prove that to

Europeans these possessed little real value. After acquiring the style of official papers, the new students turned their attention to a more attractive pursuit, the popular literature of the Chinese, as contained in their Drama, their Novels and Romances, and their Poetry. The French, meanwhile, were not idle. Without any material interests in China comparable to our own, M. Abel Rémusat had been appointed Professor of the Chinese language in Paris.

Having thus enumerated the earliest pioneers of this branch of Asiatic literature among us, we may proceed first to review the *philological* works which appeared in aid of Chinese studies, and then conclude with short critical notices of the *translations* which have served to elucidate and exemplify this entirely new field of oriental literature. The late Professor Wilson took an extensive retrospect of all branches except the Chinese, and he then took occasion to call on the late Sir George Staunton and myself to perform our part. I alone survive to respond, however imperfectly, to the call, and with reference to the professor's illustrious memory may add—

"Et fungar inani munere."

The first printed dictionary appeared at Paris in 1813, being the one already mentioned as issued under the order of Napoleon I. This gigantic monument of typography, in above eleven hundred folio pages, loses some of its usefulness from bulk alone, and has none of the Chinese character in the definitions; nothing except the words to be defined, and those in an

immense type ; while the dictionaries which have been
since printed in China abound with examples in the
original character.   The arrangement is under the
Roots, perhaps the best of all, though sometimes it is
phonetic even in native dictionaries.

There is a singular parallel to the first printed
Chinese dictionary in the first printed Sanscrit grammar.   " It formed," says Professor Wilson, " an immense volume, extending to a thousand quarto pages.
This is in great part ascribable to the size of the
Sanscrit types employed, which, in the first stages of
Sanscrit printing in India, were of unnecessarily gigantic dimensions."   It is thus that children are taught
their A B C.

In the article which follows this in the present volume
is a classification of all the Roots, and an account of
their threefold functions ; and having there provided a
systematic description of the construction of the language, we may here proceed to consider what has been
done to elucidate and display its contents, during the
eventful first half of the present century.   The dictionary next in importance to Dr. Morrison's, already
noticed, is that of Dr. Medhurst, completed in 1848.
It came in opportunely for our more intimate intercourse with China, and being in octavo is more handy
than its predecessor.   The accurate learning of the
author was a guarantee for its correctness, and it may
be fairly designated as a most important and valuable
work.   The first two volumes are Chinese and English,
and the two next English and Chinese.

A very valuable and useful dictionary by Padre Gon-salves, of the College of St. José, in Macao, was printed by him some time before his death in 1844. From being unfortunately composed in Portuguese, the language least known in Europe, this work has suffered much in value, but all those who have been able to avail themselves of its assistance have concurred in very highly praising it. The typography was what might have been expected from the backward state of the arts in a distant Portuguese colony; but the author's literary merits were acknowledged at Lisbon by his being enrolled as a member of the National Institute. This worthy man was driven by the colonial govern-ment of Macao, on account of his liberal tendencies, to take shelter on board the British merchant shipping in China, and he always spoke in grateful terms of the hospitality he there experienced, but complained of being obliged to comply with the odious English custom of washing himself, and wearing a clean shirt every day.

Among works compiled in aid of Chinese literature was one printed by Dr. Morrison in 1817, and called a "View of China for Philological Purposes." This was a curious title for a quarto volume on geography, chro-nology, &c., and the work was executed in a manner not less unusual, for the chronology is *inverted*, that is, beginning at the end, it ends at the beginning; as if one should compile a history of England, of which the narrative commenced with Queen Victoria and ended with the Norman Conquest. Our ordinary notions of the succession of time are turned completely upside down, and it was suggested that, in consulting such a work, one should adopt a corresponding posture, and stand on one's head.

I depart from the rule I had laid down, not to include in these notices the very latest aids to Chinese literature (though it is out of the first half-century by only four years), to mention the singular instance of a work which was published at the expense and with the care of a gentleman who had no professional call to study the language. The Hon. Henry Stanley edited and printed, in 1854, a most useful elementary work prepared long ago by a Frenchman in manuscript. It consists of 1500 of the most useful Chinese phrases, with a French and English translation, the latter substituted by the editor for the Latin in the manuscript, and as the sentences are of the most familiar kind they are an ample supply for common use. The characters are not printed, but taken by the new anastatic process from the writing of an Englishman with a common pen. It would have been better could types have been procured, but they are generally quite correct and easily decipherable; and this useful elementary work possesses the singularity of coming from one whose abstract and disinterested love of knowledge led him to assist others in a department where he himself had no personal interest whatever.

A very useful volume by Dr. Morrison was printed at Macao in 1816, called "Dialogues and Detached Sentences in the Chinese Language," a language which is rather to be acquired by examples than by rules of grammar. This work has become extremely scarce, from the greater portion of the impression being lost in the *Alceste* frigate, which was wrecked homeward bound with Lord Amherst, in 1817.

A collection of two hundred Chinese moral maxims appeared in 1823, the original characters being inserted, with a verbal and a free translation; and this, perhaps, is the best mode of teaching the grammatical structure of the language. It has been pretty generally admitted that the proverbs and moral maxims of China possess considerable merit. The intrinsic goodness of some Chinese apophthegms has been extolled, among many others, by no less an authority than Lord Brougham himself. With reference to one of these maxims, his Lordship observes, " It is an admirable precept, *to judge ourselves with the severity we apply to others, and to judge others as indulgently as we do ourselves.*" [1]

Our first object in England being naturally to increase our own acquaintance with the language, few attempts have as yet been made to prepare works for the instruction of the Chinese. In 1840, however, Mr. Thom, who afterwards became H.M.'s first consul at the new port of Ningpo, edited a translation into Chinese of Æsop's and other fables. Among the rest, this apologue from Horace :—

" Cervus equum pugnâ melior communibus herbis
    Pellebat, donec minor in certamine longo,
    Imploravit opes hominis, frænumque recepit ;
    Sed, postquam victor violens discessit ab hoste,
    Non equitem dorso, non frænum depulit ore."

___

[1] Polit. Philosophy, vol. i., p. 172.

Not the least useful part of Mr. Thom's work is a preface wherein much information is conveyed as to the grammar and writing of the language. As might have been expected, this book of fables, so new to the people of the Celestial Empire, took great hold of their imaginations. The mandarins, however, with the suspicion that always accompanies guilt, saw in the fable of the wolf and the lamb, and others like it, a disagreeable resemblance to their own treatment of the people, and became hostile. Our first war was just commencing, persecution and proscription of the English were the chief study of the government, and Mr. Thom's book was condemned; but he succeeded in completing it at some risk to himself. Mr. Thom was my own official subordinate in China at the time of his death in 1846, and I have not forgotten the regret which the loss of so much industry and talent in the public service occasioned to all who knew him.

The principal early aids to the study of Chinese have now been noticed, and as the purport of this paper does not extend beyond the first in point of *date*, it becomes superfluous to enumerate the later and better known results of a more extended range of inquiry among a much greater number of Sinologues. These are fully detailed in Professor Summers' preface to his " Handbook of the Chinese Language," printed at Oxford in 1862; the first work of the kind ever published at home, and in itself one of the most useful to students.

Our successful wars have entirely removed the barriers with which the native government formerly so long opposed all progress; and the growing exigencies of the Queen's service have given rise to many very able Sinologues, among whom the names of the late R. Morrison (son of the doctor), of Meadows, Medhurst, Wade, Parker, Lay, and Summers, figure conspicuously. Professor Summers, of King's College, London, has printed, as already noticed, a most useful handbook for beginners, containing a free use of the original character. He has also commenced a periodical called "The Chinese and Japanese Repository," which promises to supply the loss of the former "Chinese Repository," a valuable work, that will be noticed at the end of this paper.

China and Japan must now be treated in very near connection. Sir Rutherford Alcock observes that Japanese pictures have generally their titles attached in Chinese, and that to learn Japanese it is expedient, if not necessary, to commence with its prototype as the foundation. In Sir Rutherford's work I can often read the Japanese titles to the illustrations. The silver coin, called *itzebu*, is distinctly stamped with four Chinese characters.

Le premier pas qui coûte has long been surmounted, and it is perhaps desirable to place on record the difficulties and obstacles which beset the paths of the first explorers. In proof of the discouragement which opposed the acquisition of the language in the earliest times, we need only advert to the case of Mr. Flint, · who, with the very slight and imperfect knowledge that could be acquired towards the end of the last century, was long imprisoned by the Chinese Government, specifically on account of that knowledge, and the legitimate

uses to which he endeavoured to apply it. Our three
wars have changed all this. A large population in one
of our newest but most flourishing colonies, Hongkong,
necessitates the daily use of Chinese. We have a mint
there stamping coins with the Queen's head, and
Chinese characters on the obverse ; as well as postage
stamps so marked, which convey letters coastwise to
Peking, to the far extension of Sir Rowland Hill's fame.

Adverting next to the earlier translations from
Chinese literature, we may class them roughly under
these two heads :—I. Classical and historical, including
their sacred books. II. Belles-lettres, or drama,
poetry, romances and novels. Travels out of China
are of course few, and the little science they possess has
not attracted much notice. Their industrious arts, on
the other hand, might probably be investigated with considerable profit, now that we have such free access to
the interior.

The "Four Books" of Confucius, and the "Five
King," or canonical works, constitute, from the universal reverence paid to the great national teacher, a
species of sacred writings ; and they have, for this
reason, rather than their intrinsic merits, met with considerable notice in England and on the Continent.
The earlier Jesuits at Peking had naturally turned their
attention to these works, and Latin versions of the "Four
Books" were sent to Europe, but remained generally
unknown, except to the learned who could read them.

Confucius certainly influenced the opinions and des-
tinies of a larger portion of mankind than any other

human teacher. Nor is he now a mere *nominis umbra*, but substantially represented by lineal descendants in his native province—Shantung. No other family might presume to adopt, under pain of death, the sacred patronymic of *Koong*, the first syllable of Koong-foo-tse, or Confucius. The " descendants of the most holy teacher of antiquity," as they call him, have certain privileges, which the jealous government has taken care should (with his name) be exclusively monopolized. A lineal and undisputed descent of more than 2200 years may certainly be claimed as the oldest in the world; and it happened to myself to come into a sort of official collision with one of them when I was Her Majesty's representative in China. The treasurer of Canton, for the time being, was one of the sacred and privileged family of *Koong*, and I have preserved the envelope of his dispatch, bearing the much revered monosyllable.

The *Lun-yu*, or " Conversations " of Confucius, which I have in another place ventured to call the Chinese Boswell, is somewhat like the record of our English sage, as transmitted by his humble admirer. The *Ta-heo*, or " Study for Grown Persons," commencing with the government of one's self, deduces therefrom the government of a family, and thence extends the principle to the government of a state, and of the whole empire—which in Chinese estimate once meant the whole world, until we first disabused them of the error. The *Ta-heo* properly stands at the head of the " Four Books," and the next to it in ordinary sequence is *Choong-yoong*, the infallible medium or *juste milieu*, —ʽΗ μέσοτης ἐν πᾶσιν ἀσφαλεστερα.

The last of the "Four Books" is *Meng-tse*, the work of Mencius, the most eminent of the disciples of Confucius, and contains maxims of government and political economy much in advance of that early age, and far more in keeping with our modern notions than even the sayings of Confucius. I have in another place remarked some just observations of Mencius on the division of labour, and on the necessity for distinctions of social rank. "Those who labour with their minds (he says) rule ; those who labour with their bodies are ruled." The "Four Books" have during the first half of this century been more than once edited, in both English and French. The *Ta-heo*, or "School of Adults," was published so long ago as 1814, by Dr. Marshman, of Serampore, and is rendered more useful by the presence of the original text. The whole of the "Four Books" were published in English by Dr. Collie of Malacca in 1828. A more complete and elaborate edition than ever yet appeared is now in progress by Dr. Legge at Hong-kong, two volumes only out of seven being completed.

With the "Four Books" come the *Woo-king* or "Five Canonical Works," Confucius having been the author or compiler of all of them. For a detailed account of these I must refer to my work on China. The *Yě-king*, or "Book of Changes in Nature," having long ago been translated into Latin by Père Regis, was edited by Mohl, and published at Stuttgard in 1834. Mohl had before edited an older Latin translation of the *Shi-king*, or

"Book of Odes" in 1830. De Guignes had, as long ago as 1770, published his French edition of the *Shoo-king,* or "Historical Classic," and an English edition was printed by Dr. Medhurst, at Shanghae, in 1846, having the advantage of being coupled with the original text. The *Chun-tsieu,* a history of his own times by Confucius, has, I believe, never yet been wholly translated into a European language; and the *Le-ke,* or "Book of Rites and Ceremonies," was rendered into French, accompanied with the text, by the late M. Callery.

Three smaller and more modern works are associated with the above in the business of education, and in fact form its threshold. These are, 1. The *San-tse-king,* or "Trimetrical Classic," as it has been called since I adopted that name for it in a treatise on Chinese poetry and versification. 2. The *Tsien-tse wun,* or "Thousand Character Essay," and, 3. The *Seao-heo,* or "Youthful Study." These were all three translated by Dr. Bridgman and others. The first consists of the rudiments of knowledge in rhyming lines of three words each, calculated to help the memory. The second is an ingenious composition of one thousand different characters, forming sense together, and said to have blanched at once, from the difficulty of the task, the head of the composer. These have been lately printed in Paris by Professor Stanislas Julien, with translations in Latin and French. The third is, as its name imports, a rudimentary book for beginners.

All the foregoing works have of course less attraction for Europeans than literature of a lighter and more

F

popular kind : but as the more considerable ones constitute the basis of Chinese morals and politics, it would
be impossible to exclude them in a compendious survey,
or to deny them the first place in it. Their general
principles are inculcated in the " Sacred Instructions "
of the Emperor to the people, already mentioned as
having been translated by the late Dr. Milne from the
original. There is no better book for learning and com-
paring the two styles of Chinese composition. The work
consists of a text in the higher literary style, and a
commentary in a more diffuse and popular phraseology,
calculated for the masses. It is used as a kind of
sermon for the people. On the 1st and 15th of every
moon, one of the sixteen sections, under its proper
text, is publicly recited by the proper officer ; but this
may easily be supposed to have become a mere trite
formality, which it really is.

One of the most voluminous Chinese Histories,
Tung-kien-kang-mo, was translated as long ago as
1770 by the Jesuit Mailla at Peking, and printed at
Paris in twelve quarto volumes ; but the profit of
such a work was hardly commensurate with the labour,
and though in the course of so many years a good
deal of reference has been made to it, the work remains
little known except to Sinologues. The *San-kwŏ-che*,
which is rather a historical novel than a history, has
not been much noticed. An untranslated Latin version, in the possession of the Royal Asiatic Society, has
never been rendered into English. Thus it must ever be
with the internal annals of a nation hitherto segregated

from the rest of the world. The Buddhist religion having a connection with India, its history has excited more attention. M. Abel Rémusat translated the *Fŏ-kwŏ-ky*, or "Account of the Buddhist Countries," and the work was published in 1836, after his death. It is one of the most interesting notices of the country and the inhabitants of Eastern Asia extant, rendered especially curious as the production of a travelled Chinese. Something analogous on this score is the narrative of the Chinese Embassy to the Khan of the Tourgouth Tartars, translated by Sir George Staunton, and published in 1821. An embassy despatched by the Chinese government through Russian Tartary, was a rare occurrence, and the narrative loses nothing in interest from the way in which the ambassador himself has recorded it. M. Stanislas Julien in 1842 translated the Sacred Book of the Taou sect, or " Rationalists," called *Taou-tĕ-king*, or the " Scripture of the Way and of Virtue," by *Laou-tze*, their founder. The introduction by the translator does much to illustrate the tenets of this obscure sect. M. Julien has since translated a very entertaining book, also of the Taou sect, entitled *Kan-ying peen*, or the "Book of Rewards and Punishments," by *Tae shang*, or the "greatly exalted" author of the Taou philosophy, the above-mentioned *Laou-tze*. It is founded on the popular notion that every act committed by a man during his life has its reward or punishment, either in his own person or those of his descendants until the third and fourth generation. This might seem to exclude the notion of a future state, but there do occasionally occur the denunciations of a hell for the wicked.

The most favourable reception has perhaps been given to the lighter literature of China, or its belles lettres, comprising the Drama, Poetry, and Romances or Novels. The first specimen of their drama was given by Prémare, a Jesuit at Peking, already mentioned as author of the "*Notitia Linguæ Sinicæ.*" The "Orphan of Chaou" excited enough notice in Europe to become the groundwork of Voltaire's "Orphelin de la Chine." The second specimen, in order of date, was my translation of "The Heir in Old Age," in 1817. This play illustrates the importance which the Chinese attach to having a son to worship at the tombs of his family. A childless old man takes a second wife (or handmaid), with this object, and the jealousies and intrigues which arise on the birth of an heir make up the plot of the piece, at the same time that they display the domestic troubles which often naturally result from this oriental practice of having more than one partner, even in the subordinate position of the inferior wife. This specimen of the Chinese stage had the advantage of being edited, during my absence from England, by the late Sir John Barrow, of the Admiralty.

Six or eight translations of plays by different hands have since followed, and all have appeared in both French and English. The "Chalk Circle" was the version of M. Stanislas Julien, handsomely printed by the Oriental Translation Fund, as was also a second drama, called "The Sorrows of Hán." The story of

the "Chalk Circle" is virtually the same as the celebrated judgment of Solomon. Two women lay claim to
a child, and the judge declares it must belong to which-
ever shall succeed in dragging it out of the chalk circle,
but awards it at last to her who, from tenderness and
fear of injuring the child, fails to do so. M. Bazin
translated four or five other specimens of the Chinese
stage. Nearly all the above were selected from the
Yuen-jin-pĕ-choong, or "Hundred Plays of the Yuen,"
or Mongol dynasty. These in many respects resemble
the European drama, and are mostly divided into five
acts, or "breaks," as they call them.

In one of M. Bazin's translated plays a scene of
genuine humour occurs in the person of a miser, which,
as far as it goes, may fairly be compared with the
"Avare" of Molière.

One might not be prepared to find that the poetry of
such a language as that in question possessed, in common with others so differently constituted, the proper-
ties of accent, metrical numbers, a cæsural pause in
the longer verses, and terminal rhymes, and was, moreover, distinguished by what Bishop Lowth has elabo-
rately treated in reference to Hebrew poetry, under the
name of *parallelism*. Couplets are thus distinguished,
either by equivalence or antithesis of sense, or by an
exact correspondence in verbal construction. This constitutes the merit of those ornamental labels with which
the Chinese decorate their houses; for their characters
admit of an extent and variety of calligraphy to which
our few formal letters must of necessity be strangers,

with the addition of an epigrammatic sense heightens the value of such *mauvais dizains*, especially when they are the autographs and gifts of a friend. I have such labels, as well as inscribed fans, from the late Imperial Minister Keying, a relative of the Emperor, who knew that I should prize them more than things of greater intrinsic value. The Royal Asiatic Society did me the honour, in 1829, to print in their quarto Transactions[1] a treatise in which I endeavoured to exhaust the subject of the construction and literary character of Chinese poetry, and in the course of more than thirty years I have not found that I could add very much to the information therein contained.

There is rather a favourable specimen of poetry, with the original character added, in the eighth volume of the "Chinese Repository," p. 195. The subject of it is "Gathering Tea-leaves among the Hills" in spring time, and the young girl who is supposed to sing the ballad describes the scenery, the weather, her own dress, her feelings, &c., in the most natural and therefore pleasing manner.

It has been already observed that the poetry in question possesses the qualities of accent, measured numbers, and terminal rhymes, in common with other languages so differently constituted, and it is still more remarkable that they practise the somewhat refined amusement of what the French call *bouts-rimés*. A drawing on silk, in the Chinese style, was sent to me

---

[1] Vol. ii., p. 398.

by one of the captors of Peking, and I found on examination that it was a case of this description. The Emperor had given two or three of his favourite officers the *Yuen yun*, or "Original Rhymes," which they were to fill up on a prescribed subject. This subject was the *Heang-Shan*, or "Fragrant Hills," being the inner and more secluded portion of the park of the Summer Palace (which was burned down by our forces in 1860, in just, though bloodless, retribution for the murder of our countrymen), and, as it turned out, the birthplace of the reigning Emperor. The following account was given of it by an eyewitness :[1]—"Another collection of buildings, embosomed in trees, and girt round by a serpentine wall, which ran up the face of the hills, took a turn over their tops, and again descended to the plain. This was called *Heang-Shan*, or the 'Fragrant Hills,' and formed the fourth or innermost park of the Emperor. The arrangement of these Heang-Shan pleasure grounds was even more complete than that of the three before visited. The flights of stone steps leading from palace to palace, with the rural summer-houses, shady bowers, and delightful terraces, made the spot quite unique, and of a perfect loveliness all its own." A view of this place, as above described, forms the subject of the drawing on silk, which is stamped in red with the Emperor's private seal.

We come, lastly, to the lighter literature of romances and novels, on the subject of which I have always

---

[1] Swinhoe's Narrative.

agree with the following opinion by Professor Julien,
of the French Institute :—" Il me semble qu'avant de
traiter des questions de haute érudition, qui ne peuvent
être comprises et goûtées que d'un petit nombre de
personnes, il importe de traduire les ouvrages les plus
répandus qui peuvent faire comprendre l'histoire, les
religions, les mœurs, les usages, et la littérature des
Chinois." With similar sentiments, the late Professor
Rémusat undertook the translation of a novel, which
he styled " Les Deux Cousines," though that is not the
precise meaning of its Chinese title. The whole story
turns very much upon verse-making and *bouts-rimés*,
and is not a bad illustration of their notions of poetry
as an accomplishment, female as well as male. The
mere outline of a rather celebrated romance, called
Haou-kew-chuen, the history of the " Fortunate or
Well-assorted Union," had been published by Bishop
Percy, from a MS. sent from Canton, being translated
afterwards into French, and published at Lyons in
1766. On examining the original work, and observing
how little of its merits were apparent in this brief and
imperfect abstract, abounding as it did in the most palpable mistakes, a version of the whole was undertaken,
and printed by the Oriental Translation Committee
in 1829, being published in two volumes. Though
a most faithful description of Chinese manners in the
upper and more enlightened classes, there is nothing
in the plot to shock European sentiment; such, for
instance, as the hero espousing two wives, in the
ancient oriental, and modern occidental fashion among

the Mormons. M. Rémusat observes, in his preface (written in 1826) to the "Deux Cousines," "Un homme qui aime deux femmes à la fois est une sorte de monstre qu'on n'a jamais vu qu'au fond de l'Asie, et dont l'espèce est tout-a-fait inconnue dans l'Occident." He was little aware how soon events in North America would render his observations antiquated and inapplicable to the present time.

Mr. Wade, our Secretary of Legation at Peking, and a first-rate Chinese scholar, has taken advantage of his residence at the Chinese capital to print a larger and more correct edition of the original *Haou-kew-chuen* than ever has been seen before. His object is, that, for the use of students, it should accompany the translation, in two volumes, made thirty-five years ago; and the recognition, in such a quarter, of the general accuracy of the translation, is of course a source of satisfaction. Mr. Wade has opened an easy way to the Peking dialect by his " Book of Experiments," one of the most useful elementary works yet published.

" Blanche et Bleue, ou les Deux Couleuvres Fées," translated by M. Julien, is a curious specimen of a fairy tale, wherein two young females are transformed into serpents, and, after a long penance in that condition, are compensated at length for their sufferings by being restored to their original state. This is a tale of the *Taou* sect, or Rationalists. M. Pavie has translated seven tales, illustrative of the popular Chinese superstitions, under the title of "Choix de Contes et Nouvelles." Mr. Robert Thom, during the same state of persecution

under which he published his Chinese version of Æsop's
Fables, contrived to print, at Canton, during the
troubles of 1839, a translation from a short tale, containing the adventures of a talented heroine. He then
spoke feelingly of the degraded condition of Europeans
in China ; but, in three years from that time, was
appointed Her Majesty's Consul at one of the new ports,
under a state of things brought about by our successful
war, which completely revolutionized the old system of
exclusiveness and restraint.

Mr. Thom's Chinese version of Æsop's Fables had
been chiefly effected by the aid of an educated native,
and this translation from English into the native language was, not long after, followed by a native Chinese
named *Tsin-shen*, translating from his own language
into English a work called the "Travels of the Emperor Chingteh in Keang-nan." The story relates to
the commencement of the Ming, or Chinese dynasty,
which succeeded the Mongols. To any one who has
read the *San-kwŏ-che*, or "History of the Three
Kingdoms," this will appear to be an imitation, on a
reduced scale. The conclusion of the tale abounds in
descriptions of those strange magical practices to be
found in the older work, nor can anything more extravagant exist in the wildest Arabian fiction. The translation was revised and published by Dr. Legge of
Malacca in 1843.

In concluding this summary view of the principal
aids to the Chinese language, and the most considerable translated works which have marked its rise and

early progress, not only in this country but in France, it becomes impossible to pass in silence a most valuable and meritorious periodical, the " Chinese Repository," which occupied the twenty years between 1831 and 1850. Published at Canton in monthly numbers, by Dr. Bridgman, an American, this became the common receptacle for contributions from Chinese scholars of all countries ; while the font of Chinese types which had been made for Morrison's Dictionary rendered it easy to print a great deal in the original character. The fate of this valuable work, however, was to a considerable extent that of the Sibyl's books. One of those frequent fires which desolated Canton caused the destruction of the greater portion of the impression, and the value of the remaining parts has become, of course, enhanced in proportion. A very imperfect copy, minus several volumes, has been marked in a bookseller's catalogue at £20, but a few individuals, including myself, are fortunate enough to hold perfect and entire copies, the value of which, in this particular branch of literature, is not easily appreciable.

NOTE.—With reference to the observations at page 63, on the existing descendants of Confucius, the following notice by Gibbon has been found in his Autobiography, published by Lord Sheffield :—

" The family of Confucius is in my opinion the most illustrious in the world. After a painful ascent of eight or ten centuries, our barons and princes of Europe are lost in the darkness of the middle ages ; but in the vast equality of the empire of China the posterity of Confucius have maintained, above two thousand two hundred years, their peaceful honours and perpetual succession."—Miscellaneous Works, vol. i., p. 4.

IV.

THE ROOTS OF THE LANGUAGE,

WITH THEIR THREEFOLD USES.

(From the Proceedings of the Philological Society.)

IT is pretty generally known that, under 214 Roots or *radical and original* characters, the whole of the Chinese language is arranged in the dictionaries. It is not easy to overrate the importance of these roots, when we consider that they enter into the composition, and influence the meaning of every word in that language.

The late M. Abel Rémusat of Paris remarked, that in addition to their other uses (which will be presently noticed) these roots singly represent or express the leading objects or ideas that men have occasion to communicate in the infancy of their knowledge ; comprising within their number the heads of genera and classes in nature, and thus affording the elements and means of a philosophic system of arrangement. A fortunate instinct led the framers of the language, instead of forming characters altogether new and arbitrary, to express new objects or ideas by the ingenious combination of those elementary symbols which they already possessed. Thus among the roots we find *horse, dog, metal,* &c., and the addition of some other significant symbol, expressive of some peculiar property or characteristic, serves to designate the different *species* comprised under the different *genera,* as *horse-ass, horse-mule; dog-wolf, dog-fox; metal-iron, metal-silver;* the elementary or generic words, horse, dog, metal, being those under which the compounds are ranged in the dictionary.

The obvious analogy which this system (however imperfect in its details) bears to the principle of the Linnæan nomenclature led M. Rémusat to classify that portion of the 214 roots, consisting of only about thirty in all, which had reference to genera in the animal, vegetable, and mineral kingdoms. Whatever might be the results in a scientific point of view, and in regard to natural history only, this sort of classification appeared to me to possess considerable interest and utility on the score of general philology, and with a view to the particular study of the language in question. I have accordingly attempted to perform for the whole 214 roots what M. Rémusat did for that small portion to which he confined his attention. In so doing I have nearly retained M. Rémusat's classification under the heads of the three natural kingdoms, but extended the number to thirty-three roots ; and the following are, in the first place, the general heads under which the whole 214 roots seem most readily to arrange themselves :—

Classes.			Classes.
Human kind and its relations	14	Objects in early art . .	41
Mammalia	8	Numbers	5
Other animals . . .	7	Actions (verbs) . . .	37
Vegetables	13	Qualities (adjectives) . .	30
Minerals	5	Undefined	1
Parts of animals . . .	28		
Other objects in nature .	25		214

Whatever additional interest and importance our more intimate relations may now attach to the language of China on the score of utility alone, its very singular structure entitles it to attention as a part of the history of the human mind, and of philology in general. I have accordingly been tempted to extend this examination from the mere classification of the roots to a computation of the proportion in which each separate root enters into the construction of the whole language. The dictionary which was selected for this purpose contained about 11,600 words, the really useful and practical part of the language. The following tables exhibit each root, arranged under its own particular class, and numbered on the left (for facility of reference) according to its numerical order in all the dictionaries, by which it may be immediately found in the table of Morrison's Dictionary. The column of figures on the right shows the total number of compound words to be found under each root :—

Human Kind and its Relations.			*Mammalia.*	
No.	Compounds.	No.		Compounds.
9. Man	478	38. Woman . . .		243
10. (Another form) . .	24	39. Son		31
33. Scholar, sage . .	10	44. Corpse		39

No.	Compounds.
48. Workman . . .	7
49. Self	12
83. Family, kindred . .	3
88. Father	3
131. Minister, servant .	4
132. Self	5
158. Body, person .	158
194. Ghost, spirit .	25
93. Ox	54
94. Dog . . .	136
123. Sheep . . .	39
141. Tiger . . .	18
152. Hog . . .	33
187. Horse . . .	127
198. Deer . . .	23
208. Rat or mouse .	21

Other Animals.

142. Insect . . .	225
153. Reptile .	38
172. Bird . . .	35
195. Fish . . .	106
196. Large birds . .	160
205. Toad or frog . .	13
213. Tortoise .	5

Vegetables.

45. Bud or sprout .	4
65. Branch . .	3
75. Tree, wood . .	493
97. Melon tribe . .	16
115. Grain in husk .	144
118. Bamboo .	200
119. Rice . . .	72
140. Grass, herbs . .	470
151. Bean . . .	16
179. Onion, leek . .	6
199. Wheat . . .	15
200. Hemp . . .	7
202. Millet . . .	6

Minerals.

32. Earth, soil . .	222
96. Jade, gem . .	127
112. Stone, rock . .	135

No.	Compounds.
167. Metal	207
197. Salt	4

Parts, &c., of Animals.

30. Mouth . . .	437
58. Head of a hog . .	8
59. Long hair or feathers .	11
61. Heart . . .	467
64. Hand . . .	492
29. (Another form) .	21
82. Fur of animals .	30
84. Breath, vapour .	4
87. Nail, claw . .	7
92. Teeth . . .	3
104. Disease . .	192
107. Skin . . .	13
109. Eye . . .	186
124. Wing feathers .	43
126. Hair of the face .	8
128. Ear . . .	36
130. Flesh . . .	222
135. Tongue . .	10
143. Blood . .	10
148. Horn . . .	31
157. Foot . . .	155
176. Face . . .	9
181. Head . . .	84
185. Head, chief . .	2
188. Bone . . .	47
190. Hair of the head .	43
209. Nose . . .	9
211. Teeth . . .	37

Other Objects in Nature.

3. Point, dot . .	5
13. Wilderness, desert .	4
15. Icicle . . .	46
17. Pit, receptacle .	6
22. Depository . .	19
23. Hiding-place .	8
27. Shelter . .	29
36. Evening, twilight .	11
46. Hill, mountain .	142
47. Water-course, stream	9

No.	Compounds.	No.	Compounds
54. Journey, road	5	110. Spear, barbed	8
72. Sun	154	111. Arrow	18
74. Moon	21	120. Silk	269
85. Water	548	121. Pottery	20
86. Fire	200	122. Net	35
91. Splinter	14	127. Plough	16
114. Footprint, trace	8	129. Pencil	6
116. Cavern	51	134. Mortar	16
150. Valley	11	137. Boat	48
154. Pearl	90	145. Garment	184
163. Territory, city	88	159. Wheel, carriage	127
170. Mound	101	164. Wine	66
173. Rain	67	166. Mile	5
180. Sound, intonation	9	169. Door	71
182. Wind	23	177. Leather, undressed	73
212. Dragon, Hydra	2	178. Dressed leather	24
Objects in Art.		192. Sacrificial wine	4
16. Table	8	193. Perfume pot	6
18. Knife, sword	115	206. Tripod	4
21. Spoon	9	207. Drum	8
26. Seal	19	214. Wind instrument, flute	4
31. Enclosure	45	*Numbers.*	
41. Inch, tenth of a cubit	17	1. One	23
50. Napkin	86	5. (Another form)	11
51. Shield	6	7. Two	12
56. Dart	6	12. Eight	15
57. Bow	35	24. Ten [1]	18
62. Lance, spear	37	*Actions (verbs).*	
63. Inner, or single door	16	2. To descend	9
67. Letters inscribed	6	11. To enter	10
68. Measure of capacity	10	14. To cover	15
69. Measure of weight	15	20. To fold, envelop	17
80. Separation, privation	7	25. To divine	7
98. Tiles, earthenware	30	34. To follow	3
102. Field, enclosed	16	35. To walk slow	12
103. Measure of length	5	40. To collect, cover	99
108. Dish	42	53. To cover, protect	82

[1] All the other numerals, to nine inclusive, are derived from these, with the exception of Four, and that was also in its original form. The Chinese numerals 1, 2, 3, and 10, are the Roman numerals I., II., III., and X., turned the other way.

No.	Compounds.		No.	Compounds.
55. To join hands	14		19. Strong	66
60. To pace, walk	69		28. Crooked, perverse	7
66. To touch lightly	70		37. Great	49
73. To say, speak	14		42. Little	11
76. To owe, want	56		43. Distorted	11
77. To stop, cease	19		52. Slender, young	4
79. To kill	18		70. Square	29
81. To compare	7		71. Defective, wanting	3
89. To imitate	4		78. Bad, rotten	53
100. To produce, give life	6		90. Inclining	7
101. To use	4		95. Dark-coloured	3
105. To stride, issue forth	3		99. Sweet	10
113. To admonish, by omen	97		106. White	29
117. To erect, establish	26		125. Aged	8
136. To disturb, oppose	4		133. Extreme, reaching to	5
144. To do, to act	15		138. Disobedient	3
146. To overshadow	6		139. Coloured	4
147. To see	28		155. Red	10
149. To speak, express	373		160. Bitter	11
156. To walk	45		168. Long, extended	2
161. To mark time	4		171. Reaching to	3
162. To walk swiftly	145		174. Azure, blue	8
165. To separate, divide	4		175. False	10
183. To fly	3		186. Fragrant	10
184. To eat	90		189. High	4
191. To fight	10		201. Yellow	8
204. To embroider	3		203. Black	26
Qualities (Adjectives).			210. Even, adjusted	5
4. Inclined, biassed	16		*Undefined.*	
6. Hooked	5		8. Used only in composition	10

Some of the results of the preceding tables are curious, especially the disproportionate importance of different roots in the general construction of the language. It appears that, of the total number of 11,600 words, no less than 8,200 are comprised under only 33 roots, viz. :—

	Compounds.			Compounds.
Man	478	Body		153
Woman	243	Mouth		437

	Compounds.		Compounds.
Heart	467	Jade, gem	127
Hand	492	Metals	207
Disease . . .	192	Earth	222
Eye	186	Hill	142
Flesh	222	Sun	154
Foot	155	Water	548
Dog	136	Fire	200
Horse	127	Mound	101
Insect	225	Knife, cutting instrument	115
Fish	106	Silk	269
Bird	160	Garment . . .	184
Tree, wood . . .	493	Wheat	127
Grain	144	Speak	373
Bamboo . . .	200	Walk swiftly . . .	145
Grass, herbs	470		

An extended analysis shows that the small proportion of only seven roots comprehend under them no less than 3,385 words.

	Compounds.		Compounds.
Man	478	Tree, wood . . .	493
Mouth	437	Grass, herbs . . .	470
Heart	467	Water	548
Hand	492		

It is apparent that the bulk of these 214 roots, or primitive words, consists of nouns substantive, the names of the principal objects in nature or early art; and their *generic* character seems to corroborate the opinion of Dr. Adam Smith, in an essay concerning the first formation of languages, appended to his work on the Theory of Moral Sentiments. He observes that the assigning particular names to denote particular objects, that is, the institution of *nouns substantive*, would probably be one of the first steps towards the formation of language. The objects most familiar to two aborigines would have particular names given to them, as *a cave, a tree, a river.* Where they met with other objects, altogether similar to these, they would give the same names rather than invent new ones ; and thus these words, which were originally the proper names of individuals, would each of them become the common name of a multitude or class. It is this application of the name of an individual to a great multitude of similar objects that seems to have given occasion to the early formation of those comprehensive classes which we call *genera,* and which are admirably represented by the Chinese roots. With the progress of knowledge, the necessity for particularizing and distinguishing led to the construction of those thousands of compound words or characters which the Chinese ingeniously formed by the combinations of the simple roots, and which are arranged under the roots in their dictionaries as *species* under *genera.* We may add, that the same principle seems to have been finally extended by them, from sensible objects to abstract ideas —from the concrete to the abstract.

How superior such a rational, and often philosophical, *combination* of the elementary symbols, to the more rude and inartificial scheme of continuing to form new · and additional characters, altogether independent and arbitrary, and thus launching on a sea of multitudinous perplexity, to which scarcely any human intellect could ever have been equal. Such, however, has been the notion attached to the Chinese by many uninformed persons, who have in this manner most erroneously enhanced the supposed amount of labour and power of memory required for the mastery of the language, at the same time that they have ignored the extreme ingenuity by which an ideographic system has been rendered comparatively simple and easy of acquirement. Comparative simplicity, however, and facility of acquirement are not the only merits of the system. These will be best explained by considering in succession the three distinct uses which the roots serve. First, as supplying, in their simple and uncombined state, the place of an alphabet for lexicographic arrangement and reference. Secondly, as indicating, when combined, the derivation and meaning of compound words. Thirdly, as already explained, constituting the heads of a sort of Linnæan classification.

I. An alphabet the Chinese roots certainly are not, for they are not phonetic, but ideographic symbols; but they have been made to serve all the purposes of an alphabet in dictionaries. The arrangement and succession of the letters in our European alphabets would seem to be purely arbitrary. There is no reason in the nature of things why Z might not have been the first letter in our alphabet, and A the last; or why, in the Greek, Omega should not have come in time to imply " the beginning," and Alpha " the end." But a good and sufficient reason exists for the arrangement of the Chinese roots. They succeed in order strictly according to the number of strokes of which each is composed. The limited number of letters in our Western alphabets renders their arbitrary arrangement of little importance;

for the *abécédaire*, as the French term it, is easily committed to memory; but the roots in question being rather more than eight times as numerous as our phonetic elements, this disadvantage has been greatly mitigated by the numerical classification; and those ideographic elements are thus turned to in their dictionaries and found with equal facility and despatch by the above simple method. The obvious advantage of this numerical system has been extended in their dictionaries from the roots themselves to the compounds, which are arranged under them. Similar ends suggest analogous means. As the Chinese extend the arrangement by the number of strokes from the roots themselves to the compounds ranged under them, so we of the West extend the alphabetic arrangement from the letters themselves to the words ranged under them, according to the alphabetic succession of the letters in each word. In turning to the Chinese root you find the compound under it in its right place, indicated as this is by the number of distinct strokes which compose it, independent of the root. Thus in looking at the character or word which signifies *copper*, before seeking it in the dictionary, the searcher sees at a glance it is the root *kin*, or metal, with the addition of another character of six strokes, and thus easily discovers the word in its proper place, defined as the particular article " copper," under the general term " metal."

II. Our alphabetical spelling affords no indication of the meaning of a word to him who has never met with it before. The first letter, M, or the first syllable, Man,

would be no clue to the import of the word Mandate.
But when a Chinese sees that 人 *jhin*, " a man," is the
root of a character, he knows the word has a reference
to the human race in some one or other of its relations ;
and this at once assists his conception of the meaning,
and helps him to remember it.   The writing of his
country conveys at once its impression through the
eye ; every character is a visible representation, however
unlike, of the thing meant, and produces a more vivid
and lasting effect on the mind than by the less direct
phonetic medium ; for—

> " Segniùs irritant animos demissa per aurem,
>   Quam quæ sunt oculis subjecta fidelibus."

For this reason the 214 Chinese roots are remembered
with little difficulty ; but an alphabet of 214 elements
of mere sound (if this were necessary, or even possible)
would be a serious affair.   A Chinese has at first no
conception of the use of our letters.   He sees on the
page a perpetual repetition (to use a school-boy phrase),
of a few pothooks and hangers.   He is astonished to
hear that we have only about twenty-six characters in
all ; and if he proceeds to learn them his previous
literary notions are completely upset.   To him the
grand difficulty is the trying to acquire mere elements
of sound instead of symbols of ideas.   In his own
language he had learnt that the root 日 , *jih*, meant
the sun, and the root 月 , *yue*, the moon, and as these

bore some real or fancied resemblance to the objects
he easily remembered them. When, again, he learned
that the combination of these two elements signified 明,
ming, bright, enlightened, the relation was obvious,
and he did not forget it. This in some measure com-
pensates for the disadvantage of so many as 214 ideographic symbols, in lieu of only 26 of a phonetic description. The present is not intended as a piece of
special pleading to prove that their system is better
than ours, which it certainly is not, nor nearly as good;
but to show that the case of the Chinese is not so bad
as has been supposed, or guessed at.

III. The third and most interesting office of the
roots is in serving not only as the elements of all compound words, but as the generic heads for their specific
classification. The associations that have governed
the formation of compounds are often obvious, and they
occasionally afford curious lessons in psychology, or
the operations of the human mind. The root "man,"
combined with "one," simply denotes *alone, deserted*;
with "thousand," a *chiliarch*, the chief of a thousand;
with "hundred," a *centurion*; with "white," an *elder*
or *senior*; with "field," a *husbandman*; with "village," a *rustic, untutored*; with "emperor," *noble,
elevated*; with "justice," *right, correct*. The root *Ta*,
"great," combined with *Koong*, "a bow," forms the
word *Ee*, "a barbarian," which once raised so much
trouble and discussion with the Chinese. On this
point of etymology, however, we have turned the tables

on them, for they retain the bow while we have advanced
to the rifle, which latter article will in time call for the
invention of a new term among them.

It may be remarked that the root *sin*, " heart," enters
into the composition of more words than most of the
others. With us, the heart is the seat of the affections
or emotions, but with them of the intellect also. Combined with *hea*, " downwards," it means literally
" downhearted ; " with *taou*, " a knife," the meaning
is *taou*, " grieved ; " with *seng*, " nature, birth," it
implies *sing*, " natural disposition ; " with *urh*, " the
ear," it forms *che*, " conscience, a sense of shame,"
thus presenting in a single word the idea conveyed by
our phrase " the whisperings of conscience."

With regard to the classification of the three kingdoms of nature, we find under the root *che*, " hog,"
the compound *seang*, " an elephant," which, as one of
the *pachydermata*, might be correct enough. Many of
the compounds, however, are very incorrectly classed,
and have not the remotest affinity with the root. Under
new, " ox," is found, *se*, " rhinoceros." The wolf and
fox are properly ranged under the root *keuen*, " dog,"
but so also is the ape, and, strange to say, the lion.

The vegetable kingdom, with the exception of a very
few instances—as rice and bamboo, which are themselves roots *par excellence*,—is arranged mainly under
the roots, *muh*, " trees," and *tsaou*, " herbs," the
former indicating not only all species of trees, but
everything composed of, or having a relation to,
wood ; the latter all herbaceous plants and vegetable

productions that are not ligneous. The cereal grains are, from their importance, arranged under a single root 禾, *ho*. From imparting their direct meaning to compounds, the roots proceed to convey a figurative signification. Thus, 禾, *ho*, "grain," in composition with 火, *ho*, "fire, or heat," means the autumn ; 冬, *tung*, "winter," is distinguished by the presence of *ping*, "icicle ; " the meaning of 春, *chun*, "spring," is indicated by the "sun" appearing from below. If Anglo-Chinese dictionaries would always point out these relations between the composition of words and their import, not only would the meaning be elucidated, but the memory of the searcher at the same time greatly assisted. He has generally been left to do this for himself.

The mineral kingdom is classed principally under 土, *too*, "earth," and 金, *kin*, "metal," and these roots also compose the names of the implements or things having a relation to those materials. A philosophical Chinese chemist, in advance of his countrymen, might arrange all alkaline substances, under the root *too*, "earth," and their metallic bases under *kin*, "metal." But their usual mode of designating any new foreign importation is by adopting the name of something native, that bears a real or fancied resemblance to it, and adding the term "foreign."

The peculiar advantages of this medium, such as they are, have rendered it a universal character, not only among the 300 millions of China, but in the kingdoms of Japan and Annam, Corea and Tungking; in fact nearly half the human race. I proceeded in 1847 with two of Her Majesty's ships to Turon Bay, in Annam (where the French have now by military pressure acquired rather an unprofitable colony), with the view of trying to conclude a commercial treaty, and there I found that without knowing a syllable of their spoken language I could correspond with the officers of government as completely as in China. With regard, also, to Japan, it is clear, from Sir Rutherford Alcock's work, that the pure Chinese character is very generally used and understood. Mr. Medhurst likewise states,— " From my recent visit to Japan I have been much struck by the general and familiar use made by the Japanese of the Chinese written language, in its own regular construction." It is no doubt the *fons et origo* of Japanese letters.

V.

THE DRAMA, NOVELS, AND ROMANCES.

(From the Quarterly Review.)

THE Chinese stand eminently distinguished from other Asiatic nations by their early possession, and extensive use, of the art of *printing*—of printing, too, in that particular shape, the stereotype, which is best calculated, by multiplying the copies and cheapening the price, to promote the circulation of every species of their literature. Hence they are, as might be expected, a *reading* people; a certain quantity of education is universal among even the lower classes—and among the higher, it is superfluous to insist on the great estimation in which letters must be held, under a system where learning forms the very threshold of the gate that conducts to fame, honours, and civil employment. Amidst the vast mass of printed books, which is the natural offspring of such a state of things, the circle of their popular literature has the best claim to our attention; and there appears no readier or more agreeable mode of becoming intimately acquainted with a people, from whom Europe can have so little to learn on the score of either moral or physical *science*, than by drawing largely from the inexhaustible stores of their lighter *literature*. The publication, by that very active association, the Oriental Translation Fund, of the Chinese tragedy, which we are to analyse in this article, furnishes an occasion of introducing some observations on the subject—of throwing, we trust, some new lights upon it, and investing it with additional interest.

The Chinese themselves make no technical distinctions between *tragedy* and *comedy* in their stage pieces;—the dialogue of which is composed in ordinary prose, while the principal performer now and then chants forth, in unison with music, a species of song or vaudeville, and the name of the tune or air is always inserted at the top of the passage to be sung.

A translator from their language seems, however, at liberty to apply those terms, according to the serious and dignified, or comic and familiar character of the composition which he selects. In choosing his own specimen from among so many, the translator of the Sorrows of Han, "was influenced by the consideration of its remarkable accordance with our own canons of criticism. The unity of action is complete, and the unities of time and place much less violated than they frequently are on the English stage. The grandeur and gravity of the subject, the rank and dignity of the personages, the tragical catastrophe, and the strict award of poetical justice, might satisfy the most rigid admirer of Grecian rules. The translator has thought it necessary to adhere to the original, in distinguishing by name the first act, or proem, from the four which follow it; but the distinction is purely nominal, and the

piece consists, to all intents and purposes, of *five* acts.
It is remarkable that this peculiar division holds true
with regard to a large number of the " Hundred Plays
of Yuen "—from which the present drama is taken.

Love and war, too, very legitimate subjects of tragedy, constitute its whole action, and the language of
the imperial lover is frequently passionate to a degree
one is not prepared to expect in such a country as
China.   The nature of its civil institutions, and the
degraded state of the female sex, might generally be
pronounced unfavourable to the more elevated strains
of the erotic muse.   The bulk of the people, it might be
thought, are too much straitened for the bare means of
subsistence, through the pressing demands of an exces-
sive population, to admit of their singing after the most
approved manner of idle shepherds and shepherdesses;
and the well-educated class, which comprehends almost
all the higher ranks, or those in the employ of the
government, too proud and unfeeling to make love the
theme of their compositions—which are doubtless
chiefly confined to moral and speculative, or descriptive
subjects.   The drama in question, however, may teach
us not to pronounce too dogmatically on such points by
reasonings *à priori*, but to wait patiently for the fruits
of actual research and experience.

The moral of this play is evidently to expose the
evil consequences of luxury, effeminacy, and supineness
in the sovereign—

> " When love was all an easy monarch's care,
>   Seldom at council, never in a war."

The subject is strictly historical, and relates to that interesting period of the Chinese annals when the declining strength of the government emboldened the Tartars in their aggressions, and gave rise to the temporising and impolitic system of propitiating those barbarians by alliances and tribute, which at last produced the downfall of the empire and the establishment of the Mongol dominion. The drama opens with the entrance of the Tartar Khan, reciting these verses :—

"The autumnal gale blows wildly through the grass, amidst our woollen tents,
    And the moon of night, shining on the rude huts, hears the lament of the mournful pipe ;
    The countless hosts, with their bended bows, obey me as their leader ;
    Our tribes are the distinguished friends of the family of Han."

This formidable Scythian displays his friendship after a singular fashion, as we shall see presently. He ends a speech, which may be considered either as a soliloquy or as an address to the audience, thus :—

"We have moved to the south, and approached the border, claiming an alliance with the Imperial race. Yesterday, I despatched an envoy, with tributary presents, to demand a princess in marriage, but know not if the Emperor will ratify the engagement with the customary oaths. The fineness of the season has drawn away our chiefs on a hunting excursion, amidst the sandy steppes : may they meet with success ! for we Tartars have no fields ; our bows and arrows are our sole means of subsistence."
[*Exit.*]

The Chinese leave more to the imagination than we do ; for they neither contrive that the action should all proceed on one spot, as in the Greek tragedy, nor do they make use of shifting scenes. "You can never bring in a wall," says Snug, the joiner—so say the Chinese ; and their contrivance, though not quite so absurd as those of the "Mechanicals" in *Midsummer Night's Dream*, are scarcely more artificial.

The next personage that appears is the minister of the emperor, and he at once displays his character by these four verses, with the recital of which he enters :—

"Let a man have the heart of a kite, and the talons of an eagle ;
Let him deceive his superiors, and oppress those below him ;
Let him enlist flattery, insinuation, profligacy, and avarice on his side,
And he will then find them a lasting assistance through life."

The falsehood of this bad morality, however, is ultimately proved in the fate of its author, who thus continues :—

"By a hundred arts of specious flattery and address, I have deceived the Emperor, until he places his chief delight in me alone. My words he listens to, and he follows my counsel. Within the precincts of the palace, as without them, who is there but bows before me, who is there but trembles at my approach? But observe the chief art which I have learned—it is this : to persuade the emperor to keep aloof from his wise counsellors, and seek all his pleasures amidst the women of his palace. Thus it is that I strengthen my power and greatness ; but in the midst of my lucubrations, here comes the emperor."

(*Enter* the Emperor Yuente, *attended by eunuchs and women.*)

"*Emp.* (*Recites verses*).—During the ten generations that have succeeded our acquisition of empire,
My race has alone possessed the four hundred districts of the world : [1]
Long have the frontiers been bound in tranquillity by the ties of mutual oaths ;
And our pillow has been undisturbed by grief or anxiety."

The worthy minister and his sovereign agree that there is no better mode of improving these piping times of peace, than by adding to the numbers of the imperial harem : the favourite is appointed on the spot commissioner of selection, desired to search diligently

---

[1] That is, of China.

through the realm for all that is most beautiful of womankind, between the ages of fifteen and twenty, and then furnish his master with portraits of each, as a means of fixing his choice. And so ends the introductory act.

The minister proceeds on his commission, and does just what Falstaff did on his recruiting service—"misuses the king's press most damnably." The Knight, however, takes money for letting off the proper objects of his selection, and discharges those likely fellows, Bullcalf and Mouldy, while he marshals in his ranks the half-faced Shadow, the forceless Feeble, and the ragged Wart. Our emissary, on the contrary, was bribed to take, and not to reject. He met at length with a maiden of uncommon attractions :—

"The brightness of her charms was piercing as an arrow! She was perfectly beautiful ; and doubtless unparalleled in the whole empire. But unfortunately her father is a cultivator of the land, not possessed of much wealth. When I insisted on a hundred ounces of gold to secure her being the chief object of the imperial choice, they first pleaded their poverty; and then, relying on her extraordinary beauty, rejected my offers altogether. I therefore left them. (*Considers awhile.*)—But no ! I have a better plan. (*He knits his brows, and matures his scheme.*) I will disfigure her portrait in such manner, that when it reaches the Emperor, it shall secure her being doomed to neglected seclusion. Thus I shall contrive to make her unhappy for life [1]—base is the man who delights not in revenge !"

We next see the lady herself, who appears soliloquizing amidst the shades of night :—

"My mother dreamed, on the day I was born, that the light of the moon shone on her bosom, but was soon cast low to the earth.[2] I was

---

[1] Because, once admitted within the precincts of the palace, she could never return home.

[2] Boding a short, but fatal distinction to her offspring.

just eighteen years of age when chosen as an inhabitant of the imperial palace : but the minister, Maouyenshow, disappointed in the treasure which he demanded on my account, disfigured my portrait in such manner as to keep me out of the emperor's presence, and now I live in neglected solitude. While at home, I learned a little music, and could play a few airs on the lute. Thus sorrowing in the stillness of midnight, let me practise one of my songs to dispel my griefs. (*Begins to play on the lute.*)

(*Enter* Emperor, *attended by a eunuch, carrying a light.*)

"*Emp.*—Since the beauties were selected to grace our palace, we have not yet discovered a worthy object on whom to fix our preference. Vexed and disappointed, we have passed this day of leisure, roaming in search of her who may be destined for our imperial choice. (*Hears the lute.*) Is not that some lady's lute?

"*Attend.*—It is ; I hasten to advise her of your Majesty's approach.

"*Emp.*—No, hold ! Keeper of the yellow gate, discover to what part of our palace that lady pertains, and bid her approach our presence ; but beware lest you alarm her.

"*Attend.* (*approaches in the direction of the sound, and speaks.*)— What lady plays there? The emperor comes ; approach to meet him. (*Lady advances.*)

"*Emp.*—Keeper of the yellow gate, see that the light burns brightly within your gauze lamp, and hold it nearer to us.

"*Lady* (*approaching*).—Had your handmaid but known it was your majesty, she would have been less tardy ; forgive, then, this delay.

"*Emp.*—Truly this is a very perfect beauty ! From what quarter come such superior charms?"

The secret is now discovered, and the lady makes known to his majesty the cruel perfidy of the minister.

"*Emp.*—Keeper of the yellow gate, bring us that picture, that we may view it. (*Sees the picture.*) Ah ! how has he dimmed the purity of the gem, bright as the waves in autumn ! (*To the attendant.*) Transmit our pleasure to the officer of the guard, to behead Maouyenshow, and report to us his execution."

The traitor, however, contrives to escape from this *tranchant* sentence, and, in the next act, flies to the Tartar camp with a true likeness of the lady (now created a princess), which he exhibits to the barbarian king, and persuades him, with ingenious villany, to demand her of the emperor. No sooner said than done: an envoy is despatched by the khan, who adds—" Should he refuse, I will presently invade the south : his hills and rivers shall be exposed to ravage. Our warriors will commence by hunting, as they proceed on their way; and thus, gradually entering the frontiers, I shall be ready to act as may best suit the occasion."

The unfortunate emperor's fondness continues to increase ; and the arrival of the Tartar envoy fills him with perplexity and despair. He calls on his servants to rid him of these invaders ; but they bewail the weakness of the empire, point out the necessity of the sacrifice, and call on his majesty to consult the peace and safety of his realms by complying with the khan's demand. He consents, after a struggle, to yield up the princess ; but insists on accompanying her a part of the way. In the following act we have the parting scene :—

" *Envoy.*—Lady, let us urge you to proceed on your way ; the sky darkens, and night is coming on.

" *Prin.*—Alas ! when shall I again behold your majesty ? I will take off my robes of distinction and leave them behind me. To-day in the palace of Hān ; to-morrow I shall be espoused to a stranger. I cease to wear these splendid vestments ; they shall no longer adorn my beauty in the eyes of men !

" *Envoy.*—Again, let us urge you, princess, to depart ; we have delayed but too long already !

" *Emp.*—'Tis done ! Princess, when you are gone, let your thoughts forbear to dwell with sorrow and resentment upon us. (*They part.*)—And am I the great monarch of the line of Hān ?

"*Presid.*—Let your majesty cease to dwell with such grief upon this subject !

"*Emp.*—She is gone ! In vain have we maintained those armed heroes on the frontiers. Mention but swords and spears, and they tremble at their hearts like a young deer. The princess has this day performed what belonged to themselves ; and yet do they affect the semblance of men !

"*Presid.*—Your majesty is entreated to return to the palace ; dwell not so bitterly, sir, on her memory ; allow her to depart !

"*Emp.*—Did I not think of her, I had a heart of iron—a heart of iron ! The tears of my grief stream in a thousand channels. This evening shall her likeness be suspended in the palace, where I will sacrifice to it ; and tapers, with their silvery light, shall illuminate her chamber."

Then comes the catastrophe. The Tartar army retires with its prize, and they proceed on their march towards the north, until they reach the banks of the river Amoor, or Saghalien, which falls into the sea of Ochotsk.

"*Princess.*—What place is this ?

"*Envoy.*—It is the river of the Black Dragon, the frontier of the Tartar territories and those of China. This southern shore is the Emperor's—on the northern side commences our Tartar dominion.

"*Princess (to the Khan).*—Great King, I take a cup of wine, and pour a libation towards the south—my last farewell to the Emperor. (*Pours the libation.*) Emperor of Hän, this life is finished ; I await thee in the next ! (*Throws herself into the river.*)"

The lady is drowned, and the khan, in great sorrow, decrees that her sepulchre shall be placed on the river's bank, and called "the verdant tomb." This is said to exist at the present day, and to remain green all the year round, while the vegetation of the desert in which it stands is parched by the summer sun. With more generosity than might have been expected from him, the Tartar remits all further demands on the emperor, and directs that the wicked cause of these misfortunes

shall be delivered over to the Chinese, to receive the
just reward of his misdeeds.

The last act opens with the grief of Yuente at his
recent loss; and the princess appears to him in a vision,
which vision, however, is not a whit more extravagant
than the similar scene in our own tragedy of Richard
III.—*cum multis aliis.* But let our readers judge for
themselves.

" *Emp.*—Since the princess was yielded to the Tartars, we have not
held an audience. The lonely silence of night increases our melancholy!
We take the picture of that fair one and suspend it here, as some small
solace to our grief. (*To the attendant.*) Keeper of the yellow gate,
behold the incense in yonder vase is burnt out; hasten, then, to add
some more. Though we cannot see her, we may at least retain this
shadow, and, while life remains, betoken our regard. But, oppressed
and weary, we would fain take a little repose. (*Lies down to sleep.*)

(*The* Princess *appears before him in a vision.*)

" *Princess.*—Delivered over as a captive to appease the barbarians, they
would have conveyed me to their northern country; but I took an occasion to elude them, and have escaped back. Is not this the Emperor,
my Sovereign?—Sir, behold me again restored.

♦   (*A* Tartar soldier *appears in the vision.*)

" *Sold.*—While I chanced to sleep, the lady, our captive, has made her
escape, and returned home. Is not this she? (*Carries her off.*)

(*The* Emperor *starts from his sleep.*)

" *Emp.*—We just saw the Princess returned; but alas, how quickly
has she vanished! In bright day she answered not to our call, but when
morning dawned on our troubled sleep, a vision presented her in this
spot. (*Hears the wild-fowl's cry.*) Hark! the passing fowl screamed
twice or thrice! Can it know there is one so desolate as I? (*Cries
repeated.*) Perhaps, worn out and weak, hungry and emaciated, they
bewail at once the broad nets of the south, and the tough bows of the
north. (*Cries repeated.*) The screams of those water-birds but increase
our melancholy!

" *Attend.*—Let your majesty cease this sorrow, and have some regard to
your sacred person.

" *Emp.*—My sorrows are beyond control. Cease to upbraid this excess
of feeling, since ye are all subject to the same. Yon doleful cry is not

the note of the swallow on the carved rafters, nor the song of the variegated bird on the blossoming tree. The Princess has abandoned her home! Know ye in what place she grieves; listening, like me, to the screams of the wild bird?

(*Enter* President.)

" *Pres.*—This day, after the close of the morning council, a foreign envoy appeared, bringing with him the fettered traitor, Maouyenshow. He announces that the renegade, by deserting his allegiance, led to the breach of truce, and occasioned all these calamities. The Princess is no more!—and the Khan wishes for peace and friendship between the two nations. The envoy attends with reverence your imperial decision.

" *Emp.*—Then strike off the traitor's head, and be it presented as an offering to the shade of the Princess! Let a fit banquet be got ready for the envoy, preparatory to his return. (*Recites these verses.*)

"At the fall of the leaf, when the wild-fowl's cry was heard in the recesses of the palace,
    Sad dreams returned to our lonely pillow—we thought of her through the night :
    Her verdant tomb remains—but where shall we seek herself?
    The perfidious painter's head shall atone for the beauty which he wronged ! "

This may, perhaps, be considered as no unfavourable specimen of dramatic taste in China. One thing, at least, is certain, that Voltaire constructed a tragedy (" L'Orphelin de la Chine") which pleased his fastidious countrymen, out of the materials afforded him by a less inviting selection from the " Hundred Plays of Yuen," translated by Père Premare. The richness of their theatre is proved by a list of two hundred volumes of plays, appended by the author to his preface. It has been very truly observed of the Chinese, that, like the rabble of imperial Rome, the two things which they most care for are—" *Panis et Circenses* "—rice and raree-shows; the policy of despotism in either case finding it convenient to fill the bellies and amuse the minds of its subjects, in order to keep them quiet. In China, no sooner does a famine take place, than revolts are immediately apprehended; and unless the cravings of the populace can be allayed by supplies from the public granaries, these apprehensions are seldom groundless. Taught, according to their paternal notions of government, to consider the good which they enjoy in prosperity as resulting from the care of the emperor and his representatives, the people very naturally refer the evils which they suffer in adversity to remissness and improvidence in the same quarter; and the government, not ignorant of the danger, is proportionably cautious in guarding against it.

Another observation or two, and we have done with the Chineses drama. In their play-books, certain words are adopted, to point out the general characteristics of the different *dramatis personæ*, and these particular words are made use of in every play indiscriminately, whether its complexion be tragic or comic. No similar usage can be found on the European stage, unless, indeed, we except the invariable terms of Harlequin, &c., copied in our English pantomime from the early Italian theatre,—still marking with precision the station and character of the several performers, however varied may be the action of the piece. The great divisions of a play, or the acts, as we style them, exist, perhaps, rather in the book than in the representation, being, on the Chinese stage, not so distinctly marked as on ours, by the lapse of a considerable interval of time. The opening act, or proem, in which the different characters introduce themselves very much after the fashion of the Greek tragedy, is called by a name which means literally *a door, or the side posts of a door*, and hence metaphorically *the opening*. The rest are styled *breaks*. The words *shang* and *hea*, to "ascend" and "descend," are used for *enter* and *exit*.

In the department of Romances and Novels, a specimen appeared under the same auspices as the play. The title of the work, correctly expressed in English, is the "Fortunate Union." The term "romance" may be properly applied to any fiction, of which the personages and incidents are above the level of ordinary life. The orthodox rule used to be, that the hero should sally forth, and fight with everything either bigger or stronger than himself; and the *preux* of the "Fortunate Union" really answers pretty nearly to this description. He is attended, too, by a follower, who does him as good service as ever was performed by trusty squire to knight-errant; and, after a multitude of adventures and scrapes, produced by the malice of foes and rivals, the heroine is happily and honourably united to her lover, in whom she originally met with a protector from her enemies. It may appear strange that any fiction on so legitimate a plan should be met with in China—such, however, is the case; and it was this circumstance, joined to the spirit of the dialogue, and the merits of the style, which induced the translator to undertake the task of making a complete version, including all the poetical passages. Of the

Haoukewchuen, for that is the Chinese title, Sir George Staunton expressed a very high opinion in his miscellaneous notices of China. It is about a century since Dr. Percy, Bishop of Dromore, edited from a manuscript, partly English and partly Portuguese, a sort of skeleton or abstract, rather than a translation of this romance, and without the poetical passages, under the title of the "Pleasing History," which is not the meaning of the original name. Although it abounded in both errors and omissions, this work, at the time when it appeared, was by far the best picture of Chinese manners and society that we possessed; and Dr. Percy was not answerable for the imperfections of his materials. He was naturally puzzled by some parts of his manuscript, and expresses his surprise in notes at a number of incongruities, which, on a reference to the original, are not found to exist. In fact, at the distance of more than one hundred years since, for that is the date of the manuscript, no countryman of ours could possibly be competent to the task of translation; and the work in question appears evidently to have been taken down in great part from the mouth of a native, probably in the imperfect jargon of English spoken at Canton.

The "Fortunate Union" may be considered as a truer picture of existing Chinese manners, inasmuch as the hero espouses but one *wife*. It is not strictly true that their laws sanction *polygamy*, although they permit *concubinage*. A Chinese can have but one *wife* properly so called, who is distinguished by a title, espoused with ceremonies, and chosen from a rank of life totally different from his handmaids or mistresses, of whom he may have as many as he pleases; and though the offspring of the latter possess many of the rights of legitimacy (ranking, however, after the children of the wife), this circumstance makes little difference as to the truth of the position. Even in the present romance the profligate rival of the hero aims at effecting his union with the heroine only by setting aside his previous marriage with her cousin as informal. Any Chinese fiction, therefore, and of these there are many, which describes a man espousing two wives, is in this respect no truer a picture of existing manners than in respect to any other amusing or silly extravagance which it may happen to contain. These observations are not hastily made, being the result of careful examination and inquiry, and the "Fortunate Union" affords sufficient corroboration, were any required. The resolution of the unfortunate scholar to suffer death rather than allow his daughter to be degraded to the rank of a handmaid, even to a noble, and the attempt of the same noble, towards the conclusion of the story, to espouse the heroine as his wife, *because* he had just lost his former spouse, are abundant confirmation of what we advance. In fact the *wife* is of equal rank with her husband by birth, and espoused with regular marriage ceremonies, possessing, moreover, certain legal rights,[1] such as they are—the *handmaid* is bought for

---

[1] Staunton's Penal Code, under the head of Marriage.

money, and received into the house like a mere domestic. The principle on which Chinese law and custom admit the offspring of concubinage to legitimate rights is obvious—the importance which attaches in that country to the securing of male descendants.

Many remarkable points of resemblance will be discovered between the "Fortunate Union" and our own novels and romances. Every chapter is headed by a few verses bearing some relation to its contents, and some appropriate lines are occasionally introduced as embellishments to the story. After a corresponding fashion, too, with the designations of persons in our own favourite fictions, we should find, on translating them literally, that most of the names in similar Chinese works have some allusion to the characters of those who bear them. Thus the hero of the Haoukewchuen is named from *iron* (*quasi* Ironside); the literal import of the heroine's name is " Icy-hearted," a term which in her country implies *chaste,* and not what we should call *cold-hearted;* her father's designation literally means " dwelling in singleness of purpose," which sufficiently expresses his inflexible character; and so of many other appellatives. The most advantageous point of comparison, however, lies in the spirit of the dialogue, for which the "Fortunate Union" is distinguished above any Chinese work of the kind hitherto translated, and we proceed to make some extracts from it. In the ninth chapter the worthless uncle of the solitary and secluded heroine hears some false rumours to the disadvantage of the hero Teihchungyu, and being a bitter enemy

of his, proceeds with great glee to inform the young
lady :—

"' 'Niece,' said he, 'have you heard the strange news?' She pleaded
the retired life of a female in her situation as a sufficient reason for being
ignorant of what was passing abroad. 'Well, then,' continued her uncle,
'you must know that when I advised you to marry Teihchungyu I had the
best opinion of his character; most fortunately, however, you refused
steadily to give a hasty assent—your happiness would otherwise have been
ruined for life: can you guess what sort of person he has proved himself
to be?' 'I know nothing of his birth and family,' replied the young lady;
'but from what I have observed of his conduct it would plainly appear
that he is a young man of extraordinary virtue.' 'Of extraordinary virtue, indeed!' exclaimed the other, impatiently; 'you used to have some
share of penetration once, niece!—what has become of it on this occasion?'
'But how has he belied his former character?' inquired Shueypingsin.
'Why, he is nothing better than a practised seducer,' replied her uncle.
'I know not what schemes he might have had in view when he pretended
sickness, and gained a lodging in this house; but you may consider it the
height of good luck on your part that he was obliged, by the sound rating
I gave him, to desist, and took his departure in an affected passion. *The
earthen pitcher*, however, *gets broken at last;* and no sooner did he
reach the neighbouring village than he betrayed himself.' 'Pray, what
was it he did to betray himself?' asked the young lady."

He now relates to her the story that he had heard,
and takes care at the same time to put in some embellishments of his own.

"' 'Well,' said his niece, smiling composedly, 'let Teihchungyu be
what you say he is; it concerns myself no more than if the favourite dis-
ciple of Confucius had really been proved to be a murderer.' 'I know
it does not concern you!' exclaimed he; 'but this event shows how very
difficult it is to be sure of a person's character on a short acquaintance;
and that, to avoid the chance of being deceived, one's knowledge must be
better founded than on a casual meeting.' 'In a matter with which I have
so little concern,' observed Shueypingsin, 'there is not much occasion to
argue the point; but what you have been pleased to say, seems intended
to ridicule my want of penetration in forming a wrong opinion of this
young man. Did it relate to any person but himself, I should not think
it worth while to say a word in reply; but, after the mutual services we
have rendered each other, the slur you throw upon his character implies

that our acquaintance was dishonest, and slanders my own reputation equally with his. I have, therefore, a good reason for repelling it.' 'I do not know,' cried her uncle, ' whether to be most angry or amused by what you say. I never had any cause of enmity towards this young man ; what should make me slander him, then ? He happens to be a libertine, and entices away a young woman. You live quietly at home, and know nothing about it ; but the people near the magistrate's office report it to me : why blame me on their account ? If you choose to say that you mistook his character, and that this was a thing you could not help, I can understand you ; but if you attempt to maintain that he really is not guilty, I suspect all the water in the Yellow River will never wash him clean from the imputation.' 'If I think it worth while to maintain anything,' replied Shueypingsin, 'it will be that he is not what you call him, and that the whole is the slanderous invention of worthless people. You may then learn that I was not deceived in my good opinion. Any other point I do not think it necessary to argue.' ' My good niece, you are very obstinate,' said Shueyun. ' That he *is* guilty, has been proved by a number of witnesses. What is there for you to say on the subject?' ' You assert that it has been proved by witnesses,' answered she ; ' and until we hear something authentic, I will not debate the point with you ; but, judging from reason and principle, I must still maintain that this young man cannot be what you say ; and though such a report may have gone abroad (admitting that it be not a fabrication altogether), there must yet be something more in it than has come to light ; for, should he really prove to be guilty of the charge, I will engage to forfeit both my eyes to you.' ' Why, the woman he carried off has been apprehended in his company,' exclaimed Shueyun, ' and taken before the village officer, who transferred them both to his superior. They are now on trial—there can be no fabrication in *this*. Your attempt to vindicate his character, after matters have reached this point, proves only that you are blinded by excess of love.' ' It is vain attempting to persuade you at present, uncle,' said the young lady ; ' but do not be too positive. Inquire a little farther, and you may arrive at the real truth.' "

The result is, as usual, the entire discomfiture and confusion of the unhappy uncle, whose character for low cunning, and mischievous intrigue, is in perfect *keeping* throughout ; and the same remark applies to all the personages of the romance, of every description. We will give one more scene, from the fourteenth chapter. The hero Teihchungyu discovers, by accident, that one of the emperor's generals, at present under sentence of death, in consequence of certain reverses which he had suffered on the frontier, is the victim of combinations and intrigues among his enemies, and full of resentment at such injustice, walks straight into the court which has condemned him (of which our hero's father, by the way, is a member), and there stoutly pleads the leader's cause.

"The three members of the triple court had not ventured, after the emperor's approval of his minister's advice, to record their dissent. At the same time, however, that they confirmed the sentence of beheading, and waited only for the Imperial warrant to execute the same, they still felt a secret uneasiness at the prisoner's fate; and when a person was seen entering the court, and thus loudly addressing them, they experienced a mixed sensation of alarm at the disturbance, regret for their sentence, and resentment at the intrusion. Discovering, on a closer view, that it was Teihchungyu, the other two members felt unwilling to be harsh; but his father struck the table with fury, and rated him in round terms, demanding how he presumed thus madly to address so high a court, assembled there by Imperial commission to decide on a capital case. 'The laws admit of no private feelings,' cried he, and ordered the intruder into custody; but Teihchungyu loudly exclaimed, 'My lord, you are mistaken! The emperor himself suspends the drum at his palace gate, and admits all to state their hardships without reserve; may I not be allowed to right the injured before this very tribunal of life and death?' 'What have you to do with the prisoner,' inquired his father, ' that *you* should right his case?' 'He is not even an acquaintance,' replied Teihchungyu. 'I can have no reasons on his own account; but the difficulty of finding his substitute impels me to intercede for one who is so worthy of being the emperor's general.' 'The emperor's general must live or die as the emperor pleases,' cried Teihying. 'What concern is it of yours, that you may behave in this mad style? Seize him instantly!' The attendants now stepped up to lay their hands on the young man, but the other two members of the court interfered. 'Hold!' cried they—and calling him up to the judgment table, they pacified Teihchungyu with good words.

"'Worthy friend, we do not blame your well-intentioned spirit; but the nation has its laws, judges their dignity, and prisoners their sentence. It is not allowable to intrude in this rude manner. The leader has already been imprisoned for more than a year, and Shueykeuyih, who recommended

him, exiled on his account. His offences being proved by several con-
current authorities, how shall he now be found guiltless by his judges?
The nation's laws, the judges' dignity, and the prisoner's case, alike forbid
this! Admitting, however, that we proposed a mitigation of his punishment, it would be impossible to remit the heaviest part of the sentence.
But the minister has advised his decapitation—the emperor has assented
—how, then, shall we attempt to oppose it?'

" ' Alas,' replied Teihchungyu, sighing, ' your lordship's words would
better become those ordinary ministers who abandon what is right for
the sake of their places, their emoluments, or their personal safety: they
pertain not to that disinterested spirit which identifies your country's
welfare with your own! Were the truth as you state it, the lowest capacity might be more than sufficient to conduct the business of the state:
what need of personages of your lordship's weight to minister for the sovereign! Let me ask you, what meant that saying of the ancient emperor,
' Thrice be death delayed,'[1] or of the ancient minister, ' In three cases
only be death inflexibly awarded?' Your reasonings, if true, would go
far to deprive these sacred characters of their reputation for wisdom.'

" The two other judges answered not a word, but his father broke
silence, ' Foolish boy, say no more! This man's death is inevitable.'
Teihchungyu, however, rejoined with warmth, ' Brave men and worthy
leaders are the rare productions of heaven: if your lordships are inflexible,
and persist in condemning Howheaou to death, let me entreat you to con-
demn me with him!' ' But his guilt and incapacity have been proved,'
said Teihying, ' it is only condemning a worthless servant: is there anything extraordinary in that?' ' Men's capacities are not so easily
known,' said his son ; ' the courage and ability of this leader are such,
that, if he be re-appointed to the frontier, he shall prove another ' wall
of a thousand leagues' [2]—no hero of the age may compare with him.'
' Allowing his capacity to be great,' observed the father, ' his delin-
quency is still greater.' ' The ablest leaders,' said Teihchungyu, ' must
ever be liable to commit errors ; and hence, it is customary for the emperor to reprieve them for a while, that they may redeem themselves by
acts of merit.' ' But in that case,' remarked one of the judges, ' some-
body must be surety; will you venture to be answerable for him?' ' If
Howheaou be restored to his command,' replied he, ' I entreat that my
own head may answer for his misconduct, as the just punishment of such

---

[1] Such is the actual practice, in
ordinary cases, at the present day ;
first, by the local magistrate, who
refers to the provincial judge ;
next, by the provincial judge, who
refers to the criminal tribunal ;
lastly, by the criminal tribunal,
which refers to the emperor.

[2] The Chinese name for their
great wall.

rashness.' The other two judges now turned to Teihying, and said, ' Since your lordship's son thus publicly tenders his personal responsibility, it befits us to make a formal representation, and request his majesty's pleasure.' Teihying was compelled, under the circumstances of the case, to assent to this: the leader was accordingly remanded to prison ; and Teihchungyu, being called upon to enter into a written engagement on the spot, was placed in custody for the time being."

This novel, or rather romance, is a favourable exposition of whatever is best in the Confucian code of philosophy and morals; and the conclusion is a complete award of ' poetical justice ' to the good and bad actors.   All parties, on account of their rank, are summoned before the " Son of heaven " himself, and receive at his hands the proper recompense of their respective deeds.

" Teihchungyu, his bride, and the assembled court then bowed down and acknowledged the imperial bounty, and the hum of joy and gratulation resembled the distant roll of thunder.   The attendants had received their orders ; and, as they filed off in pairs, the ornamental lanterns in all their radiance, the harmonious band in full sound, and the marshalled banners in their variegated splendour, escorted the renowned and happy couple as they proceeded homewards attended by a vast company.

> " The choicest bud, unblown, exhales no sweets,
>   No radiance can the untried gem display:
>   Misfortune, like the winter cold that binds
>   The embryo fragrance of the flower, doth lend
>   A fresher charm to fair prosperity."

VI.

ADDRESS TO THE CHINA BRANCH OF THE ROYAL ASIATIC SOCIETY.

ON ITS INAUGURATION AT HONGKONG.

WITHOUT abusing the patience of the Society by any diffuse or trite generalities on the advantages of those inquiries which it is the object of this new institution at once to encourage and to prosecute, I shall save their time and my own by going at once into the question of what is likely to be acquired by the future labours of our members, and by taking a rapid view of the prospects before us.

It may be remarked incidentally, that, on some points, the neighbourhood of Canton, as a field already gleaned, may probably afford less of novelty in research than the more northern localities, which have been open now for about five years,—"depuis" (to use the honest expression of a foreigner[1]) "depuis que par un noble et généreux désintéressement la Grande Bretagne a ouvert le commerce de la Chine à toutes les nations."

I will just remark, that if the cursory and imperfect sketch which is to be presented in this paper should prove to be very different from the productions of learned

---

[1] Count de Pollon.

leisure, or the furniture of "academic bowers," it will be only just to explain its defects by the constant demands on my attention of two separate public offices, from whose graver and more imperative calls such digressions can occur only as chance recreations—as *impermissa raptim gaudia*, and I may add, in the absence of my books (though not exactly in the meaning of the poet), *luminibus remotis*. At the same time, the spontaneous proposition of the Society, that I should be its first President, was at once too flattering and too congenial to my own inclinations to be declined on the ground of any other than insurmountable obstacles. I will, therefore, claim its indulgence to my imperfect services in the words of the Scottish Erasmus,—"*Accipe, sed facilis!*"

To commence with the language of China, as the key to a great deal that remains to be known. With regard to the intrinsic qualities of that very peculiar literature which constitutes the archives of this language, my own experience does not lead me to be over sanguine in expectations from the future. My old preceptor and friend, Mr. Malthus, who left behind him an European reputation, applied to some of it (judging of course from translations) a remark which is true of a great deal of Asiatic literature,—that it was "childish"; in fact, a reflex of that general condition of society and intellect in which it originates. Some of the best specimens that could be discovered of their drama, their poetry, and their prose fictions, have long ago been translated, and the chief value of these has consisted not more in their own abstract merits than in the light which they threw on a people so long self-insulated, and shut in from the reach of foreign influence or investigation. Their sacred and historical works, and more particularly the latter, which are bare chronicles of events little connected with the rest of the world, have hardly repaid the pains of translation.

Some light might possibly be obtained as to Indian history from the Buddhist books, if the records which they contain could be made out. Lord Auckland observes to me,—" I mention, as a particular object of inquiry, that Pali phrases expressed in the Chinese character are said to be found in Chinese works, and that Pali works (or copies of them) taken from India to China between the second and tenth centuries of the Christian era by Buddhist priests, are supposed to exist in the libraries of China."

In its practical uses, however, the importance of the language has lately increased in proportion to the extension of the field for its exercise. The best proof of this lies in the great accession to the number of persons who make it their study, and who have gained an extensive knowledge of it. The importance of this knowledge in promoting and aiding all our relations with China is sufficiently obvious, and Sir Henry Pottinger informs me in his last letter that there is a growing impression at home to this effect.

On the other hand, in consequence of the unpliant nature of the Chinese medium, and the difficulty of conveying foreign ideas through it, we never shall be able effectually to impart *European* information to the *Chinese*, unless they learn our language. For this purpose, however, it is remarkable that there are no less than three separate institutions already in this colony, while I am not aware of any express establishment for teaching Chinese to Europeans, here open to the public.

Abstractedly, and apart from its positive uses, the Chinese, in a merely philological view, may be considered as a species of miracle. It is, in fact, the most ingenious and nearly the most perfect application of the hieroglyphic principle that can be imagined. The classification and analysis of the characters afford a subject of endless metaphysical amusement, and a new or additional language might be constructed out of the infinite combinations of their distinct constituent portions. (See Article IV.)

I am able to hand to the Society a paper, drawn up by Sir George Staunton, of general hints as to various points of inquiry to be suggested to residents in China and at Hongkong. The consuls at the five ports have been instructed by me to give every encouragement and assistance to pursuits of this nature, in conformity with the wishes of Her Majesty's Government.

Under the head of arts, we are already too much beholden to Chinese ingenuity to be altogether without hope of something from the future. The people who appear from the best accounts to have originated among themselves the inventions of gunpowder, printing, and the compass, as well as the manufactures of silk, tea, and porcelain, must carry into the operations of their pro-

ductive industry a constitution of mind rich in results,
of which something still remains to be known.   It was
only a few days ago that I was shown some white
English porcelain very well painted at Hongkong, with
figures and flowers by Chinese workmen.

I have by me several letters from the Earl of Auckland, the active President of the Royal Asiatic Society,
in which his lordship suggests subjects on which information would be interesting.   "I may premise,"
he observes, "that in our present state of knowledge
regarding the government and people of China, and the
arts, manufactures, and agriculture of that country,
scarcely any information in detail could be given to us
which would not be regarded as valuable.   I observe
that a Medical Society has been established at Hongkong, which it is proposed shall correspond with scientific societies in England.   Might it not be of advantage
to all parties if this society were to place itself in direct
communication with the Royal Asiatic Society of London ? "   The Medical Society seems, from what I hear,
to have been the germ in which our new institution
originated, and if we should hereafter desire to be
admitted as a branch of the Royal Asiatic Society (of
which I happened to be one of the seventeen or eighteen
original members, in 1823), I cannot doubt of the
accession being welcomed by that body.

It appears to myself that one of the most promising
departments of knowledge which have been opened out
to us since the war is that of natural science, and that
the mineral, vegetable, and animal kingdoms (to take

them in the ascending series) afford a comparatively unexhausted field for research.

Geology, indeed, considered as the ancient record of our planet, "rich with the spoils of time," cannot be expected to unroll one of its most interesting or alluring pages in the east and south of China. The primary, unstratified, or non-fossiliferous rocks, which there seem almost exclusively to prevail, contain none of those remains of organized existence, vegetable and animal, in which the more recent formations of *our own island* are so rich—having given birth indeed to that remarkable rule, " that the surest way of tracing the same formation in different countries or situations, is not by the identity of structure, but the identity of the fossil remains contained in it."

Of the secondary formations—the fossiliferous strata —in which the remains of organized existence show themselves, the highest or most recent that we have yet heard of in our neighbourhood are the coal-beds, which Sir Thomas Cochrane's visits to Formosa have proved to exist near the northern extremity of that country, at Quilon or Kweiloong. Some Formosan coal (of which a specimen is on the table) was lately brought to this colony and sold at 15 rupees or about 30 shillings a ton, but will in all probability be obtained much cheaper. It is needless to insist on the importance of such resources for our steamers. Now here the *practical* value of geology may come into play, by enabling persons to follow out those certain indications which are afforded by the strata that invariably lie in immediate contiguity to coal-beds, and which are a much more infallible guide to hypogene discovery than the divining wand of Dousterswivel in " The Antiquary."

If the Primary rocks of China are in some respects deficient in geological interest, they form a class that is rich in metallic treasures, and for some time past the government of the country has evinced an extraordinary desire to discover and work additional silver mines. During my stay at Florence, in 1837, I spent some time in the Grand Duke's Museum of Natural History, where, in the department of Minerals, there is an admirably arranged series of metallic substances. It so happens that I have by me the rough notes of observations which were made on the spot, and I will produce them here to show that the sites in which metals are found, or what may be called their *habitats*, are principally the granitic and other Primary rocks. The substances with which they are usually combined or alloyed when not in a native state are added.

Platina.—Found in granite rock—native or in company with iron.

Gold.—The Primitive rocks—native and often mixed with the sands of rivers ; of course a mechanical result.

Silver.—The granite rocks, and carbonate of lime—native or combined with sulphur and antimony.

Mercury.—In quartz, and in the primary calcareous rocks—native, or combined with sulphur and sulphuric acid.

Lead.—The granite rocks, fluate of lime and carbonate of lime—combined with sulphuric acid, with crome, carbonic and phosphoric acid, and with molybdenum.

Nickel.—Found in quartz and carbonate of lime—combined with arsenic—a constituent of aërolites, or meteoric stones.

Copper.—In the granite rocks, in carbonate of lime, and about volcanoes, in union with sulphuric acid. In the natural state, when pure, nothing can exceed the fine crimson colour. It is found as an oxide, and also combined with pyrites, zinc, the arsenic, muriatic, and carbonic acids ; and as a carbonate abounds in China, in the shape of *malachite*, which is found in lime rocks.

Tin.—Exists in company with quartz and mica, two of the constituents of granite—almost always as an oxide, for we learn from experience that tin rusts almost as readily as iron.

Iron.—In the granite rocks and in carbonate of lime. It is found generally as an oxide, but the Grand Duke's museum contained some fine crystals from the Isle of Elba in the neighbourhood. These the Italians call *oligisto,* I presume from their rarity.

Zinc.—In the granite rocks—found as an oxide, and combined with carbonic and sulphuric acids.

Bismuth.—In the primary rocks—exists native, as well as combined with sulphuric acid, and also as an oxide.

Cobalt.—Found in the granite rocks, and in carbonate of lime—exists as an oxide, and in combination with arsenic acid. With this substance the Chinese prepare the blue colour of their porcelain.

I may here remark, as a motive to the Society to collect a museum, the great use of such collections in concentrating, and thus subjecting to observation in a condensed view, the more rare or interesting productions of the natural world. Buffon himself is said to have commenced his career from the moment he became intendant of the Museum of Natural History at Paris. "Des lors," says his biographer, "l'ardeur de Buffon se fixa sur un seul objet—étudier, enrichir les dépôts d'histoire naturelle, et, a côté de ces échantillons toujours si incomplets de la nature, décrire la nature elle-même, en raconter l'histoire, en expliquer les lois, en retracer les monuments." Such a depôt besides has the advantage of supplying a place of reception to many objects which would otherwise become lost or destroyed.

There is the same sort of use, as regards living

plants, in a small botanical garden, for which I should
be willing to grant (and I feel persuaded H.M.'s Government would sanction it) a moderate piece of ground.
Lord Auckland wrote to me when leaving England,—
"Since I saw you I have had some communication with
the Colonial Secretary, who seems to be most favourably
disposed to the view which I have taken, and who will,
I trust, give his official authority to the proceedings
which I have in view. I wish that he may be led to
sanction a moderate expense for a garden at Hongkong,
which may serve as a depôt for the introduction of
plants to China, and for the transmission of plants to
England." An official dispatch was subsequently
addressed to me from the Foreign Office conveying a
general authority for the encouragement of scientific and
literary pursuits in this country.

I have now in the ground attached to my house three
flourishing plants of the European olive, brought out by
Mr. Fortune of the Horticultural Society. It is satisfactory to see them thrive so perfectly in this climate,
for, according to the Grecian fable, the olive was deemed
the best gift that Minerva was able to confer on mankind; and at the close of a war, whose object it was
armis exposcere pacem,[1] this was the most appropriate
and auspicious symbol that England could send to
China.

We may hope that Mr. Fortune's last valuable collections reached home in safety with himself, as the

---

[1] On the China medal.

supplement and completion of the previous consign-
ments which he had made. But his stay was of course
too brief to exhaust the boundless stores of botany
which must still remain to reward research, in a country
to which we are already much beholden.[1] With regard
to what may now be called the old and new systems of
botanical classification, every one will choose for himself; but the scheme of Linnæus seems for some years
to have lost something of its authority in competition
with that perfected by Jussieu. Indeed, in the botanical
garden at Geneva I could not perceive any allusion to
the Linnæan plan. By an amateur of the science
they may both be valued for their respective merits.
The precision with which the Swedish naturalist divided
the vegetable world into twenty-four classes, determined
by the number, situation, or proportion of the stamens
in flowers, still further subdividing these classes into
orders, founded on the number of pistils, or their styles,
is certainly highly ingenious and attractive; and what
is perhaps most remarkable in this method, is the fact,
that it has completely comprehended, not only the plants
known to Linnæus, *but all that have been discovered
since!*

At the same time, this system is so entirely artificial,
that plants which are nearly allied in nature are sometimes widely separated in classification; while, on the
other hand, many which are classed under the same
head have not the remotest natural affinity. I may

---

[1] He repeatedly returned in search of new plants.

instance the sacred lotus of China and the poppy,—they belong not only to the same *class*, but the same *order*, in the Linnæan system : yet the one has been regarded as something sacred by the Chinese, (being in fact a symbol of Buddhism,) while the other is proscribed and its cultivation prohibited. They have not the most distant affinity in nature.

The Natural System of Jussieu is less of a mere *nomenclature*, and I may here give in a few words the outline of its principles from his French biographer. There are among vegetables certain natural families, as the *gramineous*, the *umbelliferous*, and the *leguminous*. It having been observed that in each of these families some of the distinctive organs are constant, while others are varied, the first, as the most important and useful, were made to serve as the heads of the principal divisions, and the others in their turn came in to form the subdivisions under them. By this natural procedure, one certainly arrives less easily at naming any new plant than by the artificial nomenclature of Linnæus ; but it has been found that the juices and substances of vegetables naturally allied have generally similar qualities, and hence the Natural System is a great help in materia medica and economics ; at the same time that great aids may be derived from it in gardening and agriculture, particularly with reference to grafting and the rotation of crops, on account of the similar organization and habits of plants belonging to the same natural families.

The most valuable shape for transmitting home a

new plant is of course in the living state; but there is much less difficulty, and sometimes equal utility, in sending the seeds. Dried specimens of plants answer the purposes of the hortus siccus; while fruits preserve their perfect shape, and sometimes their colour, in spirits. Some vegetable productions, as the nutmeg, are so highly antiseptic that fine specimens of the fruit and leaves of that spicy aromatic have been preserved in a bottle of plain water.

Lastly, as to the animal kingdom. The greatest encouragements are afforded by the Zoological Society of London to the transmission home of living specimens, chiefly of rare mammalia and birds. I have a letter from the Earl of Derby, the president of the society, in which his lordship suggests the promotion of their objects by transmitting home any really new or scarce animals from China in a living state, and offers to defray the charges on their being delivered at Liverpool, which is not far distant from Knowsley, his seat.

But in cases where the difficulty of transmission, or the mode of capture, renders living specimens impossible, the objects of physiology, at least, may be partially answered in other ways—by the skin or the skeleton of quadrupeds or birds, or in the case of the smallest animals (reptiles especially), by entire specimens in spirits. In this manner sporting may sometimes be made subsidiary to science, and the gun may occasionally serve as purveyor to the museum.

The minister Keying sent me from Canton an adult

male and female and a fawn of what I had hoped, before they arrived, might turn out a new species of deer; but they proved to be identical with the fallow deer which we have at home. Among the natural productions of this island, I have seen a small variety of the deer kind, a fox, and a civet cat, which last was caught among the rocks by the sea-side, a circumstance which may seem to imply that it preys occasionally upon fish. It is well that the snakes appear to be neither numerous nor of a malignantly poisonous character. A variety of the boa constrictor has been proved to exist here; but its size is fortunately not such as to render it formidable.

In the several departments of natural history the Society may look especially for assistance from its medical members, in addition to their professional contributions. In language and literature, the increased number and extended range of the new race of Chinese students ought to do something; while in arts and manufactures the ordinary channels of commerce will hardly fail to supply much that is valuable. It is at once unnecessary and impossible to particularize everything that may be comprised within the sphere of an association like this, whose objects are so general.

I have a note from Dr. Buckland, at Oxford, addressed to Sir George Staunton, conveying the request of Professor Liebig to be furnished with all possible information as to the details of Chinese agriculture, and especially the question of manures. The whole subject of field cultivation has become of momentous interest, since the failure of one of our main articles of food appears to have imposed the necessity of a sort of revolution in a long established system.   It is not likely that the productions of the extreme south of China would be suited to our climate; but we know from experience that towards the north a great variety of the cereal and other dry grains are produced in lieu of rice, and some of these might be profitably adopted as articles of food.[1]

To trespass no longer on your attention, I will merely add, that the pursuits which it is the object of this Society to encourage and to cultivate are a fertile source of amusement and occupation, and that they are respectable even when unattended with success. The useful and beneficial exercise of superior intellect is the main distinction between men and the brute creation, with which the former are so nearly allied in their animal organization, their animal wants, and their animal gratifications, as to have led an ancient philosopher to define man as a mere " bipes implumis," a two-legged creature without feathers.   But the best answer to this bad compliment is the practical one.   In a sense allied to that of the popular saying, that " the boy is father to the man," youth and middle life may, by the improvement of time and opportunities, bequeath to age a species of inheritance which is no bad com-

---

[1] The French have since culti-vated the *Holcus sorghum* with great success ; and, moreover, in-troduced the Camphor tree, *Laurus camphora.*

pensation for the loss of other advantages. Let us
believe our old teachers;

Φύσις, θέλησις, ἐπιμέλει', εὐταξία,
Σοφούς τίθησι, κ' ἀγαθούς, ἐτῶν δέ τοι
'Αριθμὸς οὐδὲν ἄλλο πλὴν γῆρας ποιεῖ.

The insulated exertions of individuals, however
strenuous, must be weak in comparison with the union
and co-operation of an associated body like this institution, which I hope will assume a sort of adventitious
maturity by being incorporated with, or grafted on, the
Royal Asiatic Society.

VII.

CHUSAN IN BRITISH OCCUPATION.

(From the Proceedings of the Royal Geographical Society.)

THE importance of this island was sufficiently demonstrated in its capture on two successive occasions by a British force, and its retention (on the last) for a period of four years, as a guarantee for the fulfilment of the stipulations of the treaty with China. If any additional considerations could augment the importance of Chusan, it would be the vicinity of the position to Japan, and its intervening between the mainland of China and that other nation which once actually occupied it, and which is fast becoming an object of interest and speculation to the civilized world. Whatever may be the result of the pending American expedition to Japan, it is certain that the new current of adventure, setting westward across the Pacific, must find Japan, with Chusan, the first outpost of the Asiatic continent in that direction; and Christian states must inevitably be involved in relations, amicable or otherwise, with those hitherto secluded regions. The object of this paper was to illustrate a map of Chusan, completed by actual survey during our last occupation of the island, when Brigadier Colin Campbell (since Lord

Clyde) had the command, and to add such other details as could be collected from various sources (chiefly through Dr. Gutzlaff) in several visits to the spot. The last was in 1846, on my surrendering Chusan to the Chinese Government, after the full payment of the indemnity, according to the provisions of the treaty of Nanking.

The Chusan group appears at first to have been occupied by fishermen. The islands were in the seventh century incorporated with China, although the control at first exercised was of a precarious nature. Tradition states, that an emperor of the Soong dynasty, who held his court at Hàng-chow during the Mongol invasion, fled to Chusan for shelter. During the Ming, or next Chinese dynasty, the Japanese, then the most commercial nation of Eastern Asia, made Chusan their entrepôt, and carried on a lucrative trade. Having afterwards gone to war, on account of the ill-treatment of their countrymen by the Chinese, they took possession of the island, and kept it for many years. This forms a singular parallel, as far as it goes, with our own case. Chusan subsequently reverted to the *Ming*, or Chinese dynasty, whose representatives, long after the Manchow Tartars had taken possession of China, sought refuge there and defended themselves. But the Manchows at length became masters of Chusan and surrounded Tinghae, the capital, with a wall. They made it, moreover, a naval station, such as it was found by our force in 1840.

The latitude of Jos-house Hill, to the right of the

landing-place, near Tinghae, is 30° 0′ 24″ N., and its
longitude 122° 6′ 24″ E. of Greenwich. The island
lies from N.W. to S.E., with a circumference of 51¼
miles, the extreme length being 20, the extreme
breadth 10, and the least breadth 6 miles. The hills,
which traverse the whole island with their various
spurs, render the divisions of the territory natural
ones; and the valleys between them contain the small
towns or villages with their population, which all
belonged to the Hien of Tinghae, dependent in its
turn on the superior district, or Foo, of Ningpo. The
town of Tinghae stands about half a mile from the
beach, of irregular form, nearest approaching a pen-
tagon; in length about 1,200 yards from N. to S., and
1,000 in average breadth. The surrounding wall is
nearly 3 miles in circuit, with four gates, each defended
by an outer gate having a side approach. The ditch on
the outside of the wall is interrupted on the N.W. side
by a spur from a neighbouring hill, which projects into
the town, and forms an easy access to an attacking
force on that side. This hill constituted the head-
quarters of the Cameronian regiment in 1840. On the
arrival of the British force in that year, the population
of Tinghae numbered from 25,000 to 30,000.

Upon the S. coast of the island, the plains consist
mainly of alluvial tracts gained from the sea, and still
on the increase. There are in some places threefold
dykes, showing the gradual encroachment of human
industry upon the deep. On the northern coast the
case is different; there the sea, unchecked by those

K

numerous islands which to the S. act as natural break-waters, beats with great violence on the shore, urged by the prevailing N.W. winds; and the inhabitants have with incredible labour reared solid stone walls in the most exposed spots, to prevent the salt water getting into their rice-fields.

The valley in which Tinghae stands is called *Yung-tung*, and is one of the most extensive in the island, being 4 miles long by 3 broad. Standing nearly on a level with the sea, and copiously irrigated by canals, it is well suited to rice cultivation. It is enclosed along the S. front by an extensive dyke. This was, in 1841, considerably raised, and converted into a line of batteries, which our force easily took in flank, much to the surprise of the Chinese, who expected us to attack them in front.

The Map of Chusan shows the direction of the mountains running principally across the breadth of the island. The greater part of the surface is hilly ground, in geological character generally corresponding with the adjacent group, and consisting chiefly of granite. No volcanic traces have yet been discovered, although several of the Japanese islands, at a short sailing distance, are of that class, and among them Sulphur Island has an actually burning crater.

On most of the hills there is a moderate coating of earth, which permits the growth of grass and fir-trees; and industry has improved these natural advantages to the production of sweet potatoes and other vegetables. The climate of the island, in 30° lat., is admirably

suited to the vine, as are also the declivities of the
hills; but the Chinese make little or no wine from the
grape. Bamboo groves are planted, notwithstanding
the comparatively high latitude. The tea-shrub grows
in many places luxuriantly. An exception occurs in
the highest ridges about *Scaou-sha*, *Chae-ho*, and *Ma
Aou*, which are comparative barrenness, fit only for
herds of goats. In some places artificial terraces have
been constructed, and, as the supply of water is considerable, the earth thus retained by stone walls
produces good crops of rice. The inhabitants have
been very diligent in the construction of paved paths
across the hills, which facilitate the communication at
all seasons of the year. There are also small Buddhist
temples built in these passes, where the passenger is
supplied with tea, the leaves of which the surrounding
peasantry contribute gratuitously.

At a distance these elevations often look very wild,
but on a nearer approach it is found that no soil has
been lost, the smallest patches having some productive
cultivation. Every poor man may choose an un-
occupied spot on the hills and prepare the soil for
trees or vegetables, paying little more than a nominal
rent, and remaining the undisputed owner as long as
he continues to cultivate it.

The ground rent of the whole island appears to be
very light. According to a return obtained by Lieut.
Shadwell, of the 98th Regiment (for some time holding
civil employ), there are three rates of rent, as in the
rest of China. The irrigated ground, or *Tien*, pays

annually per *mow*, 110 copper coins in money, and
something under 2 catties of rice. The dry ground, or
Te, where corn and vegetables are grown, pays 88
copper coins, and about 1½ catties of rice. The remaining ground, called *Shan*, or hills, pays only three
copper coins, and nothing in kind. The object of a
part payment in grain may be to preserve something
like an average corn-rent.

There are many small streams running from the
mountains and crossing the plains into the sea, of
which the largest is the Tung-keang, east of the town,
which reaches the harbour close to Jos-house Hill. At
high water the native boats can ascend this only a short
distance, to a place called Tung-keang Poo, where a
number of merchants carry on an active trade with the
neighbouring main. There is not a valley without its
stream : some with boats, sluices, and bridges. Many
are dry during the summer, but when the rains fall
they furnish sufficient water for the canals and reser-
voirs. The canals in some places form a network, and
furnish a supply to every rice-field. Though not constructed by persons of professed science, they prove to
have been laid out on the best plan, and are examples
of practical skill. It is only within the town of
Tinghae itself that these canals are noxious, exhaling
most offensively in summer. .

During part of the winter the canals of the lowest
valleys overflow and cover the fields, though most of the
roads and paths are sufficiently raised for keeping up
the communication. The inundation which occurred in

1843, at the commencement of October (during our occupation), was unprecedented. The clouds seemed to come down in a mass, and the water accumulated with such rapidity that no precautions could abate its violent effects. The western part of the island exhibited a sheet of water, out of which the hills rose as islands. Immense pieces of rock were swept down by the torrents from the mountains, bridges and causeways destroyed, some of the rivulets changed their beds, while many of the most fertile fields remained covered with gravel; but on ordinary occasions the sluices are sufficiently adapted to letting off the waters, however great the quantity. The wet and dry seasons here and at Hongkong[1] are reversed: in the south the winter is dry, and the flooding rains fall during summer. The difference of lat. about 8°.

As to climate, very accurate tables were kept during our long tenure of Chusan. Considering the position of the island, in 30° lat., the average temperature is remarkably low; but the influence of the sea tempers both the extremes in comparison with the opposite main. In the beginning of the winter of 1841, while the snow at Ningpo fell above a foot in depth, and remained on the ground for several days, there was a mere sprinkling at Chusan. North-westerly winds prevail throughout the year, and it is only during July and August that the heat is oppressive to Europeans.

---

[1] This word is often written as two separate ones; but there is no better reason for writing Hong Kong than Chu San or Lon Don.

In 1843 the weather was still so cold during some part
of May as to render a fire comfortable. Nature revives
generally about the beginning of February, when the
first blossoms of the plum-tree make their appearance.
The real flower season is in April and May, when the
whole surface of the country is decked in the brightest
colours. Cherries are ripe in May, and a great variety
of vegetables brought to market, including peas and
beans. In June the grain harvest commences, and
most of the blossoms diminish. A new cultivation
takes place this month. Crops of rice, with millet,
coriander, and other seeds, are then sown, and rain falls
to July. In September the weather is generally cool
and dry, and the temperature delightful in October,
during which the last of the rice harvest is brought in.
The sweet potatoes are ripe in September. The first
hoarfrost is seen in November, and during December it
often freezes severely; but the ice does not remain so
long as on the main. Most of the trees being deciduous,
the island looks bleak during the winter. The fan-
palm, however, grows in the open plains, and even the
plantain in sheltered nooks; but this last, though it
blossoms, brings no fruit to maturity. Opinions were
at first very unfavourable as to the healthiness of the
climate, and the terrible mortality among the troops
in 1840 seemed to justify the worst that could be
formed. Certainly the rice-fields, which are nothing
but marshes, alternately flooded and dry, might lead to
the conclusion that the exhalations must be unfavourable to European constitutions. But in 1840 much of

the ill effect might be ascribed to the influence of the war. The fever was then prevalent among the natives, and carried off large numbers of them. Subsequent experience, from 1842 to 1846, when the island was peaceably restored, convinced the most doubtful that the climate is really salubrious, and that the mortality among the troops in 1840 was caused chiefly by the want of wholesome provisions and good lodging, joined to the effects of *samshoo*, the deleterious Chinese spirit. Fevers occasionally prevail during the summer months, but they seldom resist the use of quinine. The Sepoy troops from India suffered from the cold of the winter.

In its productions Chusan does not materially differ from the adjacent mainland of Ningpo. The sleek and small cattle, and the buffaloes, larger than those in the south, are used exclusively for the plough, and never slaughtered for the use of the Chinese, so near to the head-quarters of Buddhism in the neighbouring island of Pooto. The small cultivators do not keep a bullock, but there are men who hire them out for the value of about 8*d*. a-day. There are no grazing pastures, the cattle being driven to the mountains, and receiving very little fodder besides. The soil being close and adhesive, ploughing is a difficult process; but, notwithstanding the smallness of the cattle, they are very efficient, and more than one is seldom or never seen in a plough. Horses are not used for agricultural purposes, and the Chinese Government does not allow the common people to have them in their possession. There are, however, asses of a very strong description, and a mule is occa-

sionally met with. These are used exclusively for
riding, while all burthens are either transported in
boats or on men's backs. A small species of goat is
killed for its meat; but they give very little milk, an
article of which no Chinese ever makes any use whatever. During the British occupation many flocks of
Tartar sheep were brought over from the main, and
throve extremely well, but they were killed entirely for
the consumption of the English. Pigs are not so
numerous as on the main, and are sometimes imported
from thence. The dog is of the common Chinese
breed, like the Esquimaux variety; and occasionally a
very diminutive Japanese dog is met with. The island
is too well peopled to leave much range for wild animals
—a few small deer seem to be the chief.

Fowls are of the largest description, in fact of the
Ningpo breed. Ducks are reared in immense quantities
by the peasantry. There are large establishments
where the young are artificially hatched, and sold at the
rate of forty ducklings for a dollar. Even geese are
hatched in a similar manner. A few pheasants and
woodcocks were found by English sportsmen. Wild
swans come during the winter in hundreds, and occupy
the extensive watery flats; as also wild geese and wild
ducks. Our people shot snipes in the rice stubble, but
they are not disturbed by the natives. The presence of
our force, and the demand for game, gradually induced
the Chinese to pursue it, but the principal part comes
from the main.

One of the dainties in the waters of Chusan is the

yellow, or mandarin fish, which, during April, May, and June, is caught round the island in such quantities as to occupy above a thousand boats. It is a large fish, rather flat, and of a yellowish hue, and, when fresh, nearly as handsome as the gold-fish, with a dorsal fin of the same colour. When caught it is immediately sold to merchants who are on the spot, with large boats filled with ice, in which, being carefully packed, it is taken over to the main, and thus sold all over the country. The flesh is good, and when a little seasoned with sauce possesses an excellent flavour, highly estimated by Chinese gourmands. This fishery forms an important branch of industry, and occupies a considerable portion of the islanders. A small species of shark, of a dark grey colour, is also caught during summer, and, being salted, is sent to other parts of China. The shallow, muddy seas in this neighbourhood abound in fish, and produce herring, mackerel, mullet, pomfret, ray, sole, sturgeon, and other varieties.

Of reptiles, a black snake is very common, and found in the fields, but, from the little heed taken by the natives, it may be supposed to be innocuous. There is another large snake that frequents houses, pursuing rats and other vermin with great hostility; and, as it is harmless, the natives do not discourage it. It is black on the back, with a yellowish-white belly, and grows to six or eight feet in length. The silkworm is reared by only a few families, but the position and the climate of the island would insure success in a more extensive cultivation of its produce.

Chusan does not abound in wood. This scarcity is not the fault of the soil, but owing to the thriftless habit of cutting down all the growth of the hills as it rises up. The most frequent, perhaps, is the useful tallow-tree (*Stillingia*), spared and cultivated on account of its produce. It is found principally on the banks of streams, where it blossoms in May, and the berries form in bunches, coming to maturity in October and November. By this time the leaves are of a beautiful red, the pods containing the seeds burst, and those seeds make their appearance coated with white tallow, and about the size of a pea. Suddenly the leaves fall off, and the trees, from the whiteness of their berries, look as if they were in blossom. The natives then cut the branches, gather the berries, boil and press them so as to make the tallow run into a fat, which, when congealed, resembles the animal tallow, but is less firm and consistent. The island produces a large quantity of this substance, especially in the north-western districts, and exports largely.

The varnish-tree, which somewhat resembles the fig, thrives also very well in Chusan. The oil or varnish extracted is inferior to that produced in Ganhoey, which may perhaps be from another plant. The natives excel in applying it to wood-work of all kinds. Their furniture, and the framework of the best buildings, are beautifully varnished; and the durability of the coating is such as to insure its superiority to all oil-painting and other contrivances for protecting wood against the influence of climate and time. The tree might be introduced with great advantage into Europe.

The camphor-tree also flourishes at Chusan, and will grow to a large size if permitted. The natives, however, only use the wood, and do not extract the resin as they do on the main. This tree, too, might be well introduced in Europe, being very ornamental and sufficiently hardy. A kind of elm, of which the blossoms, when dried, are used as a dye-stuff, and much esteemed by the Chinese, grows on the banks of streams. The dwarf fir and oak are as common as the full-grown trees are rare. The banian ficus is even in this latitude a beautiful tree, and, as in the interior of China, planted for religious purposes round temples and other public buildings. A slender graceful pine is cultivated for ornament; and the people show superstitious veneration for the cypress, which they plant chiefly near graves.[1] This peculiar sort is the *Cupressus pendula*, or "weeping cypress," brought to England by Mr. Fortune. The Chinese say that this tree soon decays, but the wood is firm and fragrant, and esteemed by their cabinet-makers.

The natives possess apricot, peach, plum, apple, and pear trees, but take no trouble to improve them, and the fruit is consequently of the most wretched description. The Loquat, and some kinds of oranges, grow well without much care. The best fruit in the island is what has been erroneously styled "arbutus," which it very closely resembles, both in fruit and leaves, being

---

[1] "When I am dead, inter my body on the brow of some unfrequented hill, and plant the fir and the *cypress* thickly around." — Chinese drama, "Heir in Old Age," p. 34.

at the same time quite a different tree. The Chinese call it *yangmei*, and Mr. Fortune says it is—

"A species of Myrica, allied to the Himalayan *M. sapida*, noticed by Frazer, Royle, and other writers. The Chinese variety, however, is much superior to the Indian. Indeed I believe the Chinese have both, but use the Indian as a stock for grafting on. There is a very large plantation of this tree in Chusan, and the fruit was beginning to be brought to the market during my stay. The trees were bushy, round headed, and from fifteen to twenty feet in height. They were at that time loaded with dark red fruit, not unlike, at first sight, the fruit of our arbutus, although very differently formed (internally) and much larger."

It is well worth introducing in England.

"The oil plant, *Brassica Sinensis* (Mr. Fortune observes), is in seed, and ready to be taken from the ground in the beginning of May, and there is a great demand for the oil which is pressed from its seeds. I may state that this plant is a species of cabbage, producing flower stems three or four feet high, with yellow flowers, and long pods of seed like all the cabbage tribe. In April, when the fields are in bloom, the whole country seems tinged with gold, and the fragrance which fills the air, particularly after an April shower, is delightful."

He adds—

"The flora of Chusan, and all over the mainland in this part of the province of Chekeang, is very different from that of the south. Almost all the species of a tropical character have entirely disappeared, and in their places we find others related to those found in temperate climates in other parts of the world."

That new and beautiful plant, the *Weigelia rosea*, was first discovered, Mr. Fortune tells us, in the garden of a Chinese mandarin, near the city of Tinghae, on this island. "It was loaded with its noble rose-coloured flowers, and was the admiration of all who saw it, both English and Chinese." It is fortunately quite a hardy plant, and flourishes in the open air in this country.

The tea-shrub is grown almost everywhere on the island, but treated with little care, and left almost wholly to itself. The produce is accordingly of an

inferior kind. It seldom grows above four feet in
height, and occurs sometimes wild among the mountains. The utmost care taken by the natives is to
weed a little round the plants; and so congenial does
the climate appear withal, that the plant still thrives,
and produces good crops of leaves. There are, on an
average, two gatherings in the year. The first commences in April, and comprises the young and finer
leaves. Old and young women are then busily employed in gathering them, while the mistress of the
family keeps up a slow fire under a large iron pan, into
which they are thrown. When sufficiently heated, a
strong man receives them into an oval basket, and
kneads them with all his might, in order to press out
the superfluous moisture. They are then spread out
on a large frame of wicker work, under which a little
fire is kept up. This process is repeated after an
interval, and the tea is subsequently sorted and picked,
and sold to small merchants, who export it to the main,
principally Soo-chow. The finest tea fetches about a
quarter of a dollar (or one shilling) per catty of 1⅓ lb.,
and suits the Chinese; though, on account of the
slightness of the firing, it is not calculated for the
foreign market. Chusan exports about 30,000 dollars
worth every year, besides its own consumption.

The bulk of the inhabitants give their whole time to
the cultivation of rice, the *summum bonum* of every
Chinese, who affects to pity those countries which do
not grow it. Wherever the smallest spot can be converted into a rice-field they are ready to abandon any

other culture, though it might seem more advantageous. Notwithstanding this, however, there is not sufficient produce for the consumption of the island, and one-fourth the annual supply is brought from Tae-choo. They have the white, red, and *no-me*, or old man's rice. The first resembles Carolina rice in the largeness and whiteness of the grain. The seed is first thickly sown in a small bed in the spring; thence it is transplanted into the field in bunches, and placed very exactly in rows. The greatest care is taken to provide an ample supply of water, with which the field is flooded; and the tread-wheels are constantly raising water to the different levels in dry weather. Every weed is carefully pulled up, and the appearance of any is considered discreditable to the cultivator. The grain is ripe about the month of August: after being first bent down by the farmer, it is subsequently cut off, and thrashed out by beating against the inside edge of a large basket or tub, provided with raised sides, to prevent the loss of the grain. Next it is dried, freed from straw and other impurities, and laid up for use. To disengage it from the husk they pound it in large stone mortars, and then winnow it. The coarser kinds are placed in a stone mill, which is put in motion by a bullock, and a rotatory grinding separates the chaff from the grain. The crop that has been last put into the ground arrives at maturity in October, or even as late as November; but this crop, on account of the uncertainty of the weather, is liable to be spoiled before it can be gathered in. The produce varies from twenty to thirtyfold.

One of the most graceful and prolific grains in Chusan is the Barbadoes millet, which grows to a great height, and is said to produce a hundredfold. Towards harvest time, when rice is getting scarce, it is made into cakes of a reddish hue, and thus constitutes the food of the people. The large thick stalks are used for fuel. There are besides two other kinds of millet, of a fine grain and very white, which are used instead of rice.

The wheat is of an inferior description. There are two different species, both of which have a low stalk, and one is unbearded. The Chusanites cultivate it like rice, transplanting it in bunches, but without the irrigation. Of the flour they make cakes and vermicelli, and use the grain extensively in distilleries. The barley is small, and ground down by the poorer classes to mix with their rice. Buckwheat is grown in small quantities on the most sterile lands, and also found wild.

The attempts to introduce our common potato succeeded in some measure, but the sweet potato grows so successfully on the brows of the hills, that it constitutes a cheap and excellent food for all. The yam and taro are grown, but the latter is small and insipid. The fields produce a variety of summer and winter beans, as well as green peas. The radishes, turnips, and carrots are very fine; but the variety of kitchen vegetables is not great. The brinjal (a species of solanum) grows in perfection, as well as cabbage, lettuce, and spinach, with cucumbers, melons, and pumpkins. There is the large *Petsae*, or Peking cabbage (more like a lettuce in appearance), which is salted or pickled, and eaten largely by the Chinese. Ginger, of an excellent description, is common, and the coriander seed is cultivated on ridges. The fields, to a large extent, are covered with crops of mustard, the seeds of which are exclusively used for expressing the oil, a considerable item of export.

The cotton shrub is largely cultivated near the sea, and especially on lands which have been gained from the water, and still contain saline particles. Both the white and the brown, or nankeen, cotton are grown, but the latter only in small quantities. Each is of a very fine fibre, superior to what is imported from India, but also twice as dear, and by no means of so long a staple. The *yu*, hemp plant, from which grass-cloth is made, grows almost wild, and is cut down twice or even thrice a year for the sake of the fibres. The women, however, do not work it into a texture, but merely spin it into thread, and use it for sewing, probably on account of its strength.

The only walled town in the island is the capital, Tinghae. One-third of the ground-plan of this has no habitations. The level sides of the wall are encompassed by a ditch, that stops short at the hill which enters the city on the north-west. The wall is eighteen feet high and fifteen feet thick, and on the west and east sides nearly in ruins, notwithstanding the extensive repairs by the Chinese in 1841. The parapet remains in a very few places. The hill inclosed within the wall on the north-west side is a spur from the neighbouring ridge, and was occupied in 1840 by the 26th, or Cameronian regiment, so many of whom fell victims to disease, and were buried there. The city is traversed by canals, which are a real nuisance, without any countervailing advantage. The largest street is that which runs in a straight direction between the south and north gates; the rest are small and short—many of them mere lanes. There are four gates at the cardinal points, forming the outlets of the principal streets, and also a water gate, between the west and south gates. The buildings are mostly of an inferior description, with the exception of two temples, dedicated to ancestors, and to the guardian idol of the city. In the former is the largest representation of Buddha that has been met with. A few of the richer classes have long rambling houses, walled in within a court containing a whole series of buildings. The shops of the better traders are very showy; but the common people have mere mud hovels, or paltry dwellings put together with tiles and stones, without regard to warmth, ventilation, cleanliness, or comfort. Many of them are built in squares; and in a little space, which four Englishmen would find too narrow for a habitation, there are perhaps forty Chinese huddled together. Tinghae would not, in fact, rank with a good country town in England. Before our occupation it had a suburb towards the sea, called *Taou-tow*, consisting of streets, some woodyards, distilleries, and stores, all of which were levelled with the ground, and their places supplied by barracks. Temple, or Jos-house Hill, which commands the town and harbour, and was in 1841 so diligently fortified by the Chinese, is 800 yards from the south gate, and 122 feet high, close to the beach, with a canal on the east side. The dyke along the front of *Yungtung* valley was converted by the notorious[1] Yukien into a breastwork against an attack by sea, and has since been falling into decay. During our occupation a new suburb, calculated to surpass the old one in extent and solidity, gradually rose up at Tungkeang Poo, some way up the eastern creek or canal, and houses were daily building there.

The harbour of Chusan is formed by the island itself on the north; Trumball and Macclesfield Islands on the south; Grove Island and Beacon Rock on the east; Guardhouse and Tea Island on the west. It is well landlocked, the water varying from four to eight fathoms; but the currents are strong, with not very secure holding ground; they run nine knots per hour.

The largest place next to Tinghae is the town or village of Scaousha ("Little Sandy" Valley), a manufacturing station, where they make agricultural implements. *Ta-chen* has also a small town, as also *Sekea-mun* to the east, and *Tsinkong* (or Sinkong) to the west. By far the greater portion of the population lives in villages and hamlets, which are scattered all over the island, and found in the most secluded spots. The richer landholders generally assemble their tenants in a very large inclosure, where a whole clan lives together with children and children's children, and this generally constitutes a village in itself.

---

[1] China during the War, and since the Peace, vol. i. p. 184.

The people of Chusan are shorter than the Chinese on the main land; and there is no doubt of a considerable mixture of Japanese blood ever since that people possessed the island. It is well known that the Japanese are universally of short stature. Though often strong-limbed, the Chusanites are not a fine race. Their women are particularly unattractive: for owing to the habit of drawing their hair very tight, or some other cause, they lose their hair early, and become bald. The materials of dress are generally the same in both sexes. In summer they are clothed in grass-cloth (called *Hea-poo*, or summer cloth), mostly dyed blue, and some wear next to the skin a strange garment composed of a bamboo network; that is, small sections of bamboo (like bugles) formed with string into a species of net, which prevents the upper garments coming into contact with the body. On festive occasions they are gaily decked out with the help of embroidery. The better classes wear the fine stuffs of Háng-chow and Soo-chow. Since the introduction of our calicoes the cleanliness and comfort of both sexes have advanced; and this applies to the lower orders as well as the upper. In winter they wear stuffed cotton dresses, mostly of light-blue colour; a few, also, sheep-skins, and the more respectable classes, furs, which, during our stay, gradually gave way to broadcloth and camlets. The lower orders dress by no means so extensively in woollens as the cheapness of our long-ells might lead one to expect; and this is the more surprising as contrasted with the considerable consump-

tion of English cotton goods. A thick and coarse kind
of Russian cloth was much in use; but of late the
merchants of Ningpo, as well as the people of Chusan,
seem to have preferred our manufactures, which, though
thinner, are more durable, and retain their appearance
longer than the Russian. The general introduction of
woollens must be a work of time; but, as a proof of
the growing consumption, may be mentioned the great
falling off in those silk manufactures which were formerly
used as either linings or covers for fur dresses, as these
were worn outwards or inwards.

Few ragged persons are met with; but the thrifty
housewives understand patchwork thoroughly, and the
warmth and thickness of the garment increase in proportion as it is mended. The under-garments of all
classes are generally in an abominable state; nor are
the richest ashamed of vermin and cutaneous diseases.

All classes of people are gross feeders; and, strange
to say, the only articles of food for which most of them
entertain an aversion are beef, milk, and butter. This
seems originally grounded in the old Buddhist super-
stition, in regard to the flesh at least. Rice is the basis
of the daily food of all, eked out among the poor with
barley, sweet potatoes, and millet. They have three
hot meals a day; and even the beggar has a number of
small messes with which to season his rice. The
richer classes, even on common occasions, have as many
as twenty small saucers before them, containing pickled
fish, cockles, salted vegetables, soy, and similar condi-
ments. The sea furnishes the largest quota in this

account, and the ingenuity of the people in preparing
these marine delicacies is remarkable. Whatever is
highest seasoned and most pungent pleases them best.
The consumption of meat is but small, as in the rest of
China; and even pork, in such general use elsewhere
throughout that country, is but sparingly eaten at
Chusan. On the occurrence of festivals they prepare
dishes which, in point of elaboration, might rival the
productions of finished cooks; and it is by no means
uncommon to see as many as seventy following each
other in succession. Generally, however, they are very
moderate in their habits. Even the use of the distilled
spirit called *samshoo*, so general on the arrival of the
British, very much declined subsequently, in consequence of the many restrictions it became necessary to
impose for the sake of the troops. The consumption
of opium was very small in comparison with that at
Sincapore and Hongkong.

The town of Tinghae and its suburbs had at the
commencement of 1843 about 27,500 inhabitants, including men, women, and children; a large number,
considering the small extent of buildings. But even
this large number, strange to say, under the government of foreign conquerors, increased towards 1846
(when the island was restored) to above 35,000. Our
census did not extend to the whole island, of which the
population can only be *assumed* at 200,000 besides.
Notwithstanding the general fertility, and the cultivation of rice in every available nook, considerable im-
portations of grain are required.

Dr. Gutzlaff, who was for some time civil magistrate at Chusan, reported that

"Nine-tenths of the inhabitants live from hand to mouth, upon a very miserable pittance. I have gone from cottage to cottage, from hovel to hovel, in order to satisfy myself about the means of subsistence among the majority of the labouring classes, and found it at a very low level. An artizan, who understands his work tolerably well, receives, besides his daily food, about 60 copper cash (the twentieth part of a dollar), or 2½d. With this he has to maintain his family; but they contrive to subsist upon such a pittance, and the reason is, that the wives understand how to eke out a trifle ; and the children, almost as soon as they can walk, are taught to contribute something to the common stock. Even under such pinching poverty they are seldom heard to grumble, seeming to understand their duties better than their rights, and never looking to others for aid as long as they can move themselves. The poverty met with in the houses, accompanied by unabated cheerfulness, is a characteristic of the Chusanites.[1] When, after having prohibited begging in the streets, all the paupers of the island were collected, we had about seventy individuals, and these were either old decrepit men and women, or blind and maimed people, who justly claimed our charity."

Any one in the town may carry on what business he chooses, having first served an apprenticeship, and been for some time a journeyman. In the country valleys, however, the poorer classes depend entirely upon the more prosperous landholders, and, though slavery does not exist, they have to work as hard as any slaves. There is no legal restraint; the bond is merely social, the landlord being in some measure responsible for supplying his peasantry in time of scarcity with provisions at a certain rate. There is an extraordinary restriction as to the transport of grain from one valley to another (just as there is in China, from one province to another), because it is believed

---

[1] Perhaps of the Chinese in general.

that if this transport were allowed, the price in the immediate neighbourhood would rise. Owing to this absurdity, the price of rice in Chusan itself varies sometimes surprisingly in the respective districts.

The Chusanites are not fond of the sea like the people of Fokien ; but on land they resemble their own buffaloes in the patience with which they tread day after day through their inundated rice-fields. Being able to bear much fatigue, and perfectly hardened against the inclemency of the weather, they are subject to few diseases. The two that prevail most are "jungle fever" and elephantiasis. The former is at times very malignant, and carries off numbers in a short time, as was the case in 1840, partly perhaps the consequence of the war. The latter displays itself in the swollen legs of the patient, which increase in size gradually until his death ; though this complaint, however incurable, does not seem much to shorten life, as many who are afflicted with it reach old age.

No male above twenty years of age remains single if he can help it, and the women are married as early as sixteen. An old unmarried woman is unknown, nor are old bachelors often met with. The advantages attending the married state, according to Chinese institutions and notions, keep up the population to a high-pressure state ; but there are few families with more than four or five children. The disproportion between sons and daughters cannot be ascribed to natural causes, and it is admitted that female infanticide prevails here as in other parts of China. The females, notwithstanding their cramped feet, work very hard both at home and in the fields; but the men never oblige them to plough or perform the labour of cattle, as is the case in some parts of China.

A wedding is celebrated by all with more expense and display than any other event of life. The parent of the bride receives a certain sum of money, as soon as they agree to marry their daughter, but they at the same time furnish her *trousseau*. The men are generally too poor to have more than one wife, and the conjugal tie is pretty lasting. The wives are remarkable for their quarrelsome dispositions and passionate behaviour when once roused.

They do not attend much at home to the education of their children, beyond teaching the daughters to sew. The sons at about six years of age go to school if the parent can afford it, and pay perhaps the value of two or three dollars annually to the teacher. In those establishments of course none but the most elementary knowledge is taught. The boys learn to read the sacred books of Confucius, and to write a legible hand, and leave school as early as twelve or fourteen years of age. Those who intend to repair to the public examinations, and choose a higher walk of life, continue longer at school and subsequently read at home. When we first took possession of the island, there were two colleges wherein the youth of maturer age studied to become graduates, but the sum total of the learning, as usual, did not go beyond explaining the classical books (those of Confucius), and writing essays. As

some thirty were advanced every year to the grade of
Sew-tsae (bachelor), there was a great deal of emulation
among them. A few of the elder having obtained the
rank of *Keu-jin* (licentiate), and one of them even promoted to a magistracy in Honan province, literature
was held in some esteem and reputation on the island.
Nevertheless, the mass of the population, in consequence
of their extreme poverty, can neither read nor write,
and this is the more remarkable, as in most parts of
China few of the male sex can be found entirely devoid
of an elementary education.

The character of the population comprises the usual
mixture of good and bad. It has been shown that they
are a hardworking and patient race, and easily guided
when once their confidence has been gained; but, like
their countrymen on the mainland, they are commonly
lying, thievish, and faithless. The most solemn asse-
verations amount to nothing, and nobody considers
himself obliged to perform promises unless bound by
something more cogent than a mere sense of duty.
They are fond of litigation, easily awed into obedience,
orderly and quiet; but of course ignorant and narrow-
minded, and incapable of comprehending anything
beyond the range of their very limited experience. Wo
have seen that they are patterns of contentment,
cheerful bearing, and patience under difficulties; but
in their social dealings they are knaves, and, whoever
has the power and opportunity to do it, oppresses and
takes advantage of his neighbour. During our four
years' tenure of the island as conquerors, martial law

found them very quiet and orderly subjects, and had little or nothing to do the whole time, as Brigadier Campbell reported.

Such religion as they possess consists in the forms and rites of the grossest idolatry. In the town, and in the numerous valleys, there are abundance of temples (called by our people Jos-houses) built by subscription, on nearly the same models, according to their respective sizes. These serve for the varied, and somewhat inconsistent, purposes of schools, taverns, gambling houses, and theatres. They are generally built, in the country, at some romantic or picturesque spot, in some hilly pass, or some wooded nook, and derive more of their attractions from this than from their architecture. In them are to be found a few clay images of gods or deified heroes rudely executed, and in the larger ones is a priest who subsists on alms, and rather degrades the ecclesiastical character by acting at once as tavern-keeper and waiter to the travellers or visitors. Both temples and priests belong to the Buddhist religion, and the hierophants are of the lowest order of uneducated people, satisfied with a bare subsistence. All their business is to burn incense before the images, keep the lamps trimmed, and on festive occasions light up the building; or, at other times, they are working in the field; for to some of the temples a piece of land is attached as an endowment. They exercise no influence upon the minds of the people, but are generally treated with contempt.

Altogether different from these are the preachers of

the *Taou* sect, or Rationalists,[1] of whom there are about thirty in the town of Tinghae, and some in the country. They read sermons at burials, marriages, times of sickness, and other domestic occasions, and also exercise the office of exorcists, the Chinese being especially afraid of ghosts. The punishment of hanging was viewed by the natives at Hongkong as a comparatively indifferent matter, as long as the bodies were delivered to the relatives to be interred with the usual ceremonies; but when the order was given that they should be buried within the precincts of the gaol, the terrors of both hanging and imprisonment were much increased, and with salutary effect, as was intended.

The priests of Taou wear no distinguishing badge, nor do they maintain celibacy, but lead a secular life among the people at large. In their professional capacity they recite in a drawling tone discourses which only the initiated can understand, and will go on for five days for a single dollar. The common people look upon them more as sorcerers than teachers.

In many houses there is a domestic shrine, where the inmates light a lamp and burn incense; but, subsequent to the occupation of the island by the English, idolatry of all kinds very much declined. Their gods had perhaps fallen into discredit since the untoward results of the war. Occasionally a procession might be seen winding its way through the streets; but only the rabble were to be found in its train. The mass of the

---

Described in "The Chinese," vol. ii. p. 70.

people really live without religion, totally unmindful of anything but the supply of their physical wants. The only Sabbath in the whole twelve months is the New Year; all the rest is a round of unceasing daily toil, to those who are condemned to labour. A survey of China affords the best practical argument in favour of the Sabbatical institution, and of the blessings it confers on mankind; when clear of that fanatical excess, Pharisaical rather than Christian, which was authoritatively condemned by Christ himself.

The occupation of nineteen in every twenty of the inhabitants is agriculture. A large portion of the soil is held by families, not individually, but according to the Chinese rule of domestic clubbing. On letting lands to the cultivators, a stipulation is made for one half of the produce in kind, and, when the harvest arrives, the corn, on being beaten out, is put into scales, and thus equally divided. The cultivator pays the tax to Government, according to the nature of the land, at so much per mow, a space that will produce at the most eight peculs of *paddy*, or rice in the husk. The farmer must provide all the means of cultivation, and holds his lease, as tenant at will, entirely at the pleasure of the owner, who seldom lets above ten mows to one farmer, generally only five, with the produce of which the latter must manage to subsist.

Their agricultural implements are of the most simple description. The ploughshare is a piece of cast iron; the spikes of the harrow consist of knives which cut sideways. After the second rice harvest is off, they plough the fields, allowing them either to lie in large clods, or sowing a species of clover, which is used, not for feeding cattle, but as a manure. This is confirmed by the observation of Mr. Fortune, who says :—

"After the last crop of rice has been gathered in, the ground is immediately ploughed up, and prepared to receive certain hardy green crops, such as clover, the oil plant, and other varieties of the cabbage tribe. The trefoil, or clover, is sown on ridges, to keep it above the level of the water, which often covers the valleys during the winter months. When I first went to Chusan, and saw this plant cultivated so extensively in the fields, I was at a loss to know the use to which it was applied, for the Chinese have few cattle to feed, and these are easily supplied from the roadsides and uncultivated parts of the hills. On inquiry, I found that this crop was cultivated almost exclusively for manure. The large fresh leaves of the trefoil are also picked and used as a vegetable by the natives."

Their main reliance, however, is on the most disagreeable, though perhaps the most fertile, manure so universal in China. They keep it in small waterproof tanks, and promote fermentation by throwing substances into it. They are in this respect extremely filthy, and with senses more obtuse than might be readily imagined. For peas, and some other vegetables of the pulse tribe, they use dry ashes as manure, throwing it into the drill prepared for the seed, and thus manuring the plant rather than the ground. The discovery of Liebig, that beans and peas contain *Caseine*, a substance identical with the curd of milk, has been familiar to the Chinese for centuries ; and *bean-curd*, or cheese (called by them *Tow-foo*), is commonly hawked about the streets.

They transplant almost every article from a seed bed,

no matter whether green vegetable, grain, or pulse, and assimilate the cultivation of nearly everything to that of rice. In the case of the sweet potato (a convolvulus), they cut off the sprouts and plant them, after having dug up the previous crop. These sprouts are an article of trade; and, to improve the quality of the potato, people from great distances on the coast of China come over to Chusan and plant whole tracts of hills, with a certain stipulation regarding the produce.

Chusan has but few manufactures. Some weavers make up coarse stuffs of cotton from yarn which has been spun by the cottagers; but the home-made article is not sufficient to clothe more than a portion of the population. There are some forges constantly at work in *Scaou-sha*, near Ting-hae on the N., for providing agricultural implements; and the salt works on the coast make up the total of industry apart from agriculture. Within the town of Ting-hae, during our occupation, a considerable business was carried on in the carving and varnishing work, which exists in such perfection on the opposite coast of Ningpo. Nothing can exceed the durability and neatness of furniture prepared in this manner. The greatest care is bestowed on bedsteads, or rather little tabernacles, which constitute both a bed and dressing room within themselves, and on which a profusion of carving and inlay-work is lavished. One of these obtained a prize at our Great Exhibition.

Previous to our occupation of the island, a great number of junks which traded between the N. and S.

touched at Chusan, anchoring in the harbour of Ting-hae, where the suburbs formed a depôt for merchandise. The presence of our shipping seemed to discourage this resort; but Sinkeamun, to the eastward, continued to be a place of rendezvous for a great number of vessels, chiefly fishing craft, which ranged at large among the group of islands, and along the embouchure of the Keang, manned principally by Fokien sailors. These adventures are partly carried on with the capital of the island; and some Fokien firms, who traded in company with Chusan merchants, were established in Ting-hae. Thus, the most necessary article in China next to rice, that is, fish, was provided for the adjacent main from the Chusan group, whose shallow seas and landlocked roadsteads are unusually favourable to fishing. The other principal exports were coarse black tea, cotton, vegetable tallow, sweet potatoes, and some wheat. The larger junks were driven away by our capture of the island, but the smaller craft seemed to increase. They came from Wunchow, Tacchow, Shihpoo, Seang-shan, Ningpo, Shaouhing, Hángchow, and Chapoo, bringing the produce of their respective districts, and principally rice, as well as Sycee silver; in return for which they bought our cotton manufactures, opium, a few woollens, and some Straits' produce. But the European trade at Chusan never approached the anticipations of many sanguine speculators. The neighbourhood of Shanghae and Ningpo was alone enough to attract and engross the main part at those large marts, especially the former. Compared, however, with what existed previous to our arrival, the trade was active, and many of the native traders of Tinghae became comparatively opulent; a result which they could very little have anticipated, from what they must have been accustomed originally to regard as a great calamity.

Should Japan become effectively open to European trade, Chusan, from its vicinity, must occupy a still more important position than it has ever done yet. The new whaling trade, established by the Americans in the adjacent seas, would find it a most convenient spot for refitting and supplies, for which they now resort to Hongkong. Nothing more would be then required to complete its prosperity but an increased cultivation of tea and silk, for both which products it possesses the exact geographical position and climate which are found most favourable on the opposite coast of China.

Previous to our occupation, Chusan and all the smaller islands of the group constituted a district under the jurisdiction of Ningpo. The principal civil authority was a magistrate of the rank of Hien, with two subordinates at Tinghae, and several others on the other islands under his charge. He transmitted about 10,000 tales and 30,580 shih of rice annually to the government on the main.

At the head of the military establishment there was an admiral, with about 20 to 30 war-junks, and a nominal force of 5,000 to 6,000 men. A great part of these were mere men of straw, whose pay and allow-

ances were drawn, in Chinese fashion, by the mandarins.
It was seldom that a tenth of the number could be
mustered, and it was said that at our first attack in
1840 no more than 500 men were forthcoming. Upon
the temporary evacuation in 1841 the importance of the
position was fully perceived by the Chinese Government,
and three generals, with about 10,000 men, were sent
over expressly, at the same time that a militia was
raised on the spot. On the second capture in 1841
these three generals all fell, one in action, and the two
others by their own hands. After the conclusion of
peace the Chinese Government endeavoured to retain
some authority over the island, notwithstanding our
occupation by treaty, and an officer was stationed at
Taekoshan with this view. But his improper interference became soon checked by the adoption of summary
measures, and the inhabitants were thereby taught that
no divided sway would be permitted during our occupation.[1] When British rule became extended over the
island, it was the first object of our officers to put a
stop to the violences and disorder which had prevailed
during the war. Native constables were established in
all the valleys, and these being generally men of substance and influence, and supported by our authorities,
succeeded in restoring order and ensuring the security
of person and property. There was, besides, a small
and effective police, which, being backed on occasion by
military means, expelled the thieves and robbers from

---

[1] Sir Colin Campbell sent me a too officious functionary to Hong- kong where his punishment by his own government was secured.

M

the island. In a short time crime decreased; nothing was lost that was not in time restored, or its equivalent recovered. The exemption from all taxes during our tenure of the island tended of course to conciliate the good-will of the people; and upon its evacuation in 1846 the Emperor's Government did not deem it prudent to alienate the Chusanites by demanding past arrears from them. Their experience of British rule under circumstances of military conquest can hardly have failed to convey a favourable impression; and the stimulus given to the trade and industry of the island rendered the war, in its ultimate results, a benefit rather than an infliction to the inhabitants themselves.

Chusan has since, for the third time, been in our occupation during the last Chinese war.

VIII.

ANALYSIS OF A WORK ON HUSBANDRY AND BOTANY.

(Presented to the Horticultural Society with the original work.)

DURING the four years passed by me in China, as Governor of Hongkong, I had frequent communications with an accomplished Italian, Monsignor Il Conte di Besi, Bishop *in partibus infidelium*. His long residence in the country (I had known him there in 1834), and his knowledge of the language, joined to the new facilities and immunities afforded by our treaties, had enabled him to procure valuable Chinese books, among which was a work which he was good enough to present to myself. It relates to the whole system of national husbandry, and treats at the same time largely of botany, being entitled *Noong-Ching Tseuen-shoo*, literally *De Re Rustica liber completissimus*. In a Chinese sense the title is certainly not misapplied.

Subsequent leisure has enabled me to examine it with some attention; and as the methodical arrangement of the work, together with the incidental notices, appeared to be sufficiently illustrative of the state of Chinese knowledge on an important subject, it occurred

to me that a short analytical summary of the whole
might be considered within the scope of the objects
pursued by the Horticultural Society.

The work is divided into sixty sections, and contained in twenty-four of those *brochures* which constitute the form of all Chinese books. A covering of
handsome green silk distinguishes this book from ordinary ones, and the printing and paper are of the best
description. Some hundreds of coloured woodcuts
illustrate the various objects described in the work.

Sect. I.—III. The first three sections treat of the
origin and early history of husbandry, commencing with
what is to be found in classical writers, and then proceeding to cite generally what has been said later on
the subject. " Men," it is observed, " lived entirely
on flesh until the time of Shin-Noong, ' the divine
husbandman,' who taught them to *study the seasons*
and *cultivate the earth.*" This plainly refers to the
pastoral state as preceding the agricultural, and the
first lessons of the Chinese, as of all other early
nations, consisted of what Virgil calls

" Arvorum cultus, et sidera cœli."

The third section records all that the different
dynasties of sovereigns have instituted as regulations
and customs to give importance and encouragement
to husbandry. In my work on China I had occasion to state that agriculture has always been called
the " root," and manufactures and trade only the
" branches."

Sect. IV., V. These two sections are on the con-

struction and regulation of fields and cultivated lands.
They are ranked in the threefold order of—1. Rice-
fields, or those artificially levelled or flooded, and called
Tien; 2. Those destined to the ordinary, natural, or
dry cultivation, called *Te;* 3. The hills, or more barren
and waste lands, called *Shan.* These three constituted
the divisions of Chusan during our occupation,[1] and
they pay dues to government accordingly, in a descend-
ing scale. The terrace cultivation in steps is called
Te-tien, or "Ladder-fields."

So generally have the Chinese adhered to the decimal scale, on account of its obvious advantages, that
their land measurements are squares of ten. Thus a
hundred square *poo* make a *mow,* or what has been
called a Chinese acre; a hundred *mow* make a *foo.*
The original or theoretical divisions of land were in
the style of a chess-board, which of course usually
becomes impossible in practice.

Sect. VI.—XI. The next six sections are entitled the
"Business of Husbandry." The sixth and seventh
relate to the management of farms, ploughing, and the
use of manures. It is inculcated as a maxim in farm-
ing, "Better a little land and good than much and
bad." The eighth and ninth sections are on the
breaking up and reclaiming of waste lands. The
government, as an encouragement to the cultivation
of wastes and the production of food for the people,
allows any unreclaimed lands to become the property of

---

[1] Chusan in British Occupation, page 131.

him who first brings them into tilth, and levies no taxes until such time as the produce yields a surplus. The tenth and eleventh sections treat of the four seasons and their respective productions. The twelve lunations of the Chinese year are reviewed in detail. The various natural phenomena of each period, with the plants and animals which distinguish each, are enumerated, and there is a complete collection of prognostics. The subjects are exactly those of the *Phenomena* and *Diosemeia* of the Greek poet Aratus. In the tenth section is given a curious diagram, consisting of concentric circles, after the fashion of those which surround the Chinese compass. Near the centre are the seasons, months, &c., and radiating from each of these are the natural phenomena of each period. In the outer or largest circle of all are the labours to be performed, and the products to be expected, under every season. It is in fact, a very comprehensive synopsis of " Works and Days."

Sect. XII.—XX. Considering the important part which water performs in Chinese husbandry, it is not surprising to find nine sections devoted to the " Profit (or use) of Water." After some *Tsoong Lun,* or " general observations," the work proceeds to notice the modes of irrigation in various parts of the empire ; but as the eastern and southern provinces are incontestably superior in their natural advantages to the western and northern (which are either mountainous or cold), so three sections are given to the east and south and only one to the west and north.

The seventeenth section treats of the construction and management of dams and sluices, and the various modes of raising water to a higher level. Coloured woodcuts give very clear representations of the wooden chain-pump, the (so-called) Persian wheel observed by our embassies in the interior, and other contrivances for irrigating lands lying *above* the level of the water required. This is very essential in rice cultivation, and the Chinese effect their object, as usual, with great ingenuity and success.

The eighteenth section treats of Chinese water-wheels of various descriptions, which are illustrated by coloured woodcuts; and the nineteenth and twentieth sections give some account of the water machinery of the "great west," meaning some of the practical applications of hydrostatics and hydraulics in Europe. This must have been collated from treatises in Chinese composed by the Jesuit missionaries. Coloured diagrams are interspersed, explaining the principles of lifting and forcing pumps (the latter with double alternating pistons and no air-chamber), and other European contrivances. They commonly apply the principle of the forcing-pump in their fire-engines, which are very efficiently constructed. The Chinese are shrewd enough to perceive and adopt what is really advantageous in use, though it may be foreign, and this part of the work contains the very undeniable remark that, "without the machinery for water, you cannot have the profits of water."

Sect. XXI.—XXIV. These four sections are devoted

to the description and representation of *Noong Kee,*
" The Tools or Implements of Husbandry." Here the
coloured woodcuts come in with good effect, and are
highly illustrative of about one hundred and twenty
different implements, the use of most of which is sufficiently obvious without the printed description. They
comprise varieties of ploughs, harrows (square and
diagonal), scarifiers, bush-hurdles (some loaded with
stones), rollers of different kinds for smoothing or
dibbling the ground, hoes, spades, shovels, rakes,
breast-ploughs, sickles, bill-hooks, choppers, slicers,
bamboo stages for drying corn, instruments for sepa-
rating the corn from the husk,[1] mills moved by two
mules, baskets, tubs, and vessels of many sorts, and
winnowing machines. Of the last I have already
remarked in my work on China, " They have a winnowing machine exactly like ours, and there seems to
be the best evidence for the fact that we borrowed this
useful invention from them. A model was carried from
China to Holland, and from Holland the first specimen
reached Leith."

Sect. XXV.—XXX. Six sections are devoted to all
those vegetable productions which are the subjects of
planting or cultivation. It may be remarked, incidentally, that the importance of eight of these is indicated by their names constituting eight out of the
214 *roots* of which the whole written language of
China is compounded, viz., Rice, Bamboo, Wheat,

---

[1] There is no representation of a flail.

Millet, Bean, Onion, Hemp, and Cucurbitaceous plants. They were, in fact, the original materials of food, lodging, and clothing, as derived from the earth.

The first two of the above six sections treat of the principal sorts of grain and pulse constituting the materials of food. The third comprises the different species of cucurbitaceous plants, of which the Chinese possess a great variety and make much use. The fourth is on various culinary vegetables, chiefly of the onion and leek tribes. The last two enumerate and describe the principal fruits of China, as the *leechee*, the *longan*, the myrica described by Mr. Fortune at Chusan, the grape (little cultivated in comparison with Europe), the great variety of oranges, citrons, &c. &c. I had occasion in another place to notice that the Chinese do not cultivate their fruits with quite the care and skill that they bestow on their flowers; and the practice of planting their fruit trees on the banks of streams and canals, though it has been found favourable to the trees, renders the fruit the object of depredation, and causes its being gathered immature.

Sect. XXXI.—XXXIV. These four sections are devoted to *Tsán Sáng*—" Silkworms and Mulberry-trees" —that is, the rearing of the silkworm, and the cultivation of the mulberry for that purpose. The thirty-first section commences with " general observations," and proceeds to the subject of feeding the silkworms. The thirty-second relates entirely to the planting and cultivation of the mulberry-tree. The next two sections are copiously illustrated with woodcuts, in explanation of the management of the silkworm by women, from the egg to the spinning of the cocoon by the worm, and then onward to reeling off the silk, and every other successive step to the final process of weaving.

Sect. XXXV.—XXXVI. After silk come the two cognate subjects of cotton and hemp, the first of which is treated in the thirty-fifth, and the second in the thirty-sixth section. Numerous woodcuts represent the various processes of reeling and weaving these two substances.

Sect. XXXVII.—XL. These four sections are devoted to the subject of *Choong Chĕ*—" Sowing and Planting." First come general observations, which occupy the thirty-seventh section. A great number of useful trees, among others the varnish or lacquer tree, are discussed in the thirty-eighth chapter; while the bamboo and the tea-plant occupy, *par excellence*, nearly the whole of the thirty-ninth. The fortieth section is devoted to the consideration of nineteen different varieties of useful trees and plants.

Sect. XLI. This section treats of domestic animals, either edible themselves or useful in providing or preserving food. They are in the following order:—Horses, mules, oxen, sheep and goats, pigs, dogs, cats, geese, ducks, fowls, pond-fish, and lastly bees. The Chinese, like Virgil, call the queen bee the king.

Sect. XLII. The whole of the forty-second section is

composed of a large collection of useful receipts, principally for the preparation of articles of food.

Sect. XLIII.—XLV. The remaining portion of this work is the most remarkable of all. I have endeavoured, in my work on China,[1] to explain the causes which (grounded on the encouragements to over-population) tend to make the country liable to frequent visitations of dearth and famine. For these reasons, there is no nation, perhaps, in which so much attention has been directed to extraordinary provisions against famine. To this may probably be attributed the unlimited range of the Chinese kitchen and bill of fare, as well in the vegetable world as the animal. I may quote an example from the description of a dinner at Chusan:— "Another strange ragoût proved to be the flowers of the common China (or monthly) rose, dressed whole. Here the mixture of salt, sour, and other indescribable flavours forbade a repetition." There are few instances in which *we* dress the flowers of plants. For one, at least, there is the authority of the inveterate Londoner who said, "there was no garden like Covent Garden, and no flower like a cauliflower." Artichokes are another example of eating a portion of the immature flower.

The three sections, from forty-three to forty-five, are devoted to the history of public provisions against dearth. In the last is an enumeration of 414 plants described and figured in the concluding volumes of this work, of which 138 are taken from the standard Chinese

---

[1] Vol. ii., pp. 401–414.

herbal, called *Pun-tsaou*, and 276 have been added. They are classified as follows :—

Tsaou—Herbaceous [1]	245
Mŭh—Woody	80
Me Kŭh—Grains and Pulse . . .	20
Kwo—Fruits	23
Tsae—Culinary Herbs	46
	414

A further classification of the same is given, as under :—

Leaves edible	237
Seeds edible	61
Leaves and seeds edible	43
Roots edible	28
Roots and leaves edible	17
Roots and seeds edible	5
Offshoots from roots edible	2
Roots and flowers edible	2
Flowers edible	5
Flowers and leaves edible	5
Flowers, leaves, and seeds edible . . .	2
Leaves, bark, and seeds edible	2
Stalks edible	3
Young shoots edible	1
Shoots and seeds edible . . .	1
	414

Sect. XLVI.—LIX. These fourteen sections are styled the " Provisional Herbal against Dearth," being the history of all the plants above classified, and the modes of preparing them as food. The description and coloured representation of each plant occupy two con-

---

[1] This term is extended some-times to soft-wooded or pithy plants, as the fig and the plantain, the last being really herbaceous.

tiguous pages, and are easily found. The contents of
the sections are as follows :—

Sections.

XLVI.—L.	Herbaceous plants,	leaves edible . . .	159
LI.	,,	,,	roots ,, . . .	24
LII.	,,	,,	seeds[1] ,, . . .	20
,,	,,	,,	leaves and seeds edible .	12
,,	,,	,,	roots and leaves ,, .	23
,,	,,	,,	stalks ,, . .	3
,,	,,	,,	shoots and seeds ,, .	1
LIV.	Woody plants,	leaves edible	41
LV.	,,	,,	seeds (or fruit) edible . .	20
LVI.	,,	,,	leaves and seeds ,, . .	8
,,	,,	,,	flowers ,, . .	5
,,	,,	,,	flowers and leaves edible . .	1
,,	,,	,,	flowers, leaves, and seeds edible	2
,,	,,	,,	leaves, bark, and seeds ,, .	2
,,	,,	,,	offshoots from roots ,,	1
LVII.	Grain and Pulse,	seeds edible	20
LVIII.	Fruiting plants,	fruit edible . . .	14
,,	,,	,,	leaves and fruit edible .	5
,,	,,	,,	roots ,, . .	2
,,	,,	,,	roots and fruit ,, . .	2
,,	Culinary plants,	leaves edible . .	14
LIX.	,,	,,	,, ,, . . .	19
,,	,,	,,	roots ,, . . .	2
,,	,,	,,	roots and leaves edible .	4
,,	,,	,,	leaves and seeds ,, .	5
,,	,,	,,	roots and seeds ,, . .	1
				410

The above list is, for some reason or other, short of
the preceding summary by *four*.

Sect. LX. This concludes the work, with drawings
and descriptions of sixty-three wild plants, edible in case
of famine.

As to the style of description, the following account

---

[1] The term *shĕ* is occasionally applied to either seed or fruit. It means the *essential product* of the plant.

of the native Chinese fig (Sect. LV.) is a specimen of the way in which each pictured plant is described. From my own experience, the native fig of China is very poor, and hardly advanced beyond the wild state. It would be a real benefit to send some of our European figs to Hongkong.

"The *flowerless fruit* grows in the hills and wilds. At present it is also planted in gardens. The leaves somewhat like those of the vine, but larger, stiffer, and thicker; divided into three lobes. The fruit grows at the junction of the leaf with the stalk. It is at first green and small; when ripe, of the shape of a pear and of a purple colour; taste sweet. The fruit may be gathered and eaten."

The drawings in this work, of some four hundred and sixty plants, however inferior to our own in execution, might very well serve, in combination with the appended names and descriptions, to procure specimens of the plants, of which many must be new. The localities are often, and indeed generally, mentioned. Portions of the work might be advantageously translated in detail; but two circumstances are essential: the translator must have leisure for the task, and he must be resident in China, as many points would require elucidation on the spot.

IX.

VALLEY OF THE KEANG

TO THE PORT OF HANKOW.

(From the Journal of the Royal United Service Institution.)

THE Keang, or Great River of China, or the Yang-tsze (Son of the Sea), has been laid open by the treaty of Tien-tsin up to the central mart of Hankow, a distance of more than 500 miles from its mouth below Nanking. Having myself journeyed along 300 miles of that distance, from the extremity of the Grand Canal to the Poyang Lake, I purpose to state the results of my own observations to that extent, and to supply the rest from the experience of others. The fruits of Lord Elgin's adventurous and most interesting expedition may be introduced by a condensed summary of what has been known before, and followed by a comparison between the former and present states of the country (before and since the devastations of the rebels), as the ground of our just anticipations for the future.

The whole tract in question lies, with little exception, between thirty and thirty-two degrees of north latitude, the favoured climate of tea and silk, our principal imports, and including some of the finest portions of China. Commencing by the mouth or delta of the river, we have the long alluvial island of Tsoong-ming, about thirty miles in length, and called from its shape and position *Keang-shĕ*, the " tongue of the river." A small party landed here during our first war and lost an officer, whence that spot at the west end was called Harvey Point. Its principal town, *Tsoong-ming-Hien*, on the south coast, is only a town of the third class. The canals with which the island abounds have high embankments to preserve the country from floods, especially dangerous from the low, flat, and alluvial formation of the land. The dense population has resulted as the effect of Chinese industry exerted on a naturally fertile soil. The portion least cultivated is the north side, abounding in those coarse high reeds which are found on the low shores or islands of the river higher up, and which serve, in combination with mud, to form embankments and even dwellings, as well as occasionally answering the purposes of fuel. A portion of the soil in the northern part is so saturated with sea salt as to form a fund for the supply of the whole island, with a large surplus for the main land itself.[1] The southern portion is the most fertile and cultivated division of the island, producing rice, wheat, barley, and millet.

---

[1] This article is so superabundant as to render its importation from abroad a rather profitless speculation. It was a part of my business in China to decide against its importation, in accordance with the fiscal regulations of the government, with whom it is a very important source of revenue ; and by the trade regulations appended to Lord Elgin's recent treaty at Tientsin, this decision has been confirmed, the article of salt being expressly excluded.

From the western extremity of Tsoong-ming to Chin-keang on the Grand Canal, which is the first point of much interest on the river, the total distance, with windings, is about 125 miles. That so long a tract should be comparatively destitute of large towns [1] is explained by the fact that the government, aware of the accessibility of Nanking and the Grand Canal from the sea, has always discouraged the navigation below Chin-keang, the canal itself supplying an inland transit independent of the sea-coast. This portion of the river was a profound mystery until Admiral Sir William Parker in 1842 conducted seventy men-of-war or transports to Nanking without the loss of a vessel, where no European keel had ever ploughed before. This, and the late expedition of five war steamers all the way to Hankow, in spite of difficulties generally deemed insurmountable, are exploits of which our navy may justly be proud. I have known many instances in the far east where they have had the good fortune to succour foreign ships of war in trouble; and I cannot call to mind any occasion (of a merely nautical nature) on which they have had to claim foreign aid themselves.

It is at Chin-keang that my own acquaintance with the great river begins, and continues to the Poyang Lake, about 150 miles short of our treaty limit at Hankow. Journeying in the boats of the country, the

[1] The chief towns which succeed each other on the north bank are Tung-chow, Tsing-keang-Hien, and Tae-yu-Hien; on the south bank are Too-paou-Hien and Yeh-shan-Hien,—all of them towns of the second and third order.

difficulties of the passage to a large squadron of Chinese vessels, against the stream and a contrary wind, occupied no less a time than from the 19th of October to the 14th of November, or little more than ten miles a day, leaving abundance of time for excursions and observation. It conveys some idea of the breadth of the river (when full from two to five miles in breadth) when I state that it frequently afforded a tolerable horizon for ascertaining the latitude.

The neighbourhood of Nanking has become so comparatively familiar to us that we may pass on at once to a higher and less known point, which we reached on the 29th October, namely, Se-leang-Shan, the " Western Pillar Hill," a remarkable high rock, which, with the " Eastern Pillar Hill " on the opposite shore, forms the *Gades* of the Keang, about thirty-five miles above Nanking. From the top of the western rock, a height of 500 feet, we observed the broad channel of the river, as it flows between two lines of mountains to the sea. This is a remarkable spot among the Chinese themselves (in peaceable times) ; and the well-built town at the foot of the rock seemed to owe its existence to the influx of visitors. On the 30th October the strength of the stream and the want of wind obliged us to stop at Wu-hu, a very considerable town about ten miles above the " Pillar Rocks," and dependent upon Taeping. In proof that the technical classification of Chinese towns does not always indicate their real size and importance, this appeared to be superior to many of their first-class cities ; and it was to the great inland com-

merce carried on by this town that such unusual wealth
and prosperity were to be referred. We here first
observed bales of cloth with the English mark upon
them, about 600 miles from Canton, inland.

Quitting Wu-hu on the 31st October, we started with
a north-west wind, and, our course here being sometimes due south, we made more progress than usual,
accomplishing a hundred *lees*, or thirty miles, by the
time the boats reached the mouth of a tributary river
named *Teih-Keang* on the right bank, in which we
anchored, near a small town built at the foot of some
low hills. The Emperor's desire to get rid of us by
the shortest route was the fortunate occasion of our
thus navigating the Keang between the Grand Canal
and the Poyang Lake, instead of following the beaten
track of low marshes along the remainder of the canal.
After travelling through the swamps of Shantung and
the north of Keang-nan, we were now in a country that
yields to none in the whole world, and is equalled
by very few. It was justly remarked by the late Sir
Henry Ellis, one of our party up the Keang, "However
absurd the pretensions of the Emperor of China to
universal supremacy, it is impossible to travel through
his dominions without feeling that he has the finest
country within an imperial ring-fence in the world."
After the lapse of about a fortnight we were, owing to
contrary winds and the timidity of our boatmen, not
advanced one half of the way to the lake ; but this
delay only afforded the more time for observation and

inland excursions, which met with no opposition from
our conductors.

On the 1st November, we advanced only twelve miles,
to Tsing-kea-chin, on an island which divides the
stream of the Keang, and above which the river spreads
to a breadth of nearly five miles, after describing what
appeared to us a considerable portion of a circle round
two islands.   On the 2nd, as early as nine o'clock, we
found the whole squadron of boats anchored at the considerable town of *Tung-ling Hien*[1] on the right bank,
eighteen miles from Teih-keang.   Thinking we were to
stop for the day, some of us set out as usual on a
ramble through the town into the country beyond,
but in the course of an hour the wind became fair and
the boats prepared to sail.   We had extended our
excursion to about two hours, when some Chinese came
hallooing and announcing the departure of the fleet, and
we did not conclude our chase of the boats on their
way up, until four hours after quitting them.

On the morning of the 3rd November we were
anchored at a town called *Tatung Chin*, on the right
bank, and opposite to those long islands by which the
Keang is so often divided.   We were detained here by
contrary winds for no less than five days, which were
spent in exploring those beautiful hills at the foot of
which the town lies.   Our excursions extended to cir-

---

[1] The name denotes "copper
mountains," and Du Halde speaks
of a valuable *green stone* found here
probably malachite, or copper ore.

cuits of fifteen and sixteen miles, when we often came across tea plantations, though here less frequent than in the south-east parts of *Keang-nan*, and in *Chĕ-keang* and *Fokien*.

On the morning of the 7th November it blew strong from the north-east, and we made one of our best day's journeys, arriving in the afternoon at Woosha-kea, or "Black Sand Fork," *kea* meaning one of those numerous points where the Keang forks out into two branches to compass an island in the middle. As we were about to enter again on the main stream, our conductors thought it prudent to remain until the wind moderated. Nothing was more surprising than the difference between the Chinese sailors of Canton and their "longshore" brethren of the Keang. The boats were almost as different as the boatmen; for, while the Canton boats are strongly built and capable of buffeting with the waves, these great square boxes, clamped with iron at the joinings, seemed really to justify the apprehensions of their conductors. This difference may partly be ascribed to the habit of occasionally encountering the sea near Canton, and partly to the long experience and example of Europeans at that place.

On our way to the present anchorage we passed the city of Chee-chow on the right bank. Du Halde describes this as having six dependent towns, and, though surrounded by the lofty hills which we observed from the boats, rich in territory and trade. The wind on the 8th being too strong for our clumsy craft and lubberly sailors, we remained at anchor, but early on the morning of the 9th started with a fair breeze, and after traversing about one hundred *lees*, or thirty miles, anchored on the further or western side of Ganking, an important first-class city. Du Halde describes the position of this large town as very advantageous, and states that a Tartar garrison was kept there for the command of the Keang and the neighbouring lake. We must have passed this on approaching the east side of the city, where 500 men in line made a good appearance. Our examination of the interior and suburbs conveyed a favourable impression of the place, where we found very good porcelain shops, indicating our approach to the neighbourhood of King-tih-chin, the chief place of its production.

We left Ganking at an early hour on the morning of the 10th November, and, after the best day's run since entering China, viz., 125 *lees*, or nearly forty miles, reached a place called Hwa-yuen Chin, or the "Flower-garden Station," about five miles short of Wangshan Hien, on the left bank. On our way here, we passed Tung-lew Hien, on the right bank, a walled city of the third class, but containing within its extensive enceinte fewer streets than dwellings and gardens. The most populous part of the place was on the outside of the walls, between them and the river. The houses in this part of the country were whitewashed, which gave them an European look. Parts of the river, even as high as this, appeared not less than three miles across, and huge porpoises were rolling along near our boats as they do at sea.

After being detained at Hwa-yuen Chin for a whole day, we sailed on the 12th November, and soon came to a part of the river where it is again divided by a long island into two streams, and proceeding along the south or right bank, we passed Ma-tung-shang, "Stirrup-iron Hill," a curious bluff point; and towards evening approached a very remarkable insulated rock, rising precipitously from the stream to the height of 250 feet. This (with another larger one at the entrance of the Poyang Lake) is celebrated in China by the name of Seao-koo-shan, the "Little Solitary" or "Orphan Rock." It appeared inaccessible on all points, except one, and here the Buddhist priests had contrived to erect some of their temples on terraces, rising one above the other. But the most remarkable feature was the countless swarm of pelicans, or fishing cormorants, which darkened the face of the rock by their numbers.

We had now entered the limits of the Keangse province, and the first walled town we passed, by name Peng-tse Hien, was, in point of position, the most remarkable we had seen. It lay on the right bank, nestled in a romantic valley, or rather amphitheatre, formed by the lofty hills around, but open to the river. Among native drawings of remarkable places I possess one of this town, as well as of the "Orphan Rock"—both of them especially noticed in Lord Elgin's expedition.

The weather became thick and boisterous, but we proceeded, and our boat with some difficulty reached Kin-kang-leaou, our destined resting-place, being a village of small note at the mouth of a creek on the

north or left bank of the river. We passed the 13th
also at this anchorage, which the Chinese itinerary
stated to be about sixty *lees*, or some twenty miles,
from the mouth of the Poyang Lake. We became
naturally anxious to inspect this famous inland sea,
which, however, though about seventy miles long, is
only the second of the empire in size, and yields greatly
to the Tong-ting Lake, also fed by the Keang, but
considerably above Hankow.

We set sail early on the 14th November towards the
Poyang. On the bold and hilly shore to our left
(the right bank) we passed Hu-kow, at the "Lake's
Mouth," as the name implies. Here, after little less
than a month's protracted journey over a distance, by
the Chinese itinerary, of 950 *lees*, and by our own calculation 280 miles, from the canal, we quitted the mag-
nificent Keang to cross the lake on our way towards the
south, already 400 miles from its mouth, but yet 2,000
short of its source. The entrance to the lake was about
a mile wide, and after passing this we came upon the
Ta-koo-shan, or "Great Solitary Rock," rising out of
the waters of the vast lake, and larger than the others,
but less picturesque and striking in effect.

For the rest of the route to Hankow we were indebted
(previous to Lord Elgin's expedition) to Du Halde and
M. Huc. The remaining distance from hence is about
157 miles. The first large city is Kew-keang, a few
miles past the entrance of the lake, with the lake on its
east and the river on its north side. Du Halde states,
from the Jesuits' survey, that the tide is apparent here

at new and full moon. He speaks of the porpoises, which we had ourselves observed, and states besides that salmon and sturgeon are caught as high up as this point. After averaging a westward course for about twenty miles to the mouth of a river on the right bank, flowing in from Hing-kwo, the Keang lies north-west and south-east from Hankow, the first city of consequence being Hwang-chow, on the left bank. Du Halde observes of this, that its neighbourhood to the great centre of commerce, 'Hankow, and the lakes and rivers in which the vicinity abounds, naturally render it very commercial and opulent. The country is highly cultivated, and rendered very picturesque by the hills on the north. Under its jurisdiction are eight towns of the third order (Hien), and one of the second (Chow).

Seventy or eighty miles above this city we reach the important central point where the three great towns of Wuchang, Hanyang, and Hankow lie at the confluence of the Hang-keang with the Yang-tse. This affluent of the great river is in itself no inconsiderable stream, running a course of six or seven hundred miles, including windings. The three great cities form a sort of triangle, separated only by the water from each other. Wuchang is the capital of the double province Hu-kwang (north and south), and the residence of the governor-general. Du Halde observes, "Voutchang est comme le centre de tout l'empire, et le lieu d'où il est plus aisé de se répandre dans les autres provinces." He adds, that it is "le lieu le plus peuplé et du plus grand abord de la Chine." To any one who has seen

Shanghae, this must seem surprising. It is placed opposite to the confluence of the Hankeang with the Yang-tse. "Doubtless," says Du Halde, "in viewing only the forest of masts which borders that noble river the Keang, about a league in breadth at such a distance from the sea, there is sufficient ground for admiration; but if, on mounting some height, one comes to discover that vast tract all covered over with buildings, one scarcely believes one's sight, or at least one believes it to be the finest thing in the world of its kind."

Han-yang, the second city of Hu-kwang, is separated from the above only by the Keang, and lies at the western angle made by the confluence of the Hankeang with the Yang-tse. Hankow, on the opposite angle, is the mere growth of this immense commerce, which, in China, seems often to escape from the municipal trammels of the interior of walled cities and to fix itself on the outside, in order to breathe more freely.

It is some drawback to the splendid prospect held out to our future trade, to consider that the valley of the Keang, from Chin-keang and Nanking to beyond Hankow, has been for years in the power of the rebels; and that, as their occupation and pursuit have been civil war and rapine instead of trade, the baneful effects must be very perceptible. But every one who has seen how speedily the Chinese repair the disasters of a fire, may feel sanguine as to the healing results of their indomitable industry:

> " Mox reficit rates
> Quassas, indocilis pauperiem pati."

The adventurous and most interesting visit of Lord
Elgin to Hankow now enables us to judge of the existing state of the Keang and its cities. The Retribution,
Furious, and Cruiser war-steamers, and Dove and Lee
gun-boats, left Shanghae on the 9th of November.
The shifting sands and shoals of the river had completely altered its channels as far as Chin-keang since
the survey of 1842, and the squadron did not reach that
point under a week, when, as an additional delay, the
Furious struck on a sunken rock between the south
bank and Silver Island. On the 20th of November they
reached the headquarters of the rebels at Nanking.
Having been fired on pretty sharply in passing, the
wise resolution was formed to drop down next morning
with the stream and administer such a lesson as would
prevent the Chinese repeating the aggression on the
return of the squadron ; and this was done in the com-
pletest manner. It must be remarked that the Emperor's fleet, close at hand, was encouraged thereby to
make an attack on the rebels' position immediately
afterwards, though at a safe distance ; a style of warfare
which accounts for this civil strife having dragged on in
a chronic state for so many years. The condition of
the rebels, however, is decidedly retrograde. They have
been driven from Chin-keang, which they before occupied, on the canal ; their floating force has been displaced by the Emperor's war-junks along the whole of
the Keang ; and the expedition observed that the
besieging imperial army formed a complete semicircle
about Nanking by land.[1]

---

[1] Nanking has since been taken, thanks to Colonel Gordon.

The lesson at headquarters was probably the cause of amicable overtures being made from the rebel city of Tae-ping, on the right bank; and when our squadron reached Wu-hu on the 23rd, after serious detentions by shoals, here again their fame had preceded them, and they were civilly received by the insurgents, whose appearance and condition conveyed anything but a favourable impression of their character and resources.

Lord Elgin's expedition was just one month later in the season than that in which I was a traveller, and the fallen condition of the river obliged the Retribution to remain at Kew-hein, literally " old town," some twenty-five miles above Wu-hu, and almost the only place at that time in possession of the Emperor's forces on the south bank, from Nanking to the highest point of rebel occupation towards the lake.

On the 26th November the expedition reached Gan-king, the last post of the rebels to the westward. Being on the north or left bank, and the insurgents having no means of communication across, while the city was actually beleaguered by the Imperialists, the proceedings at Nanking and elsewhere were probably unknown, and hence a fire was opened on our expedition, which was soon silenced. The Emperor's force again at this place was encouraged by what took place to attack the rebels after the steamers passed on. These indications have an important bearing on what may be anticipated in the future. They denote a due appreciation of our power by the Imperial government, and must induce them to have us rather as friends than enemies. The sandbanks again impeded the navigation on approaching

the Poyang Lake; thereabouts a few trading junks were
for the first time observed, and the expedition was as
much struck by the appearance of the Orphan or
Solitary Rock (before described) as we had been so
many years previously. After passing the lake's mouth
on the way to Hankow, the city of Kew-keang, on the
south bank, was found in a state of complete desolation,
though for some time abandoned by the rebels. At
Kechow, further on, was observed the boldest and finest
scenery on the river, which is here contracted within a
gorge formed by the mountains on both sides.

It was not until the 6th December that the expedition
reached Hankow, little less than a month after quitting
Shanghae : but still not much longer than I was myself
travelling (under Chinese conduct) only from Chin-keang
to the Poyang, about half the distance.

After previous accounts the actual condition of
Hankow was especially disappointing. Every dwelling
and building in the place had been demolished during
the previous occupation by the rebels ; but still much
had been restored. The shops and warehouses in one
quarter are stated to have been unusually large, and
well furnished with a surprising supply of English and
European goods. The opposite city of Hanyang was
still a waste of ruins ; but Wuchang, the provincial
city, on the south shore, appeared in a much better
condition, and corresponded more nearly with former
accounts—exciting, indeed, considerable admiration in
the expedition.

The population had, of course, suffered by the re-

morseless civil war, almost to extinction, and could afford
no ground whatever for an estimate of its former numbers. The reception given by the governor-general of the
two provinces to Lord Elgin was a very handsome one,
promoted to some extent, no doubt, by what had been
done to the rebels on the way up; and the people
showed the greatest curiosity and desire to trade.

On the 11th December the expedition quitted Hankow
on its return, and, after proceeding about thirty miles,
found that the river was rapidly falling. After a week's
incessant labour in working the steamers over the shoals
only 130 miles had been accomplished, and on reaching
the bar at the Poyang Lake not more than eleven feet
of water remained, the Furious drawing fifteen feet. In
fact, seven feet of water had fallen since they went up.
Here the Furious and Cruiser were left, while Lord
Elgin and suite proceeded in the Dove and Lee to join
the Retribution lower down. On the 29th December
the three steamers reached Nanking.

The rebels displayed, as might have been expected, a
very peaceful disposition after their previous chastise-
ment; and a visit being paid to the rebel chief, the
interior of Nanking exhibited the same scene of ruin
and desolation as the other places occupied by the rebels,
whose sole business seems to be destruction without
any reproduction. It was evident they were hard
pressed by the Emperor's force, and one of the chiefs
made secret proposals to the English party to be allowed
to desert his colours. Arrangements were effected for
safe communication with the two ships up the river, and

the mission reached Shanghae on the 1st January, after more than seven weeks' absence.

It was impossible to anticipate any other than the best results from this well-timed expedition by Lord Elgin. It seems to have tested with success the good intentions of the Peking Government, if we may judge from the conduct of their representative, the viceroy of Hu-kwang. But had it produced no other result than to establish a proper understanding with the rebels, and show them the folly of aggressive measures towards our people, this alone was worth having. The court of Peking probably hopes from us something better for itself than perfect neutrality towards the rebels, and may have been confirmed in this hope by what the squadron, in mere self-defence, was compelled to do against them up the river. Should this tend to secure good faith and practical sincerity in the observance of the new treaty we may accept the results with satisfaction, without troubling ourselves as to the disinterestedness and purity of the motives. If the authorities are encouraged to strenuous exertion, and put a final end to the rebellion which has desolated the country and paralyzed trade, this will be a great common benefit.

THE END.

Woodfall and Kinder, Printers, Milford Lane, Strand, London, W.C.

STREET, LONDON,
January, 1865.

MR. MURRAY'S

GENERAL LIST OF WORKS.

ALBERT (Prince). THE SPEECHES AND ADDRESSES on Public Occasions of H.R.H. THE PRINCE CONSORT: with an Introduction giving some Outlines of his Character. Portrait. 8vo. 10s. 6d.; or Popular Edition, fcap. 8vo, 1s.

ABBOTT'S (Rev. J.) Philip Musgrave; or, Memoirs of a Church of England Missionary in the North American Colonies. Post 8vo. 2s.

ABERCROMBIE'S (John) Enquiries concerning the Intellectual Powers and the Investigation of Truth. 16th Edition. Fcap. 8vo. 6s. 6d.

———— Philosophy of the Moral Feelings. 12th Edition. Fcap. 8vo. 4s.

ACLAND'S (Rev. Charles) Popular Account of the Manners and Customs of India. Post 8vo. 2s.

ÆSOP'S FABLES. A New Translation. With Historical Preface. By Rev. Thomas James. With 100 Woodcuts, by Tenniel and Wolf. 50th Thousand. Post 8vo. 2s. 6d.

AGRICULTURAL (The) Journal. Of the Royal Agricultural Society of England. 8vo. Published half-yearly.

AIDS TO FAITH: a Series of Essays. By various Writers. Edited by William Thomson, D.D., Lord Archbishop of York. 8vo. 9s.

CONTENTS.

Rev. H. L. Mansel—Miracles.

Bishop of Killaloe—Christian Evidences.

Rev. Dr. McCaul—Prophecy and the Mosaic Record of Creation.

Rev. Canon Cook — Ideology and Subscription.

Rev. George Rawlinson—The Pentateuch.

Archbishop of York—Doctrine of the Atonement.

Bishop of Ely.—Inspiration.

Bishop of Gloucester and Bristol.—Scripture and its Interpretation.

AMBER-WITCH (The). The most interesting Trial for Witchcraft ever known. Translated from the German by Lady Duff Gordon. Post 8vo. 2s.

ARMY LIST (The). Published Monthly by Authority. 18mo. 1s. 6d.

ARTHUR'S (Little) History of England. By Lady Callcott. 130th Thousand. Woodcuts. Fcap. 8vo. 2s. 6d.

ATKINSON'S (Mrs.) Recollections of Tartar Steppes and their Inhabitants. Illustrations. Post 8vo. 12s.

AUNT IDA'S Walks and Talks; a Story Book for Children. By a Lady. Woodcuts. 16mo. 5s.

AUSTIN'S (John) Lectures on Jurisprudence; or, the Philosophy of Positive Law. 3 Vols. 8vo. 39s.

———— (Sarah) Fragments from German Prose Writers. With Biographical Notes. Post 8vo. 10s.

B

ADMIRALTY PUBLICATIONS; Issued by direction of the Lords
   Commissioners of the Admiralty:—

   A MANUAL OF SCIENTIFIC ENQUIRY, for the Use of Travellers.
     Ed ted by Sir JOHN F. HERSCHEL, and Rev. ROBERT MAIN. *Third
     Edition.* Woodcuts. Post 8vo. 9s.

   AIRY'S ASTRONOMICAL OBSERVATIONS MADE AT GREENWICH.
     936 to 1847. Royal 4to. 50s. each.

     ASTRONOMICAL RESULTS. 1848 to 1858. 4to. 8s. each.

     APPENDICES TO THE ASTRONOMICAL OBSERVA-
     TIONS.

     1836.—I. Bessel's Refraction Tables.
        II. Tables for converting Errors of R.A. and N.P.D. }8s.
           into Errors of Longitude and Ecliptic P.D.
     1837.—I. Logarithms of Sines and Cosines to every Ten }
          Seconds of Time. }8s.
        II. Table for converting Sidereal into Mean Solar Time.
     1842.—Catalogue of 1439 Stars. 8s.
     1845.—Longitude of Valentia. 8s.
     1847.—Twelve Years' Catalogue of Stars. 14s.
     1851.—Maskelyne's Ledger of Stars. 6s.
     1852.—I. Description of the Transit Circle. 5s.
        II. Regulations of the Royal Observatory. 2s.
     1853.—Bessel's Refraction Tables. 3s.
     1854.—I. Description of the Zenith Tube. 3s.
        II. Six Years' Catalogue of Stars. 10s.
     1856.—Description of the Galvanic Apparatus at Greenwich Ob-
        servatory. 8s.

     MAGNETICAL AND METEOROLOGICAL OBSERVA-
     TIONS. 1840 to 1847. Royal 4to. 50s. each.

     — ASTRONOMICAL, MAGNETICAL, AND METEOROLO-
     GICAL OBSERVATIONS, 1848 to 1862. Royal 4to. 50s. each.

     — ASTRONOMICAL RESULTS. 1848 to 1862. 4to.

     MAGNETICAL AND METEOROLOGICAL RESULTS.
     1848 to 1862. 4to. 8s. each.

     — REDUCTION OF THE OBSERVATIONS OF PLANETS
     1750 to 1830. Royal 4to. 50s.

     ——— ——— LUNAR OBSERVATIONS. 1750
     to 1830. 2 Vols. Royal 4to. 50s. each.

     ——————————— 1831 to 1851. 4to. 20s.

   BERNOULLI'S SEXCENTENARY TABLE. *London,* 1779. 4to.

   BESSEL'S AUXILIARY TABLES FOR HIS METHOD OF CLEAR-
     ING LUNAR DISTANCES. 8vo.

       FUNDAMENTA ASTRONOMIÆ: *Regiomontii,* 1818. Folio. 60s.

   BIRD'S METHOD OF CONSTRUCTING MURAL QUADRANTS.
     London, 1768. 4to. 2s. 6d.
     —— METHOD OF DIVIDING ASTRONOMICAL INSTRU-
     MENTS. *London,* 1767. 4to. 2s. 6d.

   COOK, KING, AND BAYLY'S ASTRONOMICAL OBSERVATIONS.
     London, 1782. 4to. 21s.

   ENCKE'S BERLINER JAHRBUCH, for 1830. *Berlin,* 1828. 8vo. 9s.

   GROOMBRIDGE'S CATALOGUE OF CIRCUMPOLAR STARS.
     4to. 10s.

   HANSEN'S TABLES DE LA LUNE. 4to. 20s.

   HARRISON'S PRINCIPLES OF HIS TIME-KEEPER. PLATES
     1767. 4to. 5s.

ADMIRALTY PUBLICATIONS—*continued.*

HUTTON'S TABLES OF THE PRODUCTS AND POWERS OF NUMBERS. 1781 Folio. 7*s.* 6*d.*

LAX'S TABLES FOR FINDING THE LATITUDE AND LONGITUDE. 1821. 8vo. 10*s.*

LUNAR OBSERVATIONS at GREENWICH. 1783 to 1819. Compared with the Tables, 1821. 4to. 7*s.* 6*d.*

MASKELYNE'S ACCOUNT OF THE GOING OF HARRISON'S WATCH. 1767. 4to. 2*s.* 6*d.*

MAYER'S DISTANCES of the MOON'S CENTRE from the PLANETS. 1822, 3*s.*; 1823, 4*s.* 6*d.* 1824 to 1835, 8vo. 4*s.* each.

———— THEORIA LUNÆ JUXTA SYSTEMA NEWTONIANUM. 4to. 2*s.* 6*d.*

———— TABULÆ MOTUUM SOLIS ET LUNÆ. 1770. 4to. 6*s.*

———— ASTRONOMICAL OBSERVATIONS MADE AT GOTTINGEN, from 1756 to 1761. 1826. Folio. 7*s.* 6*d.*

NAUTICAL ALMANACS, from 1767 to 1868. 8vo. 2*s.* 6*d.* each.

———— SELECTIONS FROM THE ADDITIONS up to 1812. 8vo. 5*s.* 1834-54. 8vo. 5*s.*

———— SUPPLEMENTS, 1828 to 1833, 1837 and 1838. 8vo. 2*s.* each.

———— TABLE requisite to be used with the N.A. 1781. 8vo. 5*s.*

POND'S ASTRONOMICAL OBSERVATIONS. 1811 to 1835. 4to. 21*s.* each.

RAMSDEN'S ENGINE for DIVIDING MATHEMATICAL INSTRUMENTS. 4to. 5*s.*

———— ENGINE for DIVIDING STRAIGHT LINES. 4to. 5*s.*

SABINE'S PENDULUM EXPERIMENTS to DETERMINE THE FIGURE OF THE EARTH. 1825. 4to. 40*s.*

SHEPHERD'S TABLES for CORRECTING LUNAR DISTANCES. 1772. Royal 4to. 21*s.*

———— TABLES, GENERAL, of the MOON'S DISTANCE from the SUN, and 10 STARS. 1787. Folio. 5*s.* 6*d.*

TAYLOR'S SEXAGESIMAL TABLE. 1780. 4to. 15*s.*

———— TABLES OF LOGARITHMS. 4to. 3*l.*

TIARK'S ASTRONOMICAL OBSERVATIONS for the LONGITUDE of MADEIRA. 1822. 4to. 5*s.*

———— CHRONOMETRICAL OBSERVATIONS for DIFFERENCES of LONGITUDE between DOVER, PORTSMOUTH, and FALMOUTH. 1823. 4to. 5*s.*

VENUS and JUPITER: OBSERVATIONS of, compared with the TABLES. London, 1822. 4to. 2*s.*

WALES' AND BAYLY'S ASTRONOMICAL OBSERVATIONS. 1777. 4to. 21*s.*

WALES' REDUCTION OF ASTRONOMICAL OBSERVATIONS MADE IN THE SOUTHERN HEMISPHERE. 1764—1771. 1768. 4to. 10*s.* 6*d.*

BABBAGE'S (CHARLES) Economy of Machinery and Manufactures. *Fourth Edition.* Fcap. 8vo. 6*s.*

——— Reflections on the Decline of Science in England, and on some of its Causes. 4to. 7*s.* 6*d.*

BAIKIE'S (W. B.) Narrative of an Exploring Voyage up the Rivers Quorra and Tshadda in 1854. Map. 8vo. 16s.

BANKES' (George) Story of Corfe Castle, with documents relating to the Time of the Civil Wars, &c. Woodcuts. Post 8vo. 10s. 6d.

BARBAULD'S (Mrs.) Hymns in Prose for Children. With 112 Original Designs. Small 4to. 5s.

BARROW'S (Sir John) Autobiographical Memoir, including Reflections, Observations, and Reminiscences at Home and Abroad. From Early Life to Advanced Age. Portrait. 8vo. 16s.

———— Voyages of Discovery and Research within the Arctic Regions, from 1818 to the present time. 8vo. 15s.

———— Life and Voyages of Sir Francis Drake. With numerous Original Letters. Post 8vo. 2s.

BATES' (H. W.) Records of a Naturalist on the River Amazons during eleven years of Adventure and Travel. Second Edition. Illustrations. Post 8vo. 12s.

BEES AND FLOWERS. Two Essays. By Rev. Thomas James. Reprinted from the "Quarterly Review." Fcap. 8vo. 1s. each.

BELL'S (Sir Charles) Mechanism and Vital Endowments of the Hand as evincing Design. Sixth Edition. Woodcuts. Post 8vo. 6s.

BERTHA'S Journal during a Visit to her Uncle in England. Containing a Variety of Interesting and Instructive Information. Seventh Edition. Woodcuts. 12mo.

BIRCH'S (Samuel) History of Ancient Pottery and Porcelain : Egyptian, Assyrian, Greek, Roman, and Etruscan. With 200 Illustrations. 2 Vols. Medium 8vo. 42s.

BLUNT'S (Rev. J. J.) Undesigned Coincidences in the Writings of the Old and New Testament, an Argument of their Veracity : containing the Books of Moses, Historical and Prophetical Scriptures, and the Gospels and Acts. 8th Edition. Post 8vo. 6s.

———— History of the Church in the First Three Centuries. Third Edition. Post 8vo. 7s. 6d.

———— Parish Priest; His Duties, Acquirements and Obligations. Fourth Edition. Post 8vo. 7s. 6d.

———— Lectures on the Right Use of the Early Fathers. Second Edition. 8vo. 15s.

———— Plain Sermons Preached to a Country Congregation. Second Edition. 3 Vols. Post 8vo. 7s. 6d. each.

———— Essays on various subjects. 8vo. 12s.

BISSET'S (Andrew) History of England during the Interregnum, from the Death of Charles I. to the Battle of Dunbar, 1648–50. Chiefly from the MSS. in the State Paper Office. 8vo. 15s.

BLAKISTON'S (Capt.) Narrative of the Expedition sent to explore the Upper Waters of the Yang-Tsze. Illustrations. 8vo. 18s.

BLOMFIELD'S (Bishop) Memoir, with Selections from his Correspondence. By his Son. 2nd Edition. Portrait, post 8vo. 12s.

BOOK OF COMMON PRAYER. Illustrated with Coloured Borders, Initial Letters, and Woodcuts. A new edition. 8vo. 18s. cloth; 31s. 6d. calf; 36s. morocco.

BORROW'S (George) Bible in Spain; or the Journeys, Adventures, and Imprisonments of an Englishman in an Attempt to circulate the Scriptures in the Peninsula. 3 Vols. Post 8vo. 27s.; or Popular Edition. 16mo, 3s. 6d.

———— Zincali, or the Gipsies of Spain; their Manners, Customs, Religion. and Language. 2 Vols. Post 8vo. 18s.; or Popular Edition, 16mo, 3s. 6d.

———— Lavengro; The Scholar—The Gipsy—and the Priest. Portrait. 3 Vols. Post 8vo. 30s.

———— Romany Rye; a Sequel to Lavengro. Second Edition. 2 Vols. Post 8vo. 21s.

BOSWELL'S (James) Life of Samuel Johnson, LL.D. Including the Tour to the Hebrides. Edited by Mr. Croker. Portraits. Royal 8vo. 10s.

BRACE'S (C. L.) History of the Races of the Old World. Designed as a Manual of Ethnology. Post 8vo. 9s.

BRAY'S (Mrs.) Life of Thomas Stothard, R.A. With Personal Reminiscences. Illustrated with Portrait and 60 Woodcuts of his chief works. 4to.

BREWSTER'S (Sir David) Martyrs of Science, or the Lives of Galileo, Tycho Brahe, and Kepler. Fourth Edition. Fcap. 8vo. 4s. 6d.

———— More Worlds than One. The Creed of the Philosopher and the Hope of the Christian. Eighth Edition. Post 8vo. 6s.

———— Stereoscope: its History, Theory, Construction, and Application to the Arts and to Education. Woodcuts. 12mo. 5s. 6d.

———— Kaleidoscope: its History, Theory, and Construction, with its application to the Fine and Useful Arts. Second Edition. Woodcuts. Post 8vo. 5s. 6d.

BRINE'S (Capt.) Narrative of the Rise and Progress of the Taeping Rebellion in China. Plans. Post 8vo. 10s. 6d.

BRITISH ASSOCIATION REPORTS. 8vo. York and Oxford, 1831-32, 13s. 6d. Cambridge, 1833, 12s. Edinburgh, 1834, 15s. Dublin, 1835, 13s. 6d. Bristol, 1836, 12s. Liverpool, 1837, 16s. 6d. Newcastle, 1838, 15s. Birmingham, 1839, 13s. 6d. Glasgow, 1840, 15s. Plymouth, 1841, 13s. 6d. Manchester, 1842, 10s. 6d. Cork, 1843, 12s. York, 1844, 20s. Cambridge, 1845, 12s. Southampton, 1846, 15s. Oxford, 1847, 18s. Swansea, 1848, 9s. Birmingham, 1849, 10s. Edinburgh, 1850, 15s. Ipswich, 1851, 16s. 6d. Belfast, 1852, 15s. Hull, 1853, 10s. 6d. Liverpool, 1854, 18s. Glasgow, 1855, 15s.; Cheltenham, 1856, 18s.; Dublin, 1857, 15s.; Leeds, 1858, 20s. Aberdeen, 1859, 15s. Oxford, 1860, 25s. Manchester, 1861, 1's. Cambridge, 1862, 20s. Newcastle, 1863.

BRITISH CLASSICS. A New Series of Standard English Authors, printed from the most correct text, and edited with notes. 8vo.

Already Published.

I. GOLDSMITH'S WORKS. Edited by PETER CUNNINGHAM, F.S.A. Vignettes. 4 Vols. 30s.

II. GIBBON'S DECLINE AND FALL OF THE ROMAN EMPIRE. Edited by WILLIAM SMITH, LL.D. Portrait and Maps. 8 Vols. 60s.

III. JOHNSON'S LIVES OF THE ENGLISH POETS. Edited by PETER CUNNINGHAM, F.S.A. 3 Vols. 22s. 6d.

IV. BYRON'S POETICAL WORKS. Edited, with Notes. 6 vols. 45s.

In Preparation.

WORKS OF POPE. With Life, Introductions, and Notes, by REV. WHITWELL ELWIN. Portrait.

HUME'S HISTORY OF ENGLAND. Edited, with Notes.

LIFE AND WORKS OF SWIFT. Edited by JOHN FORSTER.

BROUGHTON'S (LORD) Journey through Albania and other Provinces of Turkey in Europe and Asia, to Constantinople, 1809—10. *Third Edition.* Illustrations. 2 Vols. 8vo. 30s.

———————— Visits to Italy. *3rd Edition.* 2 vols. Post 8vo. 18s.

BUBBLES FROM THE BRUNNEN OF NASSAU. By an Old MAN. *Sixth Edition.* 16mo. 5s.

BUNYAN (JOHN) and Oliver Cromwell. Select Biographies. By ROBERT SOUTHEY. Post 8vo. 2s.

BUONAPARTE'S (NAPOLEON) Confidential Correspondence with his Brother Joseph, sometime King of Spain. *Second Edition.* 2 vols. 8vo. 26s.

BURGON'S (REV. J. W.) Memoir of Patrick Fraser Tytler. *Second Edition.* Post 8vo. 9s.

——— Letters from Rome, written to Friends at Home. Illustrations. Post 8vo. 12s.

BURN'S (LIEUT.-COL.) French and English Dictionary of Naval and Military Technical Terms. *Fourth Edition.* Crown 8vo. 15s.

BURNS' (ROBERT) Life. By JOHN GIBSON LOCKHART. Fifth Edition. Fcap. 8vo. 3s.

BURR'S (G. D.) Instructions in Practical Surveying, Topographical Plan Drawing, and on sketching ground without Instruments. *Fourth Edition.* Woodcuts. Post 8vo. 6s.

BUTTMAN'S LEXILOGUS; a Critical Examination of the Meaning of numerous Greek Words, chiefly in Homer and Hesiod. Translated by Rev. J. R. FISHLAKE. *Fifth Edition.* 8vo. 12s.

BUXTON'S (SIR FOWELL) Memoirs. With Selections from his Correspondence. By his Son. Portrait. *Fifth Edition.* 8vo. 16s. *Abridged Edition*, Portrait. Fcap. 8vo. 2s. 6d.

BYRON'S (Lord) Life, Letters, and Journals. By Thomas Moore. Plates. 6 Vols. Fcap. 8vo. 18s.

 Life, Letters, and Journals. By Thomas Moore. Portraits. Royal 8vo. 9s.

 — Poetical Works. Portrait. 6 Vols. 8vo. 45s.

 Poetical Works. Plates. 10 Vols. Fcap. 8vo. 30s.

 Poetical Works. 8 Vols. 24mo. 20s.

 Poetical Works. Plates. Royal 8vo. 9s.

 — — Poetical Works. Portrait. Crown 8vo. 6s.

 — - —— Childe Harold. With 80 Engravings. Small 4to. 21s.

 Childe Harold. With 30 Vignettes. 12mo. 6s.

 Childe Harold. 16mo. 2s. 6d.

 Childe Harold. Vignettes. 16mo. 1s.

 Childe Harold. Portrait. 16mo. 6d.

 — .. Tales and Poems. 24mo. 2s. 6d.

- Miscellaneous. 2 Vols. 24mo. 5s.

 Dramas and Plays. 2 Vols. 24mo. 5s.

 Don Juan and Beppo. 2 Vols. 24mo. 5s.

 Beauties. Selected from his Poetry and Prose. Portrait. Fcap. 8vo. 3s. 6d.

CARNARVON'S (Lord) Portugal, Gallicia, and the Basque Provinces. From Notes made during a Journey to those Countries. *Third Edition.* Post 8vo. 3s. 6d.

 ———— Recollections of the Druses of Lebanon. With Notes on their Religion. *Third Edition.* Post 8vo. 5s. 6d.

CAMPBELL'S (Lord) Lives of the Lord Chancellors and Keepers of the Great Seal of England. From the Earliest Times to the Death of Lord Eldon in 1838. *Fourth Edition.* 10 Vols. Crown 8vo. 6s. each.

 — - · Lives of the Chief Justices of England. From the Norman Conquest to the Death of Lord Tenterden. *Second Edition.* 3 Vols. 8vo. 42s.

 — Shakspeare's Legal Acquirements Considered. 8vo. 5s. 6d.

 — ——— Life of Lord Chancellor Bacon. Fcap. 8vo. 2s. 6d.

 — ——. (George) Modern India. A Sketch of the System of Civil Government. With some Account of the Natives and Native Institutions. *Second Edition.* 8vo. 16s.

 India as it may be. An Outline of a proposed Government and Policy. 8vo. 12s.

 ——— (Thos.) Short Lives of the British Poets. With an Essay on English Poetry. Post 8vo. 3s. 6d.

CALLCOTT'S (Lady) Little Arthur's History of England. 130th *Thousand.* With 20 Woodcuts. Fcap. 8vo. 2s. 6d.

CASTLEREAGH (The) DESPATCHES, from the commencement
of the official career of the late Viscount Castlereagh to the close of his
life. Edited by the MARQUIS OF LONDONDERRY. 12 Vols. 8vo. 14s. each.

CATHCART'S (Sir George) Commentaries on the War in Russia
and Germany, 1812-13. Plans. 8vo. 14s.

CAVALCASELLE AND CROWE'S New History of Painting in
Italy, from the Second to the Sixteenth Century, from recent researches in the Archives, as well as from personal inspection of the
Works of Art in that Country. With 70 Illustrations. Vols. I. and II.
8vo. 42s.

——— ——— Notices of the Lives and Works
of the Early Flemish Painters. Woodcuts. Post 8vo. 12s.

CHAMBERS' (G. F.) Handbook of Descriptive and Practical
Astronomy. Illustrations. Post 8vo. 12s.

CHARMED ROE (The); or, The Story of the Little Brother and
Sister. By OTTO SPECKTER. Plates. 16mo. 5s.

CHURTON'S (Archdeacon) Gongora. An Historical Essay on the
Age of Philip III. and IV. of Spain. With Translations. Portrait.
2 Vols. Small 8vo. 15s.

CLAUSEWITZ'S (Carl Von) Campaign of 1812, in Russia.
Translated from the German by LORD ELLESMERE. Map. 8vo. 10s. 6d.

CLIVE'S (Lord) Life. By Rev. G. R. Gleig, M.A. Post 8vo. 3s. 6d.

COLCHESTER (The) PAPERS. The Diary and Correspondence
of Charles Abbott, Lord Colchester, Speaker of the House of Commons,
1802-1817. Edited by His Son. Portrait. 3 Vols. 8vo. 42s.

COLERIDGE'S (Samuel Taylor) Table-Talk. *Fourth Edition.*
Portrait. Fcap. 8vo. 6s.

COLONIAL LIBRARY. [See Home and Colonial Library.]

COOK'S (Rev. Canon) Sermons Preached at Lincoln's Inn Chapel,
and on Special Occasions. 8vo. 9s.

COOKERY (Modern Domestic). Founded on Principles of Economy
and Practical Knowledge, and adapted for Private Families. By a
Lady. *New Edition.* Woodcuts. Fcap. 8vo. 5s.

CORNWALLIS (The) Papers and Correspondence during the
American War,—Administrations in India,—Union with Ireland, and
Peace of Amiens. Edited by CHARLES ROSS. *Second Edition.* 3 Vols.
8vo. 63s.

COWPER'S (Mary Countess) Diary while Lady of the Bedchamber
to Caroline Princess of Wales, 1714—20. *Second Edition.* Portrait.
8vo. 10s. 6d.

CRABBE'S (Rev. George) Life, Letters, and Journals. By his Son.
Portrait. Fcap. 8vo. 3s.

—— Life and Poetical Works. Plates. 8 Vols. Fcap.
8vo. 24s.

—— Life and Poetical Works. Plates. Royal 8vo. 7s.

CROKER'S (J. W.) Progressive Geography for Children. *Fifth Edition.* 18mo. 1s. 6d.

———— Stories for Children, Selected from the History of England. *Fifteenth Edition.* Woodcuts. 16mo. 2s. 6d.

———— Boswell's Life of Johnson. Including the Tour to the Hebrides. Portraits. Royal 8vo. 10s.

———— Essays on the Early Period of the French Revolution. 8vo. 15s.

———— Historical Essay on the Guillotine. Fcap. 8vo. 1s.

CROMWELL (OLIVER) and John Bunyan. By ROBERT SOUTHEY. Post 8vo. 2s.

CROWE'S AND CAVALCASELLE'S Notices of the Early Flemish Painters; their Lives and Works. Woodcuts. Post 8vo. 12s.

———— History of Painting in Italy, from 2nd to 16th Century. Derived from Historical Researches as well as inspection of the Works of Art in that Country. With 70 Illustrations. Vols. I. and II. 8vo. 42s.

CUNNINGHAM'S (ALLAN) Poems and Songs. Now first collected and arranged, with Biographical Notice. 24mo. 2s. 6d.

CURETON (REV. W.) Remains of a very Ancient Recension of the Four Gospels in Syriac, hitherto unknown in Europe. Discovered, Edited, and Translated. 4to. 24s.

CURTIUS' (PROFESSOR) Student's Greek Grammar, for the use of Colleges and the Upper Forms. Translated under the Author's revision. Edited by DR. WM. SMITH. Post 8vo. 7s. 6d.

———— Smaller Greek Grammar for the use of the Middle and Lower Forms, abridged from the above. 12mo. 3s. 6d.

———— First Greek Course; containing Delectus, Exercise Book, and Vocabularies. 12mo. 3s. 6d.

CURZON'S (HON. ROBERT) ARMENIA AND ERZEROUM. A Year on the Frontiers of Russia, Turkey, and Persia. *Third Edition.* Woodcuts. Post 8vo. 7s. 6d.

CUST'S (GENERAL) Annals of the Wars of the 18th & 19th Centuries. 9 Vols. Fcap. 8vo. 5s. each.

———— Lives and Characters of the Warriors of All Nations who have Commanded Fleets and Armies before the Enemy. 8vo.

DARWIN'S (CHARLES) Journal of Researches into the Natural History of the Countries visited during a Voyage round the World. Post 8vo. 9s.

———— Origin of Species by Means of Natural Selection; or, the Preservation of Favoured Races in the Struggle for Life. Post 8vo. 14s.

———— Fertilization of Orchids through Insect Agency, and as to the good of Intercrossing. Woodcuts. Post 8vo. 9s.

DAVIS'S (NATHAN) Visit to the Ruined Cities of Numidia and Carthaginia. Illustrations. 8vo. 16s.

DAVY'S (SIR HUMPHRY) Consolations in Travel; or, Last Days of a Philosopher. *Fifth Edition.* Woodcuts. Fcap. 8vo. 6s.

———— Salmonia; or, Days of Fly Fishing. *Fourth Edition.* Woodcuts. Fcap. 8vo. 6s.

DELEPIERRE'S (OCTAVE) History of Flemish Literature. From the Twelfth Century. 8vo. 9s.

DENNIS' (GEORGE) Cities and Cemeteries of Etruria. Plates. 2 Vols. 8vo. 42s.

DERBY'S (EDWARD EARL OF) Translation of the Iliad of Homer into English Blank Verse. 2 Vols. 8vo. 24s.

DIXON'S (HEPWORTH) Story of the Life of Lord Bacon. Portrait. Fcap. 8vo. 7s. 6d.

DOG-BREAKING; the Most Expeditious, Certain, and Easy Method, whether great excellence or only mediocrity be required. By LIEUT.-GEN. HUTCHINSON. *Fourth and Revised Edition.* With additional Woodcuts. Crown 8vo.

DOMESTIC MODERN COOKERY. Founded on Principles of Economy and Practical Knowledge, and adapted for Private Families. *New Edition.* Woodcuts. Fcap. 8vo. 5s.

DOUGLAS'S (GENERAL SIR HOWARD) Life and Adventures; From Notes, Conversations, and Correspondence. By S. W. FULLOM. Portrait. 8vo. 15s.

———— On the Theory and Practice of Gunnery. *5th Edition.* Plates. 8vo. 21s.

———— Military Bridges, and the Passages of Rivers in Military Operations. *Third Edition.* Plates. 8vo. 21s.

———— Naval Warfare with Steam. *Second Edition.* 8vo. 8s. 6d.

———— Modern Systems of Fortification, with special reference to the Naval, Littoral, and Internal Defence of England. Plans. 8vo. 12s.

DRAKE'S (SIR FRANCIS) Life, Voyages, and Exploits, by Sea and Land. By JOHN BARROW. *Third Edition.* Post 8vo. 2s.

DRINKWATER'S (JOHN) History of the Siege of Gibraltar, 1779-1783. With a Description and Account of that Garrison from the Earliest Periods. Post 8vo. 2s.

DU CHAILLU'S (PAUL B.) EQUATORIAL AFRICA, with Accounts of the Gorilla, the Nest-building Ape, Chimpanzee, Crocodile, &c. Illustrations. 8vo. 21s.

DUFFERIN'S (LORD) Letters from High Latitudes, being some Account of a Yacht Voyage to Iceland, &c., in 1856. *Fourth Edition.* Woodcuts. Post 8vo. 9s.

DYER'S (THOMAS H.) History of Modern Europe, from the taking of Constantinople by the Turks to the close of the War in the Crimea. 4 Vols. 8vo. 60s.

EASTLAKE'S (SIR CHARLES) Italian Schools of Painting. From the German of KUGLER. Edited, with Notes. *Third Edition.* Illustrated from the Old Masters. 2 Vols. Post 8vo. 30s.

EASTWICK'S (E. B.) Handbook for Bombay and Madras, with Directions for Travellers, Officers, &c. Map. 2 Vols. Post 8vo. 24s.

EDWARDS' (W. H.) Voyage up the River Amazon, including a Visit to Para. Post 8vo. 2s.

ELDON'S (Lord) Public and Private Life, with Selections from his Correspondence and Diaries. By Horace Twiss. *Third Editi n.* Portrait. 2 Vols. Post 8vo. 21s.

ELLIS (Rev. W.) Visits to Madagascar, including a Journey to the Capital, with notices of Natural History, and Present Civilisation of the People. *Fifth Thousand.* Map and Woodcuts. 8vo. 16s.

—— (Mrs.) Education of Character, with Hints on Moral Training. Post 8vo. 7s. 6d.

ELLESMERE'S (Lord) Two Sieges of Vienna by the Turks. Translated from the German. Post 8vo. 2s.

—— Campaign of 1812 in Russia, from the German of General Carl Von Clausewitz. Map. 8vo. 10s. 6d.

—— Poems. Crown 4to. 24s.

—— Essays on History, Biography, Geography, and Engineering. 8vo. 12s.

ELPHINSTONE'S (Hon. Mountstuart) History of India—the Hindoo and Mahomedan Periods. *Fourth Edition.* Map. 8vo. 18s.

ENGEL'S (Carl) Music of the Most Ancient Nations; particularly of the Assyrians, Egyptians, and Hebrews; with Special Reference to the Discoveries in Western Asia and in Egypt. With 100 Illustrations. 8vo. 16s.

ENGLAND (History of) from the Peace of Utrecht to the Peace of Versailles, 1713–63. By Lord Mahon (Earl Stanhope). *Library Edition,* 7 Vols. 8vo. 93s.; or *Popular Edition,* 7 Vols. Post 8vo. 35s.

—— From the First Invasion by the Romans, down to the 14th year of Queen Victoria's Reign. By Mrs. Markham. 118th *Edition.* Woodcuts. 12mo. 6s.

—— (The Student's Hume). A History of England from the Earliest Times. Based on the History by David Hume. Corrected and continued to 1858. Edited by Wm. Smith, LL.D. Woodcuts. Post 8vo. 7s. 6d.

ENGLISHWOMAN IN AMERICA. Post 8vo. 10s. 6d.

ESKIMAUX and English Vocabulary, for Travellers in the Arctic Regions. 16mo. 3s. 6d.

ESSAYS FROM "THE TIMES." Being a Selection from the Literary Papers which have appeared in that Journal. *Seventh Thousand.* 2 vols. Fcap. 8vo. 8s.

EXETER'S (Bishop of) Letters to the late Charles Butler, on the Theological parts of his Book of the Roman Catholic Church; with Remarks on certain Works of Dr. Milner and Dr. Lingard, and on some parts of the Evidence of Dr. Doyle. *Second Edition.* 8vo. 16s.

FAMILY RECEIPT-BOOK. A Collection of a Thousand Valuable and Useful Receipts. Fcap. 8vo. 5s. 6d.

FARRAR'S (Rev. A. S.) Critical History of Free Thought in reference to the Christian Religion. Being the Bampton Lectures, 1862. 8vo. 16s.

—— (F. W.) Origin of Language, based on Modern Researches. Fcap. 8vo. 5s.

FEATHERSTONHAUGH'S (G. W.) Tour through the Slave States of North America, from the River Potomac to Texas and the Frontiers of Mexico. Plates. 2 Vols. 8vo. 26s.

FERGUSSON'S (James) Palaces of Nineveh and Persepolis Restored. Woodcuts. 8vo. 16s.

———— History of the Modern Styles of Architecture, completing the above work. With 312 Illustrations. 8vo. 31s. 6d.

FISHER'S (Rev. George) Elements of Geometry, for the Use of Schools. Fifth Edition. 18mo. 1s. 6d.

—— First Principles of Algebra, for the Use of Schools. Fifth Edition. 18mo. 1s. 6d.

FLOWER GARDEN (The). By Rev. Thos. James. Fcap. 8vo. 1s.

FONNEREAU'S (T. G.) Diary of a Dutiful Son. Fcap. 8vo. 4s. 6d.

FORBES' (C. S.) Iceland; its Volcanoes, Geysers, and Glaciers. Illustrations. Post 8vo. 14s.

FORD'S (Richard) Handbook for Spain, Andalusia, Ronda, Valencia, Catalonia, Granada, Gallicia, Arragon, Navarre, &c. Third Edition. 2 Vols. Post 8vo. 30s.

—— Gatherings from Spain. Post 8vo. 3s. 6d.

FORSTER'S (John) Arrest of the Five Members by Charles the First. A Chapter of English History re-written. Post 8vo. 12s.

— —— Grand Remonstrance, 1641. With an Essay on English freedom under the Plantagenet and Tudor Sovereigns. Second Edition. Post 8vo. 12s.

———— Oliver Cromwell, Daniel De Foe, Sir Richard Steele, Charles Churchill, Samuel Foote. Third Edition. Post 8vo. 12s.

FORSYTH'S (William) Life and Times of Cicero. With Selections from his Correspondence and his Orations. Illustrations. 2 Vols. Post 8vo. 18s.

FORTUNE'S (Robert) Narrative of Two Visits to the Tea Countries of China, 1843-52. Third Edition. Woodcuts. 2 Vols. Post 8vo. 18s.

—— Third Visit to China. 1853-6. Woodcuts. 8vo. 16s.

———— Yedo and Peking. With Notices of the Agriculture and Trade of Japan and China. Illustrations. 8vo. 16s.

FOSS' (Edward) Judges of England. With Sketches of their Lives, and Notices of the Courts at Westminster, from the Conquest to the Present Time. 9 Vols. 8vo. 114s.

FRANCE (History of). From the Conquest by the Gauls to the Death of Louis Philippe. By Mrs. Markham. 56th Thousand. Woodcuts. 12mo. 6s.

— —— (The Student's History of). From the Earliest Times to the Establishment of the Second Empire, 1852. By W. H. Pearson. Edited by Wm. Smith, LL.D. Woodcuts. Post 8vo. 7s. 6d.

FRENCH (The) in Algiers; The Soldier of the Foreign Legion— and the Prisoners of Abd-el-Kadir. Translated by Lady Duff Gordon. Post 8vo. 2s.

GALTON'S (Francis) Art of Travel; or, Hints on the Shifts and Contrivances available in Wild Countries. *Third Edition.* Woodcuts. Post 8vo. 7s. 6d.

GEOGRAPHY (The Student's Manual of Ancient). By Rev. W. L. Bevan. Edited by Wm. Smith, LL.D. Woodcuts. Post 8vo. 7s. 6d.

————— Journal of the Royal Geographical Society of London. 8vo.

GERMANY (History of). From the Invasion by Marius, to the present time. By Mrs. Markham. *Fifteenth Thousand.* Woodcuts. 12mo. 6s.

GIBBON'S (Edward) History of the Decline and Fall of the Roman Empire. *A New Edition.* Preceded by his Autobiography. Edited, with Notes, by Dr. Wm. Smith. Maps. 8 Vols. 8vo. 60s.

————— (The Student's Gibbon); Being an Epitome of the above work, incorporating the Researches of Recent Commentators. By Dr. Wm. Smith. *Ninth Thousand.* Woodcuts. Post 8vo. 7s. 6d.

GIFFARD'S (Edward) Deeds of Naval Daring; or, Anecdotes of the British Navy. New Edition. Fcap. 8vo. 3s. 6d.

GOLDSMITH'S (Oliver) Works. A New Edition. Printed from the last editions revised by the Author. Edited by Peter Cunningham. Vignettes. 4 Vols. 8vo. 30s. (Murray's British Classics.)

GLADSTONE'S (Right Hon. W. E.) Financial Statements of 1853, 60, 63, and 64; also his Speeches on Tax-Bills, 1861, and on Charities, 1863. *Second Edition.* 8vo. 12s.

————— Wedgwood: an Address delivered at Burslem. Woodcuts. Post 8vo. 2s.

GLEIG'S (Rev. G. R.) Campaigns of the British Army at Washington and New Orleans. Post 8vo. 2s.

————— Story of the Battle of Waterloo. Post 8vo. 3s. 6d.

————— Narrative of Sale's Brigade in Affghanistan. Post 8vo. 2s.

————— Life of Robert Lord Clive. Post 8vo. 3s. 6d.

————— Life and Letters of Sir Thomas Munro. Post 8vo 3s. 6d.

GORDON'S (Sir Alex. Duff) Sketches of German Life, and Scenes from the War of Liberation. From the German. Post 8vo. 3s. 6d.

————— (Lady Duff) Amber-Witch: A Trial for Witchcraft. From the German. Post 8vo. 2s.

————— French in Algiers. 1. The Soldier of the Foreign Legion. 2. The Prisoners of Abd-el-Kadir. From the French. Post 8vo. 2s.

GOUGER'S (Henry) Personal Narrative of Two Years' Imprisonment in Burmah. *Second Edition.* Woodcuts. Post 8vo. 12s.

GRAMMAR (The Student's Greek.) For Colleges, and the Upper Forms. By Professor Curtius. Translated under the Revision of the Author. Edited by Wm. Smith, LL.D. Post 8vo. 7s. 6d.

————— (The Student's Latin). For Colleges and the Upper Forms. By Wm. Smith, LL.D. Post 8vo. 7s. 6d.

GREECE (The Student's History of). From the Earliest Times to the Roman Conquest. By Wm. Smith, LL.D. Woodcuts. Post 8vo. 7s. 6d.

GRENVILLE (THE) PAPERS. Being the Public and Private
Correspondence of George Grenville, including his PRIVATE DIARY.
Edited by W. J. SMITH. 4 Vols. 8vo. 16s. each.

GREY (EARL) on Parliamentary Government and Reform. A New
Edition, containing Suggestions for the Improvement of our Representative System, and an Examination of the Reform Bills of 1859—61.
8vo. 9s.

GREY'S (SIR GEORGE) Polynesian Mythology, and Ancient
Traditional History of the New Zealand Race. Woodcuts. Post
8vo. 10s. 6d.

GROTE'S (GEORGE) History of Greece. From the Earliest Times
to the close of the generation contemporary with the death of Alexander
the Great. *Fourth Edition.* Maps. 8 vols. 8vo. 112s.

—— —— PLATO, and the other Companions of Socrates. 3
Vols. 8vo.

(MRS.) Memoir of Ary Scheffer. Post 8vo. 8s. 6d.

———————— Collected Papers. 8vo. 10s. 6d.

GUIZOT'S (M.) Meditations on Christianity. Containing 1.
NATURAL PROBLEMS. 2. CHRISTIAN DOGMAS. 3. THE SUPERNATURAL.
4. LIMITS OF SCIENCE. 5. REVELATION. 6. INSPIRATION OF HOLY
SCRIPTURE. 7. GOD ACCORDING TO THE BIBLE. 8. JESUS CHRIST
ACCORDING TO THE GOSPELS. Post 8vo. 9s. 6d.

HALLAM'S (HENRY) Constitutional History of England, from the
Accession of Henry the Seventh to the Death of George the Second.
Seventh Edition. 3 Vols. 8vo. 30s.

—— —— History of Europe during the Middle Ages.
Tenth Edition. 3 Vols. 8vo. 30s.

—— Literary History of Europe, during the 15th, 16th and
17th Centuries. *Fourth Edition.* 3 Vols. 8vo. 36s.

—— Literary Essays and Characters. Fcap. 8vo. 2s.

—— Historical Works. Containing History of England,
—Middle Ages of Europe,—Literary History of Europe. 10 Vols.
Post 8vo. 6s each.

—— (ARTHUR) Remains; in Verse and Prose. With Preface, Memoir, and Portrait. Fcap. 8vo. 7s. 6d.

HAMILTON'S (JAMES) Wanderings in North Africa. Post 8vo. 12s.

HART'S ARMY LIST. (*Quarterly and Annually.*) 8vo. 10s. 6d.
and 21s each.

HANNAH'S (Rev. Dr.) Bampton Lectures for 1863; the Divine
and Human Elements in Holy Scripture. 8vo. 10s. 6d.

HAY'S (J. H. DRUMMOND) Western Barbary, its wild Tribes and
savage Animals. Post 8vo. 2s.

HEAD'S (SIR FRANCIS) Horse and his Rider. Woodcuts. Post 8vo. 5s.

———————— Rapid Journeys across the Pampas. Post 8vo. 2s.

———————— Bubbles from the Brunnen of Nassau. 16mo. 5s.

———————— Emigrant. Fcap. 8vo. 2s. 6d.

———————— Stokers and Pokers; or, N.-Western Railway. Post
8vo. 2s.

———————— Fortnight in Ireland. Map. 8vo. 12s.

———————— (SIR EDMUND) Shall and Will; or, Future Auxiliary
Verbs. Fcap. 8vo. 4s.

HAND-BOOK—TRAVEL-TALK. English, German, French, and Italian. 18mo. 3s. 6d.

—— NORTH GERMANY, Holland, Belgium, and the Rhine to Switzerland. Map. Post 8vo. 10s.

—— KNAPSACK GUIDE TO BELGIUM AND THE RHINE. Post 8vo. (*In the Press.*)

—— SOUTH GERMANY, Bavaria, Austria, Styria, Salzberg, the Austrian and Bavarian Alps, the Tyrol, Hungary, and the Danube, from Ulm to the Black Sea. Map. Post 8vo. 10s.

KNAPSACK GUIDE TO THE TYROL. Post 8vo. (*In the Press.*)

— — -— PAINTING. German, Flemish, and Dutch Schools. Edited by Dr. Waagen. Woodcuts. 2 Vols. Post 8vo. 24s.

LIVES OF THE EARLY FLEMISH PAINTERS, with Notices of their Works. By Crowe and Cavalcaselle. Illustrations. Post 8vo. 12s.

—— SWITZERLAND, Alps of Savoy, and Piedmont. Maps. Post 8vo. 9s.

—— KNAPSACK GUIDE TO SWITZERLAND. Post 8vo. 5s.

—— FRANCE, Normandy, Brittany, the French Alps, the Rivers Loire, Seine, Rhone, and Garonne, Dauphiné, Provence, and the Pyrenees. Maps. Post 8vo. 10s.

— -— KNAPSACK GUIDE TO FRANCE. Post 8vo. (*In the Press.*)

— —— PARIS and its Environs. Map. Post 8vo. 5s.

—— -—— SPAIN, Andalusia, Ronda, Granada, Valencia, Catalonia, Gallicia, Arragon, and Navarro. Maps. 2 Vols. Post 8vo. 30s.

-- PORTUGAL, Lisbon, &c. Map. Post 8vo.

NORTH ITALY, Piedmont, Liguria, Venetia, Lombardy, Parma, Modena, and Romagna. Map. Post 8vo. 12s.

—— CENTRAL ITALY, Lucca, Tuscany, Florence, The Marches, Umbria, and the Patrimony of St. Peter's. Map. Post 8vo. 10s.

ROME and its Environs. Map. Post 8vo. 9s.

— SOUTH ITALY, Two Sicilies, Naples, Pompeii, Herculaneum, and Vesuvius. Map. Post 8vo. 10s.

KNAPSACK GUIDE TO ITALY. Post 8vo. 6s.

SICILY, Palermo, Messina, Catania, Syracuse, Etna, and the Ruins of the Greek Temples. Map. Post 8vo. 12s.

— PAINTING. The Italian Schools. From the German of Kugler. Edited by Sir Charles Eastlake, R.A. Woodcuts. 2 Vols. Post 8vo. 30s.

—— —— LIVES OF THE EARLY ITALIAN PAINTERS, and Progress of Painting in Italy, from Cimabue to Bassano. By Mrs. Jameson. Woodcuts. Post 8vo. 12s.

HAND-BOOK—DICTIONARY OF ITALIAN PAINTERS. By
A LADY. Edited by RALPH WORNUM. With a Chart. Post 8vc. 6s. 6d.

———— GREECE, the Ionian Islands, Albania, Thessaly,
and Macedonia. Maps. Post 8vo. 15s.

TURKEY, Malta, Asia Minor, Constantinople,
Armenia, Mesopotamia, &c. Maps. Post 8vo. (In the Press.)

———— EGYPT, Thebes, the Nile, Alexandria, Cairo,
the Pyramids, Mount Sinai, &c. Map. Post 8vo. 15s.

———— SYRIA & PALESTINE, Peninsula of Sinai, Edom,
and Syrian Desert. Maps. 2 Vols. Post 8vo. 24s.

———— BOMBAY AND MADRAS. Map. 2 Vols. Post
8vo. 24s.

———— NORWAY. Map. Post 8vo. 5s.

DENMARK, SWEDEN and NORWAY. Maps. Post
8vo. 15s.

———— RUSSIA, THE BALTIC AND FINLAND. Maps. Post
8vo. 12s.

———— MODERN LONDON. A Complete Guide to all
the Sights and Objects of Interest in the Metropolis. Map. 16mo.
3s. 6d.

———————— WESTMINSTER ABBEY. Woodcuts. 16mo. 1s.

———————— KENT AND SUSSEX, Canterbury, Dover, Rams-
gate, Sheerness, Rochester, Chatham, Woolwich, Brighton, Chichester,
Worthing, Hastings, Lewes, Arundel, &c. Map. Post 8vo. 10s.

———— SURREY, HANTS, Kingston, Croydon, Reigate,
Guildford, Winchester, Southampton, Portsmouth, and Isle of Wight.
Maps. Post 8vo. 7s. 6d.

———— BERKS, BUCKS, AND OXON, Windsor, Eton,
Reading, Aylesbury, Uxbridge, Wycombe, Henley, the City and Uni-
versity of Oxford, and the Descent of the Thames to Maidenhead and
Windsor. Map. Post 8vo. 7s. 6d.

———— WILTS, DORSET, AND SOMERSET, Salisbury,
Chippenham, Weymouth, Sherborne, Wells, Bath, Bristol, Taunton,
&c. Map. Post 8vo. 7s. 6d.

———— DEVON AND CORNWALL, Exeter, Ilfracombe,
Linton, Sidmouth, Dawlish, Teignmouth, Plymouth, Devonport, Tor-
quay, Launceston, Truro, Penzance, Falmouth, &c. Maps. Post 8vo.
7s. 6d.

———— NORTH AND SOUTH WALES, Bangor, Car-
narvon, Beaumaris, Snowdon, Conway, Menai Straits, Carmarthen,
Pembroke, Tenby, Swansea, The Wye, &c. Maps. 2 Vols. Post 8vo.
12s.

———— CATHEDRALS OF ENGLAND—Southern Divi-
sion, Winchester, Salisbury, Exeter, Wells, Chichester, Rochester,
Canterbury. With 110 Illustrations. 2 Vols. Crown 8vo. 24s.

———— CATHEDRALS OF ENGLAND—Eastern Divi-
sion, Oxford, Peterborough, Norwich, Ely, and Lincoln. With 90
Illustrations. Crown 8vo. 18s.

———— CATHEDRALS OF ENGLAND—Western Divi-
sion, Bristol, Gloucester, Hereford, Worcester, and Lichfield. With 50
Illustrations. Crown 8vo. 16s.

———— FAMILIAR QUOTATIONS. From English Authors.
Third Edition. Fcap. 8vo. 5s.

HEBER'S (BISHOP) Journey through India. *Twelfth Edition.* 2 Vols. Post 8vo. 7s.

———— Poetical Works. *Sixth Edition.* Portrait. Fcap. 8vo. 6s.

HERODOTUS. A New English Version. Edited, with Notes and Essays, historical, ethnographical, and geographical. By Rev. G. RAWLINSON, assisted by SIR HENRY RAWLINSON and SIR J. G. WILKINSON. *Second Edition.* Maps and Woodcuts. 4 Vols. 8vo. 48s.

HESSEY (REV. DR.). Sunday—Its Origin, History, and Present Obligations. Being the Bampton Lectures for 1860. *Second Edition.* 8vo. 16s.

HICKMAN'S (WM.) Treatise on the Law and Practice of Naval Courts-Martial. 8vo. 10s. 6d.

HILLARD'S (G. S.) Six Months in Italy. 2 Vols. Post 8vo. 16s.

HOLLWAY'S (J. G.) Month in Norway. Fcap. 8vo. 2s.

HONEY BEE (THE). An Essay. By REV. THOMAS JAMES. Reprinted from the "Quarterly Review." Fcap. 8vo. 1s.

HOOK'S (DEAN) Church Dictionary. *Ninth Edition.* 8vo. 16s.

———— (THEODORE)Life. By J. G. LOCKHART. Reprinted from the "Quarterly Review." Fcap. 8vo. 1s.

HOOKER'S (Dr. J. D.) Himalayan Journals; or, Notes of an Oriental Naturalist in Bengal, the Sikkim and Nepal Himalayas, the Khasia Mountains, &c. *Second Edition.* Woodcuts. 2 Vols. Post 8vo. 18s.

HOPE'S (A. J. BERESFORD) English Cathedral of the Nineteenth Century. With Illustrations. 8vo. 12s.

HORACE (Works of). Edited by DEAN MILMAN. With 300 Woodcuts. Crown 8vo. 21s.

—— (Life of). By DEAN MILMAN. Woodcuts, and coloured Borders. 8vo. 9s.

HUME'S (THE STUDENT') History of England, from the Invasion of Julius Cæsar to the Revolution of 1688. Corrected and continued to 1858. Edited by Dr. Wm. Smith. Woodcuts. Post 8vo. 7s. 6d.

HUTCHINSON (GEN.) on the most expeditious, certain, and easy Method of Dog-Breaking. *Fourth Edition.* Enlarged and revised, with additional Illustrations. Crown 8vo.

HUTTON'S (H. E.) Principia Græca; an Introduction to the Study of Greek. Comprehending Grammar, Delectus, and Exercise-book, with Vocabularies. *Third Edition.* 12mo. 3s. 6d.

c

HOME AND COLONIAL LIBRARY. A Series of Works adapted for all circles and classes of Readers, having been selected for their acknowledged interest and ability of the Authors. Post 8vo. Published at 2s. and 3s. 6d. each, and arranged under two distinctive heads as follows :—

CLASS A.
HISTORY, BIOGRAPHY, AND HISTORIC TALES.

1. SIEGE OF GIBRALTAR. By John Drinkwater. 2s.

2. THE AMBER-WITCH. By Lady Duff Gordon. 2s.

3. CROMWELL AND BUNYAN. By Robert Southey. 2s.

4. LIFE OF Sir FRANCIS DRAKE. By John Barrow. 2s.

5. CAMPAIGNS AT WASHINGTON. By Rev. G. R. Gleig. 2s.

6. THE FRENCH IN ALGIERS. By Lady Duff Gordon. 2s.

7. THE FALL OF THE JESUITS. 2s.

8. LIVONIAN TALES. 2s.

9. LIFE OF CONDE. By Lord Mahon. 3s. 6d.

10. SALE'S BRIGADE. By Rev. G. R. Gleig. 2s.

11. THE SIEGES OF VIENNA. By Lord Ellesmere. 2s.

12. THE WAYSIDE CROSS. By Capt. Milman. 2s.

13. SKETCHES of GERMAN LIFE. By Sir A. Gordon. 3s. 6d.

14. THE BATTLE of WATERLOO. By Rev. G. R. Gleig. 3s. 6d.

15. AUTOBIOGRAPHY OF STEFFENS. 2s.

16. THE BRITISH POETS. By Thomas Campbell. 3s. 6d.

17. HISTORICAL ESSAYS. By Lord Mahon. 3s. 6d.

18. LIFE OF LORD CLIVE. By Rev. G. R. Gleig. 3s. 6d.

19. NORTH - WESTERN RAILWAY. By Sir F. B. Head. 2s.

20. LIFE OF MUNRO. By Rev. G. R. Gleig. 3s. 6d.

CLASS B.
VOYAGES, TRAVELS, AND ADVENTURES.

1. BIBLE IN SPAIN. By George Borrow. 3s. 6d.

2. GIPSIES of SPAIN. By George Borrow. 3s. 6d.

3 & 4. JOURNALS IN INDIA. By Bishop Heber. 2 Vols. 7s.

5. TRAVELS in the HOLY LAND. By Irby and Mangles. 2s.

6. MOROCCO AND THE MOORS. By J. Drummond Hay. 2s.

7. LETTERS FROM the BALTIC. By a Lady. 2s.

8. NEW SOUTH WALES. By Mrs. Meredith. 2s.

9. THE WEST INDIES. By M. G. Lewis. 2s.

10. SKETCHES OF PERSIA. By Sir John Malcolm. 3s. 6d.

11. MEMOIRS OF FATHER RIPA. 2s.

12. 13. TYPEE AND OMOO. By Hermann Melville. 2 Vols. 7s.

14. MISSIONARY LIFE IN CANADA. By Rev. J. Abbott. 2s.

15. LETTERS FROM MADRAS. By a Lady. 2s.

16. HIGHLAND SPORTS. By Charles St. John. 3s. 6d.

17. PAMPAS JOURNEYS. By Sir F. B. Head. 2s.

18 GATHERINGS FROM SPAIN. By Richard Ford. 3s. 6d.

19. THE RIVER AMAZON. By W. H. Edwards. 2s.

20. MANNERS & CUSTOMS OF INDIA. By Rev. C. Acland. 2s.

21. ADVENTURES IN MEXICO. By G. F. Ruxton. 3s. 6d.

22. PORTUGAL AND GALLICIA. By Lord Carnarvon. 3s. 6d.

23. BUSH LIFE IN AUSTRALIA. By Rev. H. W. Haygarth. 2s.

24. THE LIBYAN DESERT. By Bayle St. John. 2s.

25. SIERRA LEONE. By a Lady. 3s. 6d.

*** Each work may be had separately.

IRBY AND MANGLES' Travels in Egypt, Nubia, Syria, and the Holy Land. Post 8vo. 2s.

JAMES' (Rev. Thomas) Fables of Æsop. A New Translation, with Historical Preface. With 100 Woodcuts by Tenniel and Wolf. *Thirty-eighth Thousand*. Post 8vo. 2s. 6d.

JAMESON'S (Mrs.) Lives of the Early Italian Painters, from Cimabue to Bassano, and the Progress of Painting in Italy. *New Edition*. With Woodcuts. Post 8vo. 12s.

JESSE'S (Edward) Gleanings in Natural History. *Eighth Edition*. Fcp. 8vo. 6s.

JOHNSON'S (Dr. Samuel) Life. By James Boswell. Including the Tour to the Hebrides. Edited by the late Mr. Croker. Portraits. Royal 8vo. 10s.

———— Lives of the most eminent English Poets. Edited by Peter Cunningham. 3 vols. 8vo. 22s. 6d. (Murray's British Classics.)

JOURNAL OF A NATURALIST. Woodcuts. Post 8vo. 9s. 6d.

KEN'S (Bishop) Life. By A Layman. *Second Edition*. Portrait. 2 Vols. 8vo. 18s.

———— Exposition of the Apostles' Creed. Extracted from his "Practice of Divine Love." Fcap. 1s. 6d.

———— Approach to the Holy Altar. Extracted from his "Manual of Prayer" and "Practice of Divine Love." Fcap. 8vo. 1s. 6d.

KING'S (Rev. S. W.) Italian Valleys of the Alps; a Tour through all the Romantic and less frequented "Vals" of Northern Piedmont. Illustrations. Crown 8vo. 18s.

———— (Rev. C. W.) Antique Gems; their Origin, Use, and Value, as Interpreters of Ancient History, and as Illustrative of Ancient Art. Illustrations. 8vo. 42s.

KING EDWARD VIth's Latin Grammar; or, an Introduction to the Latin Tongue, for the Use of Schools. *Sixteenth Edition*. 12mo. 3s. 6d.

———— ———— First Latin Book; or, the Accidence, Syntax, and Prosody, with an English Translation for the Use of Junior Classes. *Fourth Edition*. 12mo. 2s. 6d.

KIRK'S (J. Foster) History of Charles the Bold, Duke of Burgundy. Portrait. 2 Vols. 8vo. 30s.

KERR'S (Robert) GENTLEMAN'S HOUSE: or, How to Plan English Residences, from the Parsonage to the Palace. With Tables of Accommodation and Cost, and a Series of Selected Views and Plans. 8vo. 21s.

c 2

KUGLER'S Italian Schools of Painting. Edited, with Notes, by SIR CHARLES EASTLAKE. *Third Edition.* Woodcuts. 2 Vols. Post 8vo. 30s.

- German, Dutch, and Flemish Schools of Painting. Edited, with Notes, by DR. WAAGEN. *Second Edition.* Woodcuts. 2 Vols. Post 8vo. 24s.

LANGUAGE (THE ENGLISH). A Series of Lectures. By GEORGE P. MARSH. Edited, with additional Chapters and Notes, by WM. SMITH, LL.D. Post 8vo. 7s. 6d.

LATIN GRAMMAR (KING EDWARD VITH'S). For the Use of Schools. *Sixteenth Edition.* 12mo. 3s. 6d.

——— First Book (KING EDWARD VITH'S); or, the Accidence, Syntax, and Prosody, with English Translation for Junior Classes. *Fourth Edition.* 12mo. 2s. 6d.

LAYARD'S (A. H.) Nineveh and its Remains. Being a Narrative of Researches and Discoveries amidst the Ruins of Assyria. With an Account of the Chaldean Christians of Kurdistan; the Yezedis, or Devil-worshippers; and an Enquiry into the Manners and Arts of the Ancient Assyrians. *Sixth Edition.* Plates and Woodcuts. 2 Vols. 8vo. 36s.

——— Nineveh and Babylon : being the Result of a Second Expedition to Assyria. *Fourteenth Thousand.* Plates 8vo. 21s. Or *Fine Paper,* 2 Vols. 8vo. 30s.

——— Popular Account of Nineveh. *15th Edition.* With Woodcuts. Post 8vo. 5s.

LEAKE'S (COL.) Topography of Athens, with Remarks on its Antiquities. *Second Edition.* Plates. 2 Vols. 8vo. 30s.

—— Travels in Northern Greece. Maps. 4 Vols. 8vo. 60s.

—— Disputed Questions of Ancient Geography. Map. 8vo. 6s. 6d.

——— Numismata Hellenica, and Supplement. Completing a descriptive Catalogue of Twelve Thousand Greek Coins, with Notes Geographical and Historical. With Map and Appendix. 4to. 63s.

——— Peloponnesiaca. 8vo. 15s.

—— Degradation of Science in England. 8vo. 3s. 6d.

LESLIE'S (C. R.) Handbook for Young Painters. With Illustrations. Post 8vo. 10s. 6d.

——— Autobiographical Recollections, with Selections from his Correspondence. Edited by TOM TAYLOR. Portrait. 2 Vols. Post 8vo. 18s.

——— Life of Sir Joshua Reynolds. With an Account of his Works, and a Sketch of his Cotemporaries. By TOM TAYLOR. Illustrations. 2 Vols. 8vo.

LETTERS FROM THE SHORES OF THE BALTIC. By a LADY. Post 8vo. 2s.

——— MADRAS. By a LADY. Post 8vo. 2s.

——— SIERRA LEONE. By a LADY. Edited by the HONOURABLE MRS. NORTON. Post 8vo. 3s. 6d.

LEWIS' (Sir G. C.) Essay on the Government of Dependencies. 8vo. 12s.

- Glossary of Provincial Words used in Herefordshire and some of the adjoining Counties. 12mo. 4s. 6d.

-- (M. G.) Journal of a Residence among the Negroes in the West Indies. Post 8vo. 2s.

LIDDELL'S (Dean) History of Rome. From the Earliest Times to the Establishment of the Empire. With the History of Literature and Art. 2 Vols. 8vo. 28s.

-------- Student's History of Rome. Abridged from the above Work. 25th Thousand. With Woodcuts. Post 8vo. 7s. 6d.

LINDSAY'S (Lord) Lives of the Lindsays; or, a Memoir of the Houses of Crawfurd and Balcarres. With Extracts from Official Papers and Personal Narratives. Second Edition. 3 Vols. 8vo. 24s.

Report of the Claim of James, Earl of Crawfurd and Balcarres, to the Original Dukedom of Montrose, created in 1488 Folio. 15s.

Scepticism; a Retrogressive Movement in Theology and Philosophy. 8vo. 9s.

LISPINGS from LOW LATITUDES; or, the Journal of the Hon. Impulsia Gushington. Edited by Lord Dufferin. With 24 Plates, 4to. 21s.

LITERATURE (English). A Manual for Students. By T. B. Shaw. Edited, with Notes and Illustrations, by Wm. Smith, LL.D. Post 8vo. 7s. 6d.

----------------(Choice Specimens of). Selected from the Chief English Writers. By Thos. B. Shaw, M.A. Edited by Wm. Smith, LL.D. Post 8vo. 7s. 6d.

LITTLE ARTHUR'S HISTORY OF ENGLAND. By Lady Callcott. 120th Thousand. With 20 Woodcuts. Fcap. 8vo. 2s. 6d.

LIVINGSTONE'S (Rev. Dr.) Popular Account of his Missionary Travels in South Africa. Illustrations. Post 8vo. 6s.

-- Narrative of an Expedition to the Zambezi and its Tributaries; and of the Discovery of Lakes Shirwa and Nyassa. 1858-64. By David and Charles Livingstone. Map and Illustrations. 8vo.

LIVONIAN TALES. By the Author of "Letters from the Baltic." Post 8vo. 2s.

LOCKHART'S (J. G.) Ancient Spanish Ballads. Historical and Romantic. Translated, with Notes. Illustrated Edition. 4to. 21s. Or, Popular Edition, Post 8vo. 2s. 6d.

- Life of Robert Burns. Fifth Edition. Fcap. 8vo. 8s.

LONDON'S (Bishop of) Dangers and Safeguards of Modern Theology. Containing Suggestions to the Theological Student under present difficulties. Second Edition. 8vo. 9s.

LOUDON'S (Mrs.) Instructions in Gardening for Ladies. With Directions and Calendar of Operations for Every Month. Eighth Edition. Woodcuts. Fcap. 8vo. 5s.

LUCAS' (Samuel) Secularia; or, Surveys on the Main Stream of History. 8vo. 12s.

LUCKNOW: a Lady's Diary of the Siege. *Fourth Thousand.* Fcap. 8vo. 4s. 6d.

LYELL'S (Sir Charles) Elements of Geology; or, the Ancient Changes of the Earth and its Inhabitants considered as illustrative of Geology. *Sixth Edition.* Woodcuts. 8vo. 18s.

——— Geological Evidences of the Antiquity of Man. *Third Edition.* Illustrations. 8vo. 14s.

LYTTELTON'S (Lord) Ephemera. Post 8vo. 10s. 6d.

LYTTON'S (Sir Edward Bulwer) Poems. *New Edition.* Revised. Post 8vo. 10s. 6d.

MAHON'S (Lord) History of England, from the Peace of Utrecht to the Peace of Versailles. 1713—83. *Library Edition.* 7 Vols. 8vo. 93s. Popular Edition, 7 Vols. Post 8vo. 35s.

——————— "Forty-Five;" a Narrative of the Rebellion in Scotland. Post 8vo. 3s.

——————— History of British India from its Origin till the Peace of 1783. Post 8vo. 3s. 6d.

——————— Spain under Charles the Second; 1690 to 1700. *Second Edition.* Post 8vo. 6s. 6d.

——————— Life of William Pitt, with Extracts from his MS. Papers. *Second Edition.* Portraits. 4 Vols. Post 8vo. 42s.

——————— Condé, surnamed the Great. Post 8vo. 3s. 6d.

——————— Belisarius. *Second Edition.* Post 8vo. 10s. 6d.

——————— Historical and Critical Essays. Post 8vo. 3s. 6d.

——————— Miscellanies. *Second Edition.* Post 8vo. 5s. 6d.

——————— Story of Joan of Arc. Fcap. 8vo. 1s.

——————— Addresses. Fcap. 8vo. 1s.

McCLINTOCK'S (Capt. Sir F. L.) Narrative of the Discovery of the Fate of Sir John Franklin and his Companions in the Arctic Seas. *Twelfth Thousand.* Illustrations. 8vo. 16s.

McCULLOCH'S (J. R.) Collected Edition of Ricardo's Political Works. With Notes and Memoir. *Second Edition.* 8vo. 16s.

MacDOUGALL (Col.) On Modern Warfare as Influenced by Modern Artillery. With Plans. Post 8vo. 12s.

MAINE (H. Sumner) On Ancient Law: its Connection with the Early History of Society, and its Relation to Modern Ideas. *Second Edition.* 8vo. 12s.

MALCOLM'S (Sir John) Sketches of Persia. *Third Edition.* Post 8vo. 3s. 6d.

MANSEL (Rev. H. L.) Limits of Religious Thought Examined. Being the Bampton Lectures for 1858. *Fourth Edition.* Post 8vo. 7s. 6d.

MANSFIELD (Sir William) On the Introduction of a Gold Currency into India: a Contribution to the Literature of Political Economy. 8vo. 3s. 6d.

MANTELL'S (GIDEON A.) Thoughts on Animalcules; or, the Invisible World, as revealed by the Microscope. *Second Edition.* Plates. 16mo. 6s.

MANUAL OF SCIENTIFIC ENQUIRY, Prepared for the Use of Officers and Travellers. By various Writers. Edited by Sir J. F. HERSCHEL and Rev. R. MAIN. *Third Edition.* Maps. Post 8vo. 9s. *(Published by order of the Lords of the Admiralty.)*

MARKHAM'S (MRS.) History of England. From the First Invasion by the Romans, down to the fourteenth year of Queen Victoria's Reign. *156th Edition.* Woodcuts. 12mo. 6s.

———— History of France. From the Conquest by the Gauls, to the Death of Louis Philippe. *Sixtieth Edition.* Woodcuts. 12mo. 6s.

———— History of Germany. From the Invasion by Marius, to the present time. *Fifteenth Edition.* Woodcuts. 12mo. 6s.

———— History of Greece. From the Earliest Times to the Roman Conquest. By Dr. WM. SMITH. Woodcuts. 16mo. 3s. 6d.

———— History of Rome. From the Earliest Times to the Establishment of the Empire. By DR. WM. SMITH. Woodcuts. 16mo. 3s. 6d.

———— (CLEMENTS, R.) Travels in Peru and India, for the purpose of collecting Cinchona Plants, and introducing Bark into India. Maps and Illustrations. 8vo. 16s.

MARKLAND'S (J. H.) Reverence due to Holy Places. *Third Edition.* Fcap. 8vo. 2s.

MARRYAT'S (JOSEPH) History of Modern and Mediæval Pottery and Porcelain. With a Description of the Manufacture. *Second Edition.* Plates and Woodcuts. 8vo. 31s. 6d.

———— (HORACE) Jutland, the Danish Isles, and Copenhagen. Illustrations. 2 Vols. Post 8vo. 24s.

———— Sweden and Isle of Gothland. Illustrations. 2 Vols. Post 8vo. 28s.

MATTHIÆ'S (AUGUSTUS) Greek Grammar for Schools. Abridged from the Larger Grammar. By Blomfield. *Ninth Edition.* Revised by EDWARDS. 12mo. 3s.

MAUREL'S (JULES) Essay on the Character, Actions, and Writings of the Duke of Wellington. *Second Edition.* Fcap. 8vo. 1s. 6d.

MAXIMS AND HINTS on Angling and Chess. By RICHARD PENN. Woodcuts. 12mo. 1s.

MAYNE'S (R. C.) Four Years in British Columbia and Vancouver Island. Its Forests, Rivers, Coasts, and Gold Fields, and Resources for Colonisation. Illustrations. 8vo. 16s.

MELVILLE'S (HERMANN) Typee and Omoo; or, Adventures amongst the Marquesas and South Sea Islands. 2 Vols. Post 8vo. 7s.

MEREDITH'S (MRS. CHARLES) Notes and Sketches of New South Wales. Post 8vo. 2s.

MESSIAH (THE): A Narrative of the Life, Travels, Death, Resurrection, and Ascension of our Blessed Lord. By A LAYMAN. Author of the " Life of Bishop Ken." Map. 8vo. 18s.

MICHIE'S (ALEXANDER) Siberian Overland Route from Peking to Petersburg, through the Deserts and Steppes of Mongolia, Tartary, &c. Maps and Illustrations. 8vo. 16s.

MILLS' (ARTHUR) India in 1858; A Summary of the Existing Administration. *Second Edition.* Map. 8vo. 10s. 6d.

—— (REV. JOHN) Three Months' Residence at Nablus, with an Account of the Modern Samaritans. Illustrations. Post 8vo. 10s. 6d.

MILMAN'S (DEAN) History of the Jews, from the Earliest Period, brought down to Modern Times. *New Edition.* 3 Vols. 8vo. 36s.

Christianity, from the Birth of Christ to the Abolition of Paganism in the Roman Empire. *New Edition.* 3 Vols. 8vo. 36s.

—— Latin Christianity; including that of the Popes to the Pontificate of Nicholas V. *New Edition.* 9 Vols. 8vo 81s.

—— Character and Conduct of the Apostles considered as an Evidence of Christianity. 8vo. 10s. 6d.

—— Life and Works of Horace. With 300 Woodcuts. 2 Vols. Crown 8vo. 30s.

—— Poetical Works. Plates. 3 Vols. Fcap. 8vo. 13s.

—— Fall of Jerusalem. Fcap. 8vo. 1s.

—— (CAPT. E. A.) Wayside Cross. A Tale of the Carlist War. Post 8vo. 2s.

MILNES' (R. MONCKTON, LORD HOUGHTON) Poetical Works. Fcap. 8vo. 6s.

MODERN DOMESTIC COOKERY. Founded on Principles of Economy and Practical Knowledge and adapted for Private Families. *New Edition.* Woodcuts. Fcap. 8vo. 5s.

MOORE'S (THOMAS) Life and Letters of Lord Byron. Plates. 6 Vols. Fcap. 8vo. 18s.

—— Life and Letters of Lord Byron. Portraits. Royal 8vo. 9s.

MOTLEY'S (J. L.) History of the United Netherlands: from the Death of William the Silent to the Synod of Dort. Embracing the English-Dutch struggle against Spain; and a detailed Account of the Spanish Armada. Portraits. 2 Vols. 8vo. 30s.

MOUHOT'S (HENRI) Siam, Cambojia, and Lao; a Narrative of Travels and Discoveries. Illustrations. 2 vols. 8vo. 32s.

MOZLEY'S (REV. J. B.) Treatise on Predestination. 8vo. 14s.

—— Primitive Doctrine of Baptismal Regeneration. 8vo. 7s. 6d.

MUNDY'S (General) Pen and Pencil Sketches in India. *Third Edition.* Plates. Post 8vo. 7s. 6d.

(Admiral) Account of the Italian Revolution, with Notices of Garibaldi, Francis II., and Victor Emmanuel. Post 8vo. 12s.

MUNRO'S (General Sir Thomas) Life and Letters. By the Rev. G. R. Gleig. Post 8vo. 3s. 6d.

MURCHISON'S (Sir Roderick) Russia in Europe and the Ural Mountains. With Coloured Maps, Plates, Sections, &c. 2 Vols. Royal 4to.

Siluria ; or, a History of the Oldest Rocks containing Organic Remains. *Third Edition.* Map and Plates. 8vo. 42s.

MURRAY'S RAILWAY READING. Containing :—

Wellington. By Lord Ellesmere. 6d.	Mallam's Literary Essays. 2s.
Nimrod on the Chase. 1s.	Mahon's Joan of Arc. 1s.
Essays from "The Times." 2 Vols. 8s.	Head's Emigrant. 2s. 6d.
Music and Dress. 1s.	Nimrod on the Road. 1s.
Layard's Account of Nineveh. 5s.	Croker on the Guillotine. 1s.
Milman's Fall of Jerusalem. 1s.	Hollway's Norway. 2s.
Mahon's "Forty-Five." 3s.	Maurel's Wellington 1s. 6d.
Life of Theodore Hook. 1s.	Campbell's Life of Bacon. 2s. 6d.
Deeds of Naval Daring. 3s. 6d.	The Flower Garden. 1s.
The Honey Bee. 1s.	Lockhart's Spanish Ballads. 2s. 6d.
James' Æsop's Fables. 2s. 6d.	Taylor's Notes from Life. 2s.
Nimrod on the Turf. 1s. 6d.	Rejected Addresses. 1s.
Art of Dining. 1s. 6d.	Penn's Hints on Angling. 1s.

MUSIC AND DRESS. By a Lady. Reprinted from the " Quarterly Review." Fcap. 8vo. 1s.

NAPIER'S (Sir Wm) English Battles and Sieges of the Peninsular War. *Third Edition.* Portrait. Post 8vo. 10s. 6d.

Life and Letters. Edited by H. A. Bruce, M.P. Portraits. 2 Vols. Crown 8vo. 28s.

Life of General Sir Charles Napier; chiefly derived from his Journals and Letters. *Second Edition.* Portraits. 4 Vols. Post 8vo. 48s.

NAUTICAL ALMANACK. Royal 8vo. 2s. 6d. *(By Authority.)*

NAVY LIST. *(Published Quarterly, by Authority.)* 16mo. 2s. 6d.

NEW TESTAMENT (The) Illustrated by a Plain Explanatory Commentary, and authentic Views of Sacred Places, from Sketches and Photographs. Edited by Archdeacon Churton and Rev. Basil Jones. With 110 Illustrations. 2 Vols. Crown 8vo.

NEWDEGATE'S (C. N.) Customs' Tariffs of all Nations; collected and arranged up to the year 1855. 4to. 30s.

NICHOLLS' (Sir George) History of the English, Irish and Scotch Poor Laws. 4 Vols. 8vo.

(Rev. H. G.) Historical Account of the Forest of Dean. Woodcuts, &c. Post 8vo. 10s. 6d.

Personalities of the Forest of Dean, its successive Officials, Gentry, and Commonalty. Post 8vo. 3s. 6d.

NICOLAS' (Sir Harris) Historic Peerage of England. Exhibiting the Origin, Descent, and Present state of every Title of Peerage which has existed in this Country since the Conquest. By William Courthope. 8vo. 30s.

NIMROD On the Chace—The Turf—and The Road. Reprinted from the "Quarterly Review." Woodcuts. Fcap. 8vo. 3s. 6d.

O'CONNOR'S (R.) Field Sports of France; or, Hunting, Shooting, and Fishing on the Continent. Woodcuts. 12mo. 7s. 6d.

OXENHAM'S (Rev. W.) English Notes for Latin Elegiacs; designed for early Proficients in the Art of Latin Versification, with Prefatory Rules of Composition in Elegiac Metre. Fourth Edition. 12mo. 3s. 6d.

PARIS' (Dr.) Philosophy in Sport made Science in Earnest; or, the First Principles of Natural Philosophy inculcated by aid of the Toys and Sports of Youth. Ninth Edition. Woodcuts. Post 8vo. 7s. 6d.

PEEL'S (Sir Robert) Memoirs. Edited by Earl Stanhope and Mr. Cardwell. 2 Vols. Post 8vo. 7s. 6d. each.

PENN'S (Richard) Maxims and Hints for an Angler and Chess-player. New Edition. Woodcuts. Fcap. 8vo. 1s.

PENROSE'S (F. C.) Principles of Athenian Architecture, and the Optical Refinements exhibited in the Construction of the Ancient Buildings at Athens, from a Survey. With 40 Plates. Folio. 5l. 5s.

PERCY'S (John, M.D.) Metallurgy of Iron and Steel; or, the Art of Extracting Metals from their Ores and adapting them to various purposes of Manufacture. Illustrations. 8vo. 42s.

PHILLIPP (Charles Spencer March) On Jurisprudence. 8vo. 12s.

PHILLIPS' (John) Memoirs of William Smith, the Geologist. Portrait. 8vo. 7s. 6d.

——— ——— Geology of Yorkshire, The Coast, and Limestone District. Plates. 4to. Part I., 20s.—Part II., 30s.

——— ——— Rivers, Mountains, and Sea Coast of Yorkshire. With Essays on the Climate, Scenery, and Ancient Inhabitants. Second Edition, Plates. 8vo. 15s.

PHILPOTT'S (Bishop) Letters to the late Charles Butler, on the Theological parts of his "Book of the Roman Catholic Church;" with Remarks on certain Works of Dr. Milner and Dr. Lingard, and on some parts of the Evidence of Dr. Doyle. Second Edition. 8vo. 16s.

POPE'S (Alexander) Life and Works. A New Edition. Containing nearly 500 unpublished Letters. Edited with a New Life, Introductions and Notes. By Rev. Whitwell Elwin. Portraits. 8vo. (In the Press.)

PORTER'S (Rev. J. L.) Five Years in Damascus. With Travels to Palmyra, Lebanon and other Scripture Sites. Map and Woodcuts. 2 Vols. Post 8vo. 21s.

——— Handbook for Syria and Palestine: including an Account of the Geography, History, Antiquities, and Inhabitants of these Countries, the Peninsula of Sinai, Edom, and the Syrian Desert. Maps. 2 Vols. Post 8vo. 24s.

PRAYER-BOOK (The Illustrated), with 1000 Illustrations of Borders, Initials, Vignettes, &c. Medium 8vo. 18s. cloth; 31s. 6d. calf; 36s. morrocco.

PRECEPTS FOR THE CONDUCT OF LIFE. Extracted from the Scriptures. *Second Edition.* Fcap. 8vo. 1s.

PUSS IN BOOTS. With 12 Illustrations By OTTO SPECKTER. Coloured, 16mo. 2s. 6d.

QUARTERLY REVIEW (THE). 8vo. 6s.

RAMBLES in Syria among the Turkomans and Bedaweens. Post 8vo. 10s. 6d.

RAWLINSON'S (REV. GEORGE) Herodotus. A New English Version. Edited with Notes and Essays. Assisted by SIR HENRY RAWLINSON and SIR J. G. WILKINSON, *Second Edition.* Maps and Woodcut. 4 Vols. 8vo. 48s.

———————— Historical Evidences of the truth of the Scripture Records stated anew. *Second Edition.* 8vo. 14s.

Five Great Monarchies of the Ancient World. Illustrations. 4 Vols. 8vo. 16s. each.
Vols. I.—II., Chaldæa and Assyria. Vols. III.—IV., Babylon, Media, and Persia.

REJECTED ADDRESSES (THE). By JAMES AND HORACE SMITH. Fcap. 8vo. 1s., or *Fine Paper*, Portrait, fcap. 8vo. 5s.

RENNIE'S (D. F.) British Arms in Peking, 1860; Kagosima, 1862. Post 8vo. 12s.

———————— Pekin and the Pekinese: Narrative of a Residence at the British Embassy. Illustrations. 2 Vols. Post 8vo.

REYNOLDS' (SIR JOSHUA) His Life and Times. Commenced by C. R. LESLIE, R.A., and continued by TOM TAYLOR. Portraits and Illustrations. 2 Vols. 8vo.

RICARDO'S (DAVID) Political Works. With a Notice of his Life and Writings. By J. R. M'CULLOCH. *New Edition.* 8vo. 16s.

RIPA'S (FATHER) Memoirs during Thirteen Years' Residence at the Court of Peking. From the Italian. Post 8vo. 2s.

ROBERTSON'S (CANON) History of the Christian Church, from the Apostolic Age to the Concordat of Worms, A.D. 1123. *Second Edition.* 3 Vols. 8vo. 38s.

ROBINSON'S (REV. DR.) Biblical Researches in the Holy Land. Being a Journal of Travels in 1838 and 1852. Maps. 3 Vols. 8vo. 45s.

——— Physical Geography of the Holy Land. Post 8vo. 10s. 6d.

ROME (THE STUDENT'S HISTORY OF). FROM THE EARLIEST TIMES TO THE ESTABLISHMENT OF THE EMPIRE. By DEAN LIDDELL. Woodcuts. Post 8vo. 7s. 6d.

ROWLAND'S (DAVID) Manual of the English Constitution; Its Rise, Growth, and Present State. Post 8vo. 10s. 6d.

——— Laws of Nature the Foundation of Morals. Post 8vo.

RUNDELL'S (MRS.) Domestic Cookery, adapted for Private Families. *New Edition.* Woodcuts. Fcap. 8vo. 5s.

RUSSELL'S (J. Rutherfurd, M.D.) Art of Medicine—Its History and its Heroes. Portraits. 8vo. 14s.

RUXTON'S (George F.) Travels in Mexico; with Adventures among the Wild Tribes and Animals of the Prairies and Rocky Mountains. Post 8vo. 3s. 6d.

SALE'S (Sir Robert) Brigade in Affghanistan. With an Account of the Defence of Jellalabad. By Rev. G. R. Gleig. Post 8vo. 2s.

SANDWITH'S (Humphry) Siege of Kars. Post 8vo. 3s. 6d.

SCOTT'S (G. Gilbert) Secular and Domestic Architecture, Present and Future. Second Edition. 8vo. 9s.

—— (Master of Baliol) University Sermons Post 8vo. 8s. 6d.

SCROPE'S (G. P.) Geology and Extinct Volcanoes of Central France. Second Edition. Illustrations. Medium 8vo. 30s.

SELF-HELP. With Illustrations of Character and Conduct. By Samuel Smiles. 50th Thousand. Post 8vo. 6s.

SENIOR'S (N. W.) Suggestions on Popular Education. 8vo. 9s.

SHAFTESBURY (Lord Chancellor); Memoirs of his Early Life. With his Letters, &c. By W. D. Christie. Portrait. 8vo. 10s. 6d.

SHAW'S (T. B.) Student's Manual of English Literature. Edited, with Notes and Illustrations. by Dr. Wm. Smith. Post 8vo. 7s. 6d.

—————— Choice Specimens of English Literature. Selected from the Chief English Writers. Edited by Wm. Smith, LL.D. Post 8vo. 7s. 6d.

SIERRA LEONE: Described in Letters to Friends at Home. By A Lady. Post 8vo. 3s. 6d.

SIMMONS on Courts-Martial. 5th Edition. 8vo. 14s.

SMILES' (Samuel) Lives of British Engineers; from the Earliest Period to the Death of Robert Stephenson; with an account of their Principal Works, and a History of Inland Communication in Britain. Portraits and Illustrations. 3 Vols. 8vo. 63s.

—— George and Robert Stephenson; the Story of their Lives. With Portraits and 70 Woodcuts. Post 8vo. 6s.

James Brindley and the Early Engineers. With Portrait and 50 Woodcuts. Post 8vo. 6s.

- Self-Help. With Illustrations of Character and Conduct. Post 8vo. 6s.

Industrial Biography: Iron-Workers and Tool Makers. A companion volume to "Self-Help." Post 8vo. 6s.

— Workmen's Earnings—Savings—and Strikes. Fcap. 8vo. 1s. 6d.

SOMERVILLE'S (Mary) Physical Geography. Fifth Edition. Portrait. Post 8vo. 9s.

—————— Connexion of the Physical Sciences. Ninth Edition. Woodcuts. Post 8vo. 9s.

SOUTH'S (John F.) Household Surgery; or, Hints on Emergencies. Seventeenth Thousand. Woodcuts. Fcp. 8vo. 4s. 6d.

SMITH'S (Dr. Wm.) Dictionary of the Bible; its Antiquities, Biography, Geography, and Natural History. Illustrations. 3 Vols. 8vo. 105s.

—— Greek and Roman Antiquities. 2nd Edition. Woodcuts. 8vo. 42s.

———————— Biography and Mythology. Woodcuts. 3 Vols. 8vo. 5l. 15s. 6d.

·· — ———— — Geography. Woodcuts. 2 Vols. 8vo. 80s.

Classical Dictionary of Mythology, Biography, and Geography, compiled from the above. With 750 Woodcuts. 8vo. 18s.

— Latin-English Dictionary. 3rd Edition. Revised. 8vo. 21s.

— — Smaller Classical Dictionary. Woodcuts. Crown 8vo. 7s. 6d.

— Dictionary of Antiquities. Woodcuts. Crown 8vo. 7s. 6d.

— Latin-English Dictionary. 12mo. 7s. 6d.

Latin-English Vocabulary; for Phædrus, Cornelius Nepos, and Cæsar. 2nd Edition. 12mo. 3s. 6d.

Principia Latina—Part I. A Grammar, Delectus, and Exercise Book, with Vocabularies. 6th Edition. 12mo. 3s. 6d.

——— — — — — Part II. A Reading-book of Mythology, Geography, Roman Antiquities, and History. With Notes and Dictionary. 3rd Edition. 12mo. 3s. 6d.

Part III. A Latin Poetry Book. Hexameters and Pentameters; Eclogæ Ovidianæ; Latin Prosody. &c. 2nd Edition. 12mo. 3s. 6d.

Part IV. Latin Prose Composition. Rules of Syntax, with Examples, Explanations of Synonyms, and Exercises on the Syntax. Second Edition. 12mo. 3s. 6d.

Student's Greek Grammar. By Professor Curtius. Post 8vo. 7s. 6d.

——— Latin Grammar. Post 8vo. 7s. 6d.

Latin Grammar. Abridged from the above. 12mo. 3s. 6d.

Smaller Greek Grammar. Abridged from Curtius. 12mo. 3s. 6d.

STANLEY'S (Dean) Sinai and Palestine, in Connexion with their History. Map. 8vo. 16s.

Bible in the Holy Land. Woodcuts. Fcap. 8vo. 2s. 6d.

— St. Paul's Epistles to the Corinthians. 8vo. 18s.

- Eastern Church. Plans. 8vo. 12s.

Jewish Church. Vol. 1. Abraham to Samuel. Plans. 8vo. 16s.

Vol. 2. Samuel to the Captivity. 8vo. 16s.

Historical Memorials of Canterbury. Woodcuts. Post 8vo. 7s. 6d.

Sermons in the East, with Notices of the Places Visited. 8vo. 9s.

Sermons on Evangelical and Apostolical Teaching. Post 8vo. 7s. 6d.

- Addresses and Charges of Bishop Stanley. With Memoir. 8vo. 10s. 6d.

SOUTHEY'S (ROBERT) Book of the Church. *Seventh Edition.*
Post 8vo. 7s. 6d.

       Lives of Bunyan and Cromwell. Post 8vo. 2s.

SPECKTER'S (OTTO) Puss in Boots. With 12 Woodcuts. Square
12mo. 1s. 6d. plain, or 2s. 6d. coloured.

       Charmed Roe; or, the Story of the Little Brother
and Sister. Illustrated. 16mo.

ST. JOHN'S (CHARLES) Wild Sports and Natural History of the
Highlands. Post 8vo. 3s. 6d.

——————— (BAYLE) Adventures in the Libyan Desert and the
Oasis of Jupiter Ammon. Woodcuts. Post 8vo. 2s.

STANHOPE'S (EARL) Life of William Pitt. With Extracts
from his M.S. Papers. *Second Edition.* Portraits. 4 Vols. Post 8vo.
42s.

       Miscellanies. *Second Edition.* Post 8vo. 5s. 6d.

STEPHENSON (GEORGE and ROBERT). The Story of their
Lives. By SAMUEL SMILES. With Portraits and 70 Illustrations. Post
8vo. 6s.

STUDENT'S HUME. A History of England from the Invasion
of Julius Cæsar to the Revolution of 1688. By DAVID HUME, and
continued to 1858. Woodcuts. Post 8vo. 7s. 6d.
*** A Smaller History of England. 12mo. 3s. 6d.

—— ——— HISTORY OF FRANCE; from the Earliest Times
to the Establishment of the Second Empire, 1852. By W. H. PEARSON,
M.A. Woodcuts. Post 8vo. 7s. 6d.

       HISTORY OF GREECE; from the Earliest Times
to the Roman Conquest. With the History of Literature and Art. By
WM. SMITH, LL.D. Woodcuts. Crown 8vo. 7s. 6d. (Questions. 2s.)
*** A SMALLER HISTORY OF GREECE. 12mo. 3s. 6d.

    — — HISTORY OF ROME; from the Earliest Times
to the Establishment of the Empire. With the History of Literature
and Art. By Dean LIDDELL. Woodcuts. Crown 8vo. 7s. 6d.
*** A SMALLER HISTORY OF ROME. 12mo. 3s. 6d.

—— ——— GIBBON; an Epitome of the History of the Decline
and Fall of the Roman Empire. By EDWARD GIBBON. Incorporating the Researches of Recent Commentators. Woodcuts. Post 8vo.
7s. 6d.

       MANUAL OF ANCIENT GEOGRAPHY. By
Rev. W. L. BEVAN, M.A. Woodcuts. Post 8vo. 7s. 6d.

      ····· ENGLISH LANGUAGE. By GEORGE P. MARSH.
Post 8vo. 7s. 6d.

     —- ENGLISH LITERATURE. By T. B. SHAW,
M.A. Post 8vo. 7s. 6d.

     —— SPECIMENS OF ENGLISH LITERATURE.
Selected from the Chief Writers. By THOMAS B. SHAW, M.A. Post
8vo. 7s. 6d.

STOTHARD'S (Thos.) Life. With Personal Reminiscences. By Mrs. Bray. With Portrait and 60 Woodcuts. 4to. 21s.

STREET'S (G. E.) Gothic Architecture in Spain. From Personal Observations during several journeys through that country. Illustrations. Medium 8vo.

——————— Brick and Marble Architecture of Italy in the Middle Ages. Plates. 8vo. 21s.

SWIFT'S (Jonathan) Life, Letters. Journals, and Works. By John Forster. 8vo. (In Preparation.)

SYME'S (Professor) Principles of Surgery. 5th Edition. 8vo. 12s.

TAIT'S (Bishop) Dangers and Safeguards of Modern Theology. 8vo. 9s.

TAYLOR'S (Henry) Notes from Life. Fcap. 8vo. 2s.

THOMSON'S (Archbishop) Lincoln's Inn Sermons. 8vo. 10s. 6d.

THREE-LEAVED MANUAL OF FAMILY PRAYER; arranged so as to save the trouble of turning the Pages backwards and forwards. Royal 8vo. 2s.

TRANSACTIONS OF THE ETHNOLOGICAL SOCIETY OF LONDON. New Series. Vols. I. and II. 8vo.

TREMENHEERE'S (H. S.) Political Experience of the Ancients, in its bearing on Modern Times. Fcap. 8vo. 2s. 6d.

TRISTRAM (H. B.). The Great Sahara. Wanderings South of the Atlas Mountains. Map and Illustrations. Post 8vo. 15s.

TWISS' (Horace) Public and Private Life of Lord Chancellor Eldon, with Selections from his Correspondence. Portrait. Third Edition. 2 Vols. Post 8vo. 21s.

TYLOR'S (E. B.) Researches into the Early History of Mankind, and the Development of Civzation. Illustrations. 8vo.

TYNDALL'S (John) Glaciers of the Alps. With an account of Three Years' Observations and Experiments on their General Phenomena. Woodcuts. Post 8vo. 14s.

TYTLER'S (Patrick Fraser) Memoirs. By Rev. J. W. Burgon, M.A. 8vo. 9s.

VAUGHAN'S (Rev. Dr.) Sermons preached in Harrow School. 8vo. 10s. 6d.

VENABLES' (Rev. R. L.) Domestic Scenes in Russia. Post 8vo. 5s.

WAAGEN'S (Dr.) Treasures of Art in Great Britain. Being an Account of the Chief Collections of Paintings, Sculpture, Manuscripts, Miniatures, &c &c., in this Country. Obtained from Personal Inspection during Visits to England. 4 Vols. 8vo.

WALSH'S (Sir John) Practical Results of the Reform Bill of 1832. 8vo. 5s. 6d.

VAMBERY'S (Armixius) Travels in Central A ia, from Teheran across the Turk man D r, on the Eastern Shore of the Caspian to Khiva, Bokhara, and Samarcand in 1863. Map and Illustrations. 8vo. 21s.

WELLINGTON'S (The Duke of) Despatches during his various Campaigns. Compiled from Official and other Authentic Documents. By Col. Gurwood, C.B. 8 Vols. 8vo. 21s. each.

——— —— Supplementary Despatches, and other Papers. Edited by his Son. Vols. I. to XII. 8vo. 20s. each.

——— ——- Selections from his Despatches and General Orders. By Colonel Gurwood. 8vo. 18s.

——— —— Speeches in Parliament. 2 Vols. 8vo. 42s.

WILKINSON'S (Sir J. G.) Popular Account of the Private Life, Manners, and Customs of the Ancient Egyptians. New Edition. Revised and Condensed. With 500 Woodcuts. 2 Vols. Post 8vo. 12s.

——— Handbook for Egypt.—Thebes, the Nile, Alexandria, Cairo, the Pyramids, Mount Sinai, &c. Map. Post 8vo. 15s.

—— - (G. B.) Working Man's Handbook to South Australia; with Advice to the Farmer, and Detailed Information for the several Classes of Labourers and Artisans. Map. 18mo. 1s. 6d.

WILSON'S (Bishop Daniel) Life, with Extracts from his Letters and Journals. By Rev. Josiah Bateman. Second Edition. Illustrations. Post 8vo. 9s.

— (Genl. Sir Robert) Secret History of the French Invasion of Russia, and Retreat of the French Army, 1812. Second Edition. 8vo. 15s.

—— - Private Diary of Travels, Personal Services, and Public Events, during Missions and Employments in Spain, Sicily, Turkey, Russia, Poland, Germany, &c. 1812-14. 2 Vols. 8vo. 26s.

—— Autobiographical Memoirs. Containing an Account of his Early Life down to the Peace of Tilsit. Portrait. 2 Vols. 8vo. 26s.

WORDSWORTH'S (Canon) Journal of a Tour in Athens and Attica. Third Edition. Plates. Post 8vo. 8s. 6d.

—— ——— Pictorial, Descriptive, and Historical Account of Greece, with a History of Greek Art, by G. Scharf, F.S.A. New Edition. With 600 Woodcuts. Royal 8vo. 28s.

WORNUM (Ralph). A Biographical Dictionary of Italian Painters : with a Table of the Contemporary Schools of Italy. By a Lady. Post 8vo. 6s. 6d.